"Santa Clara-Silicon Valley 2006" gives a snapshot of the region — Santa Clara and Santa Cruz counties — and its cities at a time of rapid change. The central theme is useful information, presented in a readable style.

School Rankings, including latest academic rankings (STAR test) for public schools, college placements by high school, SAT scores, directory of private schools.

Community profiles. Home prices, rents. Descriptions of cities, towns and neighborhoods.

The perfect guide for parents or people shopping for homes or apartments or just interested in finding out more about Santa Clara and Santa Cruz counties, their schools and their communities.

Weather, annual rain, when to expect rain.

Hospital services and medical care. Directory of hospitals.

Child Care. Directory of infant-care and day-care centers. Most popular names for local babies.

Places to visit, things to do.

Local Colleges and Unemployment Figures.

Vital statistics. Population, education by town. Voter registration. Presidential votes. Crime, history, trivia, more.

McCormack's Guides, edited by former newspaper reporters and editors, was established in 1984 and publishes the most popular general-interest guides to California counties. For a list of our other books and an order form, see the last page. Or visit: www.mccormacks.com

Publisher and editor Don McCormack formed McCormack's Guides in 1984. A graduate of the University of California-Berkeley, McCormack joined the Contra Costa Times in 1969 and covered police, schools, politics, planning, courts and government. Later with the Richmond Independent and Berkeley Gazette, he worked as a reporter, then editor and columnist.

———

Maps illustrator Louis Liu attended Los Medanos College and the Academy of Art College in San Francisco, where he majored in illustration.

Many thanks to the people who write, edit, layout and help publish McCormack's Guides: Martina Bailey, Paul Fletcher, Mary Jennings, Meghan McCormack, John VanLandingham

DISCLAIMER

Indexed   ISBN 1-929365-78-0

SANTA CLARA
Silicon Valley
2006

12252

3211 Elmquist Court, Martinez, CA 94553
Phone: (800) 222-3602 & Fax: (925) 228-7223
bookinfo@mccormacks.com • www.mccormacks.com

Contents

Part

4

Living & Working in Santa Clara & Santa Cruz

Work Hard.
Play Hard.
Change The World.

www.genencor.com

Genencor International®
Innovative by Nature®

On the Cover:
*Genencor, one of the
major employers of
Santa Clara County*

Before you move ... buy

$13⁹⁵
SINGLE COPY
VOLUME DISCOUNTS

McCormack's Guides are published for:

• ALAMEDA-CENTRAL VALLEY • CONTRA COSTA-SOLANO
• SANTA CLARA-SANTA CRUZ-SILICON VALLEY
• SAN FRANCISCO-SAN MATEO-MARIN-SONOMA
• SAN DIEGO • ORANGE COUNTY • GREATER SACRAMENTO

Available in e-book format at www.mccormacks.com:

LOS ANGELES • RIVERSIDE • SANTA BARBARA • SAN BERNARDINO • VENTURA

Also from McCormack's Guides:
How California Schools Work

www.mccormacks.com
1•800•222•3602

SANTA CRUZ, SAN BENITO SANTA CLARA & MONTEREY COUNTIES

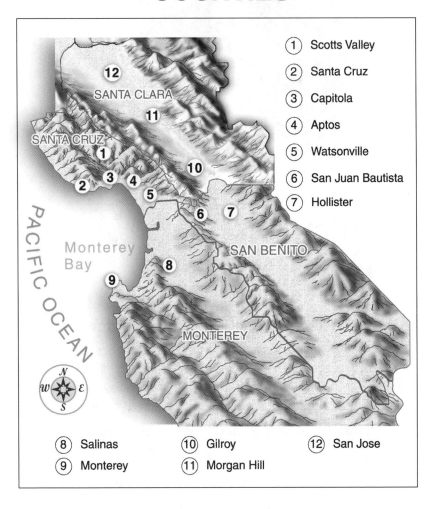

1. Scotts Valley
2. Santa Cruz
3. Capitola
4. Aptos
5. Watsonville
6. San Juan Bautista
7. Hollister
8. Salinas
9. Monterey
10. Gilroy
11. Morgan Hill
12. San Jose

Santa Clara County

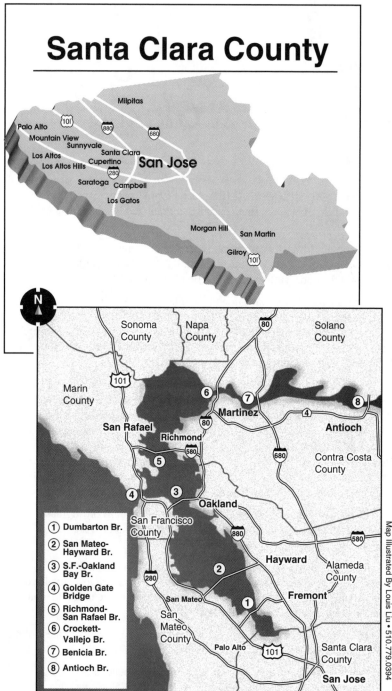

1. Dumbarton Br.
2. San Mateo-Hayward Br.
3. S.F.-Oakland Bay Br.
4. Golden Gate Bridge
5. Richmond-San Rafael Br.
6. Crockett-Vallejo Br.
7. Benicia Br.
8. Antioch Br.

Map Illustrated By Louis Liu • 510.779.0394

Chapter 1

County at A Glance

THE ORIGINAL SILICON VALLEY, Santa Clara County, population 1,759,585, is located at the south end of San Francisco Bay and includes 15 cities.

Its crime is low, its weather balmy, its school scores mixed but many quite high, its economy the envy of the globe until 2001 when the hi-tech sector, as they say in the trade, suffered a "correction." A big correction!

Since then, with the exception of Google and a few other ventures, the Valley has been saying goodbye to businesses that didn't make the cut — the old inevitable in this part of the world — squeezing its costs, refining operations and looking for the next new wave. In 2005, traffic started to increase on local freeways, a good sign that the worst is behind.

Rectangular in shape, Santa Clara covers 1,316 square miles, smaller than Delaware, slightly larger than Rhode Island. There are two Santa Claras: one, the county, encompassing everything; the second, a city, one of the largest in the county. San Jose, 944,857 residents, is the biggest and most populous city in the county. Monte Sereno, 3,505, has the fewest people. Palo Alto is the brainiest town; Los Altos Hills, the richest; San Jose, increasingly, the most dynamic and becoming recognized as the political leader of the region; Gilroy, in July, the most odoriferous. The town is famous for its garlic festival.

Palo Alto borders Stanford University, one of the most prestigious universities in the world, and the intellectual force behind the region's prosperity.

Most people reside on the flatland of the Santa Clara Valley, which stretches from the Bay down to beyond Gilroy, the southernmost city. If you want a home with a view, generally you have to head for the hills and mountains that border the bay and the valley.

In housing, Santa Clara favors the suburban tract and the steadiness of the middle class. Crime, even in the larger cities, is very low.

Single homes outnumber apartments 2-to-1. The state in 2005 counted 607,035 residential units: 332,346 single homes, 53,5753 single attached,

Santa Clara County Population

City or Area	1990	2000	2005*
Campbell	36,048	38,138	38,415
Cupertino	40,263	50,546	53,452
Gilroy	31,487	41,464	47,671
Los Altos	26,303	27,693	27,614
Los Altos Hills	7,514	7,902	8,452
Los Gatos	27,357	28,592	28,976
Milpitas	50,686	62,698	64,998
Monte Sereno	3,287	3,483	3,505
Morgan Hill	23,928	33,556	36,423
Mountain View	67,460	70,708	72,033
Palo Alto	55,900	58,598	61,674
San Jose	782,248	894,943	944,857
Santa Clara	93,613	102,361	109,106
Saratoga	28,061	29,843	30,850
Stanford**	18,097	13,315	NA
Sunnyvale	117,229	131,760	133,086
Countywide	1,497,577	1,682,585	1,759,585
California	29,760,021	33,871,648	36,810,358

Source: 1990 Census, 2000 Census. *From California Dept. of Finance, Jan. 1, 2005. **Stanford is located just outside Palo Alto city limits.

201,456 multiples, 19,658 mobiles. Santa Clara has its mansions but the typical home, the census reports, is that old workhorse, the three-bedroom unit.

In the 1990s and early 2000s, the economy boomed and home prices and rents soared. Then the economy soured but home prices, thanks mainly to low interest rates, kept rising. Modest homes, three bedrooms, often sell above $600,000. On a happier note, rents declined.

Rarely does the humidity discomfort or the thermometer drop below freezing. Rain confines itself to the winter and snow to the tops of the local mountains, of which Copernicus, 4,360 feet, is the highest.

On the down side, Santa Clara and much of coastal California straddle active faults. Earthquakes are not a matter of if, but a matter of when. For sound advice on earthquakes, read the first section of the local phone directory.

Sports, Activities, Things to Do

Stanford and two other universities greatly enrich cultural life. Movies, opera, plays, pop and rock, professional and collegiate sports, ballet, symphonies, a children's musical theater, classes of all descriptions, performances by top-notch entertainers — in Santa Clara County you can find it all. Almost every year some new cultural ornament presents itself. What you can't find, nearby San Francisco and Oakland usually can provide.

Average Household Income

City	1990	2000	*2005
Campbell	$71,000	$97,400	$98,500
Cupertino	105,900	147,300	105,200
Gilroy	68,700	91,000	97,500
Los Altos	145,300	215,000	220,400
Los Altos Hills	255,900	385,000	407,000
Los Gatos	115,900	165,100	107,300
Milpitas	88,100	112,200	114,600
Monte Sereno	195,800	215,300	226,400
Morgan Hill	89,500	107,100	115,400
Mountain View	72,000	100,200	103,700
Palo Alto	99,300	149,200	150,700
San Jose	75,400	102,300	104,300
Santa Clara	71,900	99,400	101,100
Saratoga	163,100	242,600	246,500
Sunnyvale	77,000	104,400	107,700
Remainder	100,700	138,200	141,000
Countywide	83,600	114,600	116,900

Source: Association of Bay Area Governments, *"Projections 2002."* Average income per household includes wages and salaries, dividends, interest, rent and transfer payments such as Social Security or public assistance. *Projections.

In sports, San Jose is home to the only professional ice hockey team in Northern California, the Sharks. San Jose also fields teams for professional soccer and minor league baseball. Professional football (the Forty Niners and the Raiders) and major-league baseball (the Giants and the Athletics) and NBA basketball (the Warriors) are within a short drive. Stanford and San Jose State University offer top-notch collegiate sports. Just about every town offers a smorgasbord of Little League, softball, football, swimming, gymnastics, aerobics, tennis and so on. Among children, soccer is turning into the most popular sport. Parks, large and small, are scattered throughout the county. San Francisco Bay is in the county's back yard but rarely is it used for swimming (too cold; current comes from the Arctic.)

Yosemite, Lake Tahoe and the snow country are four to six hours to the east. Most residents live within 30 to 45 minutes of the fishing boats of Half Moon Bay and Santa Cruz and the waves of the Pacific.

Because of the mild weather, outdoor sports run almost year round. Many people delight in gardening and hiking and cycling. Indoors, many a night is spent tinkering with this or that gizmo or computer. Many of the major high-tech firms are headquartered in the county — for one big reason. They want their people to tap into the energy and creativity that abounds in the region.

Silicon Valley More a Frame of Mind

Silicon Valley is a term more indicative of a frame of mind than a geographic location but it used to have fairly precise borders, generally Palo Alto

The South Bay

S A N T A   C L A R A   C O U N T Y

Map Illustrated By Louis Liu • 925.779.0394

to south San Jose. Now high-tech firms (Sun, Oracle) have jumped over the county line into Redwood City and Menlo Park, and on the east side of the Valley and across the Bay, into Milpitas, Newark, Fremont, San Ramon, Livermore, Dublin and Pleasanton, and even up to Berkeley and Richmond.

To work in Silicon Valley is to profess an interest in, often a passion for, high-tech. Here is where Stephan Wozniak, between raids on his parents' refrigerator, built the first Apple computer.

Here is where Stanford grads Bill Hewlett and David Packard, using the former's master's thesis, built in a Palo Alto garage an audio oscillator. Their first customer, Walt Disney, ordered eight for the soundtrack of "Fantasia."

Hewlett-Packard is now one of the biggies in high-tech research, development and manufacturing. Here also is where other firms pursue the golden break-throughs, the ideas that will transform the ways of multitudes and nations.

Growth Pains

Paradise? Close, but not quite. The freeways are wide and plentiful but inadequate to handle the number of vehicles. In the 1980s, the county added 239,145 people, a number equivalent then to the population of nine of its 15 cities. In the 1990s, it added 185,008. Many are the fights over development. If you strip away other fights — schools, traffic, taxes, services, rents, home prices — you will find underneath a county that is running hard to keep up with a growing population.

Many schools score high but a large number do not. After years of beggaring its schools, the state of California, thanks to the thriving economy, put up billions to lower class sizes and make other improvements. But the results may take a while to show themselves and, oh yes, California burned through its surplus and is saddled with a huge deficit. Some school cuts are inevitable. Prudent parents will take an active interest in their children's schools and try to make up the shortcomings in funding.

Crime is low, not nonexistent. You should always take precautions. In 2004, the FBI reports, homicides in Santa Clara County totaled 37. By contrast, San Francisco, with less than half the population, recorded 88 homicides.

The Loma Prieta quake in 1989 scared holy hell out of thousands, killed dozens and caused damage in the billions. But few residents quit Santa Clara County. In sum, the good, the promising and the delightful far outweigh the bad and the ominous.

A Changing Ethnic Mix

The county is changing from predominantly Caucasian to minority-majority. The sum of all minorities outnumbers or soon will outnumber Caucasians. This is often stated in a way that implies that ethnic groups form a bloc that vote, think and act in concert. They don't. A man from the highlands of Vietnam may have little in common with a man descended from people who roamed the highlands of Scotland. But he also may have little in common with a fellow recently arrived from the Mexican desert. Or conversely, what they have in common — the hope for a good life — may far outweigh their differences.

As for the politics of the county, in national elections people vote Demo-cratic, in local elections, they vote pragmatic and progressive. School bonds usually win. The city councils are populated by men and women who avoid the flamboyant and generally pay attention to filling potholes, reviewing building applications, funding parks and recreation and solving traffic problems.

The 2000 census counted 744,282 Caucasians, 403,401 people of Hispanic descent, 430,095 of Asian or Pacific Islander heritage, 47,182 African-Americans, 11,350 American Indians and 5,773 Native Hawaiian or other Pacific Islander. Many of the new immigrants are from Mexico, China and India.

Women and Minorities in Seats of Power

Women have discovered what men always knew: It is fun to give orders, command attention and respect, and pull down high salaries. The majority of students at most, if not all, of the county's colleges and universities are women, and women routinely win seats on school boards, city councils and the board of supervisors. Minorities are also showing up more on city councils and government bodies. In 1998, Ron Gonzales was elected mayor of San Jose.

A Little History

Spanish expeditions arrived in 1769 and 1776, intrepid and brave but late. Having ignored California since claiming it in the 1500s, Spain was dismayed to find other countries interested in her province. The Spanish explorers and those who followed were supposed to plant the flag, subdue and convert the Indians and colonize the land. The flag was planted, great ranches carved out, but the colonists were few and the Indians, through disease, hostility and misguided benevolence, were almost exterminated. At a critical time, Spain and Europe were diverted by the Napoleonic wars. On the other side of the continent, the United States secured its independence, bought the Midwest and heard the siren call of California. Over the mountains the Americans came, first for land, then gold. They kicked over the flag (Mexico's, Spain having been ousted) and by purchase, violence, swindles and squatting drove the rancheros into obscurity.

Left behind were city names and a fondness for romanticized Spanish architecture that has influenced the design of banks, churches, colleges and hamburger stands. Also remaining: a mild sense of guilt about seizing the land from the Mexicans, who in the perverse ways of history reestablished themselves in Santa Clara County through immigration.

Era of Rustic Happiness

The new Californians built roads, cities and railroads, cultivated the county into fabled abundance and — in the great American tradition of boosterism and speculation — spent much time and ink trying to lure others to Santa Clara County. Thousands did come but never enough to turn Santa Clara into a metropolis. Well into the 20th century, the county tended the pear, prune and tomato — an era of rustic happiness, fondly recalled in local histories.

On 13 March, 1884, Leland Stanford Jr., age 16, died of typhoid fever. His saddened mom and dad (grocer, railroad tycoon, governor) founded and endowed Stanford University in memory of their only child. Santa Clara County owes much of its prosperity to Stanford U.

Top 30 Baby Names

Santa Clara County				California			
Boys		**Girls**		**Boys**		**Girls**	
Daniel	187	Emily	165	Daniel	4157	Emily	3388
Ryan	187	Ashley	121	Anthony	3797	Ashley	2922
Andrew	166	Sophia	109	Andrew	3464	Samantha	2474
Anthony	166	Isabella	99	Jose	3379	Isabella	2435
Alexander	163	Natalie	98	Jacob	3327	Natalie	1942
Matthew	140	Samantha	95	Joshua	3292	Alyssa	1808
Michael	140	Emma	92	David	3246	Emma	1740
Ethan	138	Jasmine	83	Angel	3232	Sophia	1715
David	134	Jessica	83	Matthew	2853	Jessica	1700
Jacob	133	Sarah	79	Michael	2844	Jasmine	1666
Joshua	130	Alyssa	75	Christopher	2754	Elizabeth	1595
Jonathan	127	Jennifer	74	Jonathan	2541	Madison	1572
Jose	127	Elizabeth	70	Ryan	2511	Jennifer	1483
Nathan	125	Hannah	70	Alexander	2440	Kimberly	1460
Kevin	123	Michelle	68	Joseph	2430	Alexis	1434
Christopher	117	Lauren	64	Ethan	2356	Andrea	1374
Brandon	109	Madison	64	Nathan	2302	Abigail	1314
Nicholas	107	Abigail	63	Brandon	2208	Hannah	1310
Joseph	101	Mia	61	Kevin	2133	Sarah	1304
William	94	Nicole	60	Juan	2106	Vanessa	1299
Benjamin	88	Katherine	57	Christian	2022	Mia	1270
Bryan	88	Julia	56	Jesus	2012	Stephanie	1246
Justin	87	Olivia	56	Nicholas	1999	Brianna	1221
Angel	85	Kimberly	55	Diego	1977	Michelle	1152
James	85	Alexandra	52	Luis	1957	Olivia	1149
Jason	85	Leslie	52	Adrian	1824	Kayla	1147
Gabriel	84	Andrea	51	Dylan	1757	Leslie	1137
Dylan	82	Grace	51	Gabriel	1735	Grace	1127
Christian	81	Stephanie	51	Isaac	1722	Maria	1099
Jesus	79	Maria	50	Carlos	1638	Victoria	1083

Source: California Department of Health Services, 2004 birth records. Some names would move higher on the list if the state grouped essentially same names with slightly different spellings, for example, Sarah and Sara. But state computer goes by exact spellings.

The War Boom

On Dec. 7, 1941, the Japanese bombed Pearl Harbor, a blunder that inadvertently did more for real estate in Santa Clara County than 90 years of booster hoopla. War industries blossomed and thousands of servicemen, recalling that pleasant sunshine, returned to the county after the war. The war also made America a superpower, which entailed the support of a military establishment. For decades, defense dollars drove much of the county's economy. Down went the orchards, up went the housing tracts, slowly at first, with some wringing of hands, then rapidly as people poured in. The population, 290,000 people in 1950, doubled, then tripled.

In 1951, prompted by Fred Terman, vice president of Stanford, the university opened 700 acres for development. Electronics companies, attracted by the proximity of big brains, snapped up parcels. The result: Silicon Valley.

Tinkerers, Entrepreneurs

Actually, it wasn't quite that easy. Santa Clara County has a soft spot for the tinkerers, the Main Street whiz kids who get an idea into their heads, then spend days and weeks in their garages working it into something practical.

Hewlett and Packard, Jobs and Wozniak (Apple) epitomize the romance of the garage. They took their ideas and built industries. Of course, they drew on the work of others. The Apple could not have been built without the microprocessor, a 1971 Silicon Valley invention. The whole technological revolution would have stalled in its tracks without the transistor, developed in Bell Labs, New Jersey, but the co-inventor was William Shockley, Palo Alto native, who came home and formed a group of inventors who later split off on their own and founded some of the top businesses of the world, including Intel.

Modern Santa Clara County

Until 2001, flourishing and growing but now slowed by the economic doldrums. Still arguing over development. The days of the fast zonings and marching subdivisions are gone. San Jose has spent the last two decades putting muscle on its downtown. Many towns are going for what is called smart growth, building housing next to the jobs.

With the collapse of the Soviet Union, defense spending was sharply curtailed and this forced painful cutbacks in local industries. The Navy in 1994 quit Moffett Field, its airbase near Mountain View.

Defense industries may make a minor comeback; the world after Sept. 11 seems a more hostile place. But high-tech really is looking for its markets to spend down their inventories, capture their old confidence, and begin placing orders. In the meantime, many firms have laid off employees. The venture capitalists, burned by their own exuberance, have closed their wallets and gone fishing. One big recent exception in 2004: Google went public.

Santa Clara County has heard this story before. The county booms and inevitably gets carried away with its natural optimism then takes a tumble. But it always comes back. The people are too talented, their ideas too helpful or convenient for the county to stay down.

How Government Works

To Sacramento and Washington is where the money goes first these days and that's where much of the power resides. If you want more or less spent on roads, welfare, warfare, schools or pensions, write your congressman, senator or state legislator. Although weakened, local governments are far from penniless and enjoy considerable powers. Major agencies include:

Board of Supervisors

Five members are elected countywide, but by districts. (Gilroy, south end of the county, votes for its supervisor, Milpitas, northeast, for its supervisor and so on.) Supervisors are regional and municipal governors. They control spending for courts, animal services, many libraries, social services, public health. In their municipal hats, they build roads, decide zonings and, through the sheriff's department, provide police protection for unincorporated areas and some cities under contractual arrangements. If you live outside the limits of any city, you will be governed from San Jose, seat of county government. This sometimes gets confusing. In some areas, the county governs one side of a street and a city the other side.

City Councils

Generally five members (San Jose has 10 plus an elected mayor, the tie breaker, Palo Alto has nine), one council for each of the county's 15 cities. Councils are responsible for repairing roads, keeping neighborhoods safe, maintaining parks, providing recreation and other municipal chores. Much of their time goes to planning and development.

Special Service Districts

California grew so fast and chaotically that some regional needs, such as sewer and water, were met on an emergency basis by forming taxing districts with their own elected directors.

School Boards

Generally composed of five persons. There are 32 school districts in Santa Clara County, each with an elected board. A real hodgepodge. Trustees hire or fire principals and superintendents, negotiate teacher salaries, decide how much should be spent on computers and shop and whether the children should wear uniforms, and more.

What's in a Name

- Campbell. After Benjamin Campbell, wagon-train pioneer.

- Cupertino. At the time of Spanish expeditions, Catholic Church canonized a priest from the Italian village, Cupertino. Camped beside a stream, Spanish honored saint by calling spot "Arroyo San Jose de Cupertino."

- Gilroy. John Cameron, Scottish seaman, jumped ship and took his mother's maiden name, Gilroy. He settled near that town, married into a Spanish land grant, gambled most of it away and left his name.

- Los Altos. After developing firm, Los Altos Land Company.

- Los Gatos (The Cats). Several legends. The most popular: Men searching for water heard two wildcats fighting in the bushes.

- Milpitas. Obscure. May be Aztec for little cornfields.

Santa Clara County Voter Registration

City	Demo	Repub	NP
Campbell	9,542	6,346	4,514
Cupertino	10,233	8,308	8,025
Gilroy	9,004	5,630	3,280
Los Altos	7,691	7,788	3,751
Los Altos Hills	1,886	2,554	1,343
Los Gatos	7,831	7,683	3,648
Milpitas	10,700	6,640	7,311
Monte Sereno	877	1,124	397
Morgan Hill	7,262	6,878	3,377
Mountain View	17,948	8,596	9,395
Palo Alto	21,136	8,816	9,590
San Jose	186,911	108,088	89,919
Santa Clara	22,377	12,642	10,584
Saratoga	6,448	8,555	4,693
Sunnyvale	26,927	16,793	14,795
Unincorporated	23,837	15,785	9,953
Countywide	370,610	232,226	184,575

Source: Santa Clara Registrar of Voters, California Secretary of State's office, 2004. Key: Demo (Democrat), Repub (Republican), NP (non-partisan or independent).

Presidential Voting in Santa Clara County

Year	Democrat	D-Votes	Republican	R-Votes
1948	Truman*	41,905	Dewey	52,982
1952	Stevenson	59,350	Eisenhower*	87,554
1956	Stevenson	72,528	Eisenhower*	105,657
1960	Kennedy*	117,667	Nixon	131,735
1964	Johnson*	161,422	Goldwater	93,448
1968	Humphrey	175,511	Nixon*	163,446
1972	McGovern	208,505	Nixon*	237,329
1976	Carter*	208,023	Ford	219,188
1980	Carter	166,955	Reagan*	229,048
1984	Mondale	229,865	Reagan*	288,638
1988	Dukakis	277,810	Bush*	254,442
1992	Clinton*	276,391	Bush	155,984
1996	Clinton*	297,639	Dole	168,291
2000	Gore	328,690	Bush*	186,595
2004	Kerry	280,016	Bush*	151,660

Source: California Secretary of State's office. * Election winner nationally.

- Monte Sereno. Peaceful Mountain.

- Morgan Hill. After early rancher, Hiram Morgan Hill, but, yes, Morgan Hill does have a few hills.

- Mountain View. You can see mountains from this city, a vista that impressed an early settler.

- Palo Alto. Spanish for a tall tree. Explorers found one, a coastal redwood, over 1,000 years old, near the present site of Palo Alto city hall. Still standing but it lost part of its trunk in 1909.

- San Jose. After the patron saint of the second Spanish expedition.

- Santa Clara. At this site the Spanish built "Mission Santa Clara de Asis."

- Saratoga. Several versions, most popular: After Saratoga, New York, which has mineral springs, same as Saratoga, CA.

- Sunnyvale. Founding Realtor saw the sunshine.

Other Names to Know

- The Cardinal. What Stanford teams and rooters are called.

- The Farm. Another name for Stanford.

- Golden Bears or Bears or Old Blues. What UC Berkeley teams and rooters are called.

- Big Game. Football game, held every fall. Decides who is the better: The Cardinal or the Golden Bears. Winner gets the Ax, trophy with ax head.

- Spartans. What teams and rooters of San Jose State University are called.

- The City. San Francisco. Pretentious but appropriate.

- The Peninsula. Generally San Mateo County but some may include Palo Alto. See map of Bay Area.

- East Bay. Alameda and Contra Costa counties.

- South Bay. Santa Clara County.

- Bay Area. San Francisco, San Mateo, Santa Clara, Alameda, Contra Costa, Solano, Marin, Napa, Sonoma. All touch San Francisco Bay.

- Golden Gate. Yes it's the name of the bridge but it's also the name of the opening into San Francisco Bay.

How Santa Clara Residents Earn Their Money

City or Town	MAN-PRO	SERV	SAL-OFF	FARM	CON	MANU-TRANS
Campbell	50%	10%	25%	0%	6%	8%
Cupertino	71	4	18	0	2	4
Gilroy	29	14	28	3	11	15
Los Altos	75	4	16	0	2	3
Los Altos Hills	74	5	16	0	1	3
Los Gatos	64	5	23	0	3	3
Milpitas	46	8	23	0	6	16
Monte Sereno	70	5	20	0	0	4
Morgan Hill	45	11	25	1	10	8
Mountain View	29	13	28	1	18	11
Palo Alto	76	5	15	0	2	2
San Jose	41	12	24	0	8	14
Santa Clara	51	9	23	0	6	11
Saratoga	73	4	19	0	2	3
Stanford	75	8	15	0	0	2
Sunnyvale	60	9	19	0	4	8
Santa Clara County	49	11	23	0	7	11

Education Level of Population Age 25 & Older

Santa Clara County

City or Town	ND	HS	SC	AA	BA	Grad
Campbell	7%	17%	25%	9%	26%	13%
Cupertino	3	9	14	7	32	33
Gilroy	13	20	24	7	13	6
Los Altos	2	8	14	4	36	36
Los Altos Hills	2	4	10	5	37	41
Los Gatos	3	10	20	8	34	25
Milpitas	9	17	20	10	24	12
Monte Sereno	2	5	15	6	38	34
Morgan Hill	7	18	27	9	22	11
Mountain View	13	32	28	9	15	3
Palo Alto	2	6	12	4	31	43
San Jose	11	18	21	8	21	11
Santa Clara	7	17	20	8	26	17
Saratoga	3	8	14	6	35	34
Stanford	1	1	3	1	30	65
Sunnyvale	6	13	18	8	29	22
Santa Clara County	9	16	20	7	24	16

Source: 2000 Census. Figures are percent of population age 25 and older, rounded to the nearest whole number. **Key**: ND (Less than 9th grade or some high school but no diploma); HS (adults with high school diploma or GED only, no college); SC (adults with some college education); AA (adults with an associate degree); BA (adults with a bachelor's degree only); Grad (adults with a master's or higher degree).

Chapter **2a**

State School Rankings

HERE ARE COMPARISON RANKINGS from the 2005 STAR tests taken by almost every public-school student in California. This test is administered annually by the California Department of Education.

We have broken out the results in a way that makes comparisons between schools easy.

The rankings, based on the scores, range from 1 (the lowest) to 99 (the highest). A school that scores in the 20th percentile is landing in the bottom 20 percent of the state. A school that scores in the 95th percentile is placing among the top 5 percent of schools in the state.

These rankings should be considered rough measures of how the schools and their students are performing.

Many low- and middle-scoring schools have students who score high. Many high-scoring schools have students who land below the 25th percentile.

A few schools post average scores but turn out many high-scoring students. These schools often will have many students at the bottom and many at the top and few in the middle.

For more information, visit the school or go on the web and check out reports about individual schools. For more test results, go to www.star.cde.ca.gov. See also the school accountability reports.

To flesh out these scores, we are including in Chapter 2B a ranking system issued by the California Department of Education and in Chapter 3 the SAT scores, math and verbal, for the regular high schools. These scores and a chart that presents SAT scores by state will give you some idea of how local schools compare to schools nationwide.

Scores range from 1-99. A school scoring 75 has done better than 75 percent of other public schools in California.
Key: Eng (English), Ma (Math), Sci (Science).

Alum Rock Union Elem. School Dist.

Arbuckle Elem. (San Jose)

Grade	Eng	Ma	Sci
2	48	34	
3	11	18	
4	34	45	
5	14	37	18
6	17	20	

Cassell Elem. (San Jose)

Grade	Eng	Ma	Sci
2	52	50	
3	49	53	
4	21	18	
5	33	56	45
6	51	44	

Chavez Elem. (San Jose)

Grade	Eng	Ma	Sci
2	21	25	
3	4	11	
4	12	35	
5	9	23	5
6	10	19	

Cureton Elem. (San Jose)

Grade	Eng	Ma	Sci
2	36	34	
3	17	19	
4	32	31	
5	30	36	18

Dorsa Elem. (San Jose)

Grade	Eng	Ma	Sci
2	10	8	
3	14	17	
4	6	10	
5	13	50	16

Fischer Middle (San Jose)

Grade	Eng	Ma	Sci
6	12	27	
7	29	23	
8	19		

George Middle (San Jose)

Grade	Eng	Ma	Sci
6	16	15	
7	34	18	
8	32		

Goss Elem. (San Jose)

Grade	Eng	Ma	Sci
2	10	3	
3	7	3	
4	10	17	
5	9	16	9
6	23	23	

Hubbard Elem. (San Jose)

Grade	Eng	Ma	Sci
2	30	27	
3	29	24	
4	32	56	
5	19	26	22
6	17	30	

KIPP Heartwood Academy

Grade	Eng	Ma	Sci
5	84	99	88

Learning in an Urban Comm.

Grade	Eng	Ma	Sci
3	52	62	

Linda Vista Elem. (San Jose)

Grade	Eng	Ma	Sci
2	45	34	
3	34	35	
4	30	50	
5	56	78	50

Lyndale Elem. (San Jose)

Grade	Eng	Ma	Sci
2	43	32	
3	49	34	
4	41	55	
5	26	31	16

Mathson Middle (San Jose)

Grade	Eng	Ma	Sci
7	36	53	
8	36		

McCollam Elem. (San Jose)

Grade	Eng	Ma	Sci
2	95	95	
3	63	80	
4	58	56	
5	34	27	23

Meyer Elem. (San Jose)

Grade	Eng	Ma	Sci
2	44	48	
3	17	18	
4	15	61	
5	22	44	41

Ocala Middle (San Jose)

Grade	Eng	Ma	Sci
6	25	22	
7	32	41	
8	43		

Painter Elem. (San Jose)

Grade	Eng	Ma	Sci
2	67	76	
3	38	78	
4	57	65	
5	43	73	51

Pala Middle (San Jose)

Grade	Eng	Ma	Sci
6	19	17	
7	24	21	
8	30		

Renaissance Academy

Grade	Eng	Ma	Sci
6	47	45	

Rogers Elem. (San Jose)

Grade	Eng	Ma	Sci
2	57	38	
3	44	33	
4	37	29	
5	29	50	20

Ryan Elem. (San Jose)

Grade	Eng	Ma	Sci
2	36	3	
3	50	16	
4	26	10	
5	23	24	22
6	11	4	

San Antonio Elem. (San Jose)

Grade	Eng	Ma	Sci
2	30	25	
3	32	22	
4	23	13	
5	31	46	32
6	36	45	

Sheppard Middle (San Jose)

Grade	Eng	Ma	Sci
6	29	25	
7	44	28	
8	42		

Shields Elem. (San Jose)

Grade	Eng	Ma	Sci
2	25	11	
3	22	33	
4	5	4	
5	28	23	21

Scores range from 1-99. A school scoring 75 has done better than 75 percent of other public schools in California.
Key: Eng (English), Ma (Math), Sci (Science).

Grade	Eng	Ma	Sci
Slonaker Elem. (San Jose)			
2	9	11	
3	13	11	
4	12	22	
5	8	32	13
6	20	39	

Berryessa Union Elem. School Dist.

Grade	Eng	Ma	Sci
Brooktree Elem. (San Jose)			
2	68	74	
3	64	61	
4	67	67	
5	58	38	67
Cherrywood Elem. (San Jose)			
2	65	52	
3	69	78	
4	53	49	
5	57	48	62
Laneview Elem. (San Jose)			
2	58	53	
3	53	62	
4	71	58	
5	60	35	54
Majestic Way Elem. (San Jose)			
2	48	36	
3	45	52	
4	62	70	
5	76	83	86
Morrill Middle (San Jose)			
6	58	54	
7	68	82	
8	65		
Noble Elem. (San Jose)			
2	61	63	
3	70	73	
4	85	90	
5	86	69	81
Northwood Elem. (San Jose)			
2	70	70	
3	59	55	
4	57	52	
5	79	79	73
Piedmont Middle (San Jose)			
6	57	56	
7	78	83	
8	57		
Ruskin Elem. (San Jose)			
2	92	94	
3	97	95	
4	93	92	
5	89	90	90
Sierramont Middle (San Jose)			
6	71	65	
7	82	91	
8	69		
Summerdale Elem. (San Jose)			
2	56	57	
3	67	87	
4	47	39	
5	58	44	59

Grade	Eng	Ma	Sci
Toyon Elem. (San Jose)			
2	51	46	
3	42	43	
4	55	23	
5	53	17	56
Vinci Park Elem. (San Jose)			
2	41	55	
3	57	64	
4	46	51	
5	51	48	62

Cambrian Elem. School Dist.

Grade	Eng	Ma	Sci
Bagby Elem. (San Jose)			
2	83	91	
3	91	95	
4	83	90	
5	89	91	84
Fammatre Char. (San Jose)			
2	89	93	
3	85	82	
4	78	93	
5	87	84	90
Farnham Char. (San Jose)			
2	71	74	
3	74	73	
4	83	89	
5	71	87	83
Price Char. Middle (San Jose)			
6	86	89	
7	90	87	
8	89		
Sartorette Char. (San Jose)			
2	88	85	
3	85	89	
4	85	90	
5	93	93	90

Campbell Union Elem. School Dist.

Grade	Eng	Ma	Sci
Blackford Elem. (San Jose)			
2	27	29	
3	50	53	
4	52	46	
5	36	34	36
Campbell Middle			
5	25	17	36
6	33	26	
7	48	42	
8	36		
Capri Elem. (Campbell)			
2	68	67	
3	88	94	
4	69	67	
5	74	74	55
Castlemont Elem. (Campbell)			
2	59	71	
3	49	48	
4	82	82	
5	73	65	74

Scores range from 1-99. A school scoring 75 has done better than 75 percent of other public schools in California.
Key: Eng (English), Ma (Math), Sci (Science).

Grade	Eng	Ma	Sci
Forest Hill Elem. (San Jose)			
2	75	83	
3	75	85	
4	82	80	
5	74	85	70
Lynhaven Elem. (San Jose)			
2	56	47	
3	51	41	
4	47	60	
5	32	13	27
Marshall Lane Elem. (Saratoga)			
2	98	95	
3	93	91	
4	87	85	
5	98	97	94
Monroe Middle (San Jose)			
5	57	45	64
6	53	63	
7	53	65	
8	63		
Rolling Hills Middle (Los Gatos)			
5	87	83	93
6	89	82	
7	88	86	
8	85		
Rosemary Elem. (Campbell)			
2	31	18	
3	8	9	
4	22	28	
Sherman Oaks Elem. (San Jose)			
2	19	44	
3	36	45	
4	14	23	
5	11	15	22
6	10	69	
Village School			
2	66	30	
4	95	82	
5	86	55	69

Campbell Union High School Dist.

Grade	Eng	Ma	Sci
Boynton High (San Jose)			
10	20		
11	16		
Branham High (San Jose)			
9	81		
10	83		
11	73		
Camden Comm. Day (San Jose)			
9	14		
10	52		
Del Mar High (San Jose)			
9	63		
10	61		
11	60		
Leigh High (San Jose)			
9	91		
10	91		
11	89		

Grade	Eng	Ma	Sci
Prospect High (San Jose)			
9	81		
10	79		
11	70		
Westmont High (Campbell)			
9	79		
10	85		
11	79		

Cupertino Union School Dist.

Grade	Eng	Ma	Sci
Abraham Lincoln Elem. (Cupertino)			
2	99	99	
3	97	99	
4	98	99	
5	97	98	96
6	97	97	
Blue Hills Elem. (Saratoga)			
2	99	98	
3	98	97	
4	98	98	
5	99	99	98
6	97	99	
Collins Elem. (Cupertino)			
2	95	97	
3	98	98	
4	96	98	
5	98	98	96
6	98	99	
Cupertino Middle (Sunnyvale)			
6	93	94	
7	96	96	
8	97		
De Vargas Elem. (San Jose)			
2	71	74	
3	74	81	
4	84	95	
5	71	82	53
6	64	86	
Dilworth Elem. (San Jose)			
2	99	99	
3	99	99	
4	99	99	
5	99	99	98
Eaton Elem. (Cupertino)			
2	94	92	
3	97	97	
4	99	99	
5	97	97	96
6	95	99	
Eisenhower Elem. (Santa Clara)			
2	91	94	
3	88	89	
4	91	90	
5	88	83	93
6	89	84	
Faria Elem. (Cupertino)			
2	99	99	
3	99	99	
4	99	99	
5	99	99	99

Scores range from 1-99. A school scoring 75 has done better than 75 percent of other public schools in California.
Key: Eng (English), Ma (Math), Sci (Science).

Grade	Eng	Ma	Sci
Garden Gate Elem. (Cupertino)			
2	99	99	
3	98	97	
4	99	99	
5	98	98	97
6	97	97	
Hyde Middle (Cupertino)			
6	90	97	
7	87	90	
8	86		
Kennedy Middle (Cupertino)			
6	99	99	
7	99	99	
8	99		
McAuliffe Elem. (Saratoga)			
2	81	83	
3	72		
4	91	67	
5	96	66	90
6	90	90	
7	94	96	
Meyerholz Elem. (San Jose)			
2	93	95	
3	96	96	
4	98	97	
5	98	98	98
Miller Middle (San Jose)			
6	98	99	
7	98	99	
8	98		
Montclaire Elem. (Los Altos)			
2	99	99	
3	97	96	
4	98	99	
5	99	96	97
Muir Elem. (San Jose)			
2	93	97	
3	84	97	
4	89	96	
5	89	96	78
6	55	84	
Murdock-Portal Elem. (Cupertino)			
2	97	99	
3	99	99	
4	99	99	
5	99	99	99
Nimitz Elem. (Sunnyvale)			
2	57	75	
3	69	86	
4	75	85	
5	60	73	53
Regnart Elem. (Cupertino)			
2	97	98	
3	99	98	
4	99	99	
5	98	99	96

Grade	Eng	Ma	Sci
Sedgwick Elem. (Cupertino)			
2	77	74	
3	82	88	
4	92	92	
5	92	94	80
6	77	80	
Stevens Creek Elem. (Sunnyvale)			
2	98	98	
3	99	96	
4	97	97	
5	98	98	98
6	96	96	
Stocklmeir Elem. (Sunnyvale)			
2	97	98	
3	99	98	
4	93	88	
5	98	98	96
West Valley Elem. (Sunnyvale)			
2	95	98	
3	92	89	
4	95	96	
5	98	97	97
6	94	97	

East Side Union High School Dist.

Grade	Eng	Ma	Sci
Alt. Placement Academy			
9	3		3
10	13		6
11	11		
Apollo High (Cont.) (San Jose)			
11	20		
Escuela Popular (San Jose)			
2	1	15	
3	4	76	
4	4	3	
5	4	3	4
9	3		
10	6		
Evergreen Valley High (San Jose)			
9	90		
10	95		
11	90		
Foothill High (San Jose)			
11	15		
Genesis High (Cont.) (San Jose)			
11	62		
Hill High (San Jose)			
9	52		
10	51		
11	51		
Independence High (San Jose)			
9	66		
10	64		
11	67		
Latino College (San Jose)			
9	29		
10	25		
11	27		

Scores range from 1-99. A school scoring 75 has done better than 75 percent of other public schools in California.
Key: Eng (English), Ma (Math), Sci (Science).

Grade	Eng	Ma	Sci
Lick High (San Jose)			
9	27		
10	33		
11	37		
MACSA Academia (San Jose)			
9	21		
10	31		
11	17		
Mt. Pleasant High (San Jose)			
9	65		
10	55		
11	57		
Oak Grove High (San Jose)			
9	54		
10	59		
11	64		
Overfelt High (San Jose)			
9	36		
10	38		
11	42		
Pegasus High (Cont.) (San Jose)			
11	22		
Phoenix High (Cont.) (San Jose)			
11	3		
Piedmont Hills High (San Jose)			
9	88		
10	87		
11	89		
Santa Teresa High (San Jose)			
9	85		
10	77		
11	73		
Silver Creek High (San Jose)			
9	70		
10	71		
11	73		
Yerba Buena High (San Jose)			
9	32		
10	33		
11	37		

Evergreen Elem. School Dist.

Grade	Eng	Ma	Sci
Cadwallader Elem. (San Jose)			
2	63	60	
3	55	49	
4	53	48	
5	78	78	72
6	65	73	
Carolyn A. Clark Elem.			
2	89	93	
3	94	94	
4	97	96	
5	94	95	93
6	89	90	
Cedar Grove Elem. (San Jose)			
2	71	82	
3	81	80	
4	59	57	
5	64	74	75
6	56	46	

Grade	Eng	Ma	Sci
Chaboya Middle (San Jose)			
7	90	90	
8	86		
Dove Hill Elem. (San Jose)			
2	61	56	
3	58	72	
4	56	50	
5	55	66	49
6	38	42	
Evergreen Elem. (San Jose)			
2	92	91	
3	88	93	
4	92	94	
5	92	89	94
6	81	85	
Holly Oak Elem. (San Jose)			
2	79	69	
3	64	59	
4	72	75	
5	64	57	59
6	71	48	
Laurelwood Elem. (San Jose)			
2	76	75	
3	65	79	
4	75	82	
5	75	71	74
6	81	72	
Leyva Int. (San Jose)			
6	55	61	
7	62	78	
8	56		
Matsumoto Elem. (San Jose)			
2	97	95	
3	92	93	
4	98	98	
5	96	96	98
6	98	98	
Millbrook Elem. (San Jose)			
2	87	80	
3	76	84	
4	77	78	
5	80	81	81
6	64	64	
Montgomery Elem. (San Jose)			
2	70	78	
3	76	87	
4	47	44	
5	45	36	41
6	54	59	
Norwood Creek Elem. (San Jose)			
2	68	64	
3	75	84	
4	80	81	
5	72	72	78
6	91	89	
Quimby Oak Int. (San Jose)			
7	85	88	
8	74		

Scores range from 1-99. A school scoring 75 has done better than 75 percent of other public schools in California.
Key: Eng (English), Ma (Math), Sci (Science).

Grade	Eng	Ma	Sci
Silver Oak Elem. (San Jose)			
2	94	97	
3	97	96	
4	99	98	
5	98	97	97
6	99	99	
Smith Elem. (San Jose)			
2	99	99	
3	96	98	
4	98	98	
5	97	97	98
6	95	95	
Smith Elem. (San Jose)			
2	66	57	
3	37	42	
4	47	60	
5	57	46	47
6	60	74	
Whaley Elem. (San Jose)			
2	58	68	
3	53	69	
4	62	76	
5	57	83	69

Franklin-McKinley Elem. School Dist.

Grade	Eng	Ma	Sci
Dahl Elem. (San Jose)			
2	29	47	
3	21	26	
4	35	45	
5	16	14	34
6	41	37	
Fair Jr. High (San Jose)			
7	28	42	
8	49		
Franklin Elem. (San Jose)			
2	52	61	
3	55	74	
4	30	29	
5	47	65	46
6	40	32	
Hellyer Elem. (San Jose)			
2	50	53	
3	37	49	
4	45	45	
5	47	57	63
6	50	72	
Kennedy Elem. (San Jose)			
2	34	24	
3	26	46	
4	38	49	
5	47	64	55
6	48	40	
Los Arboles Elem. (San Jose)			
2	21	33	
3	16	21	
4	16	17	
5	3	6	7
6	15	15	

Grade	Eng	Ma	Sci
McKinley Elem. (San Jose)			
2	9	13	
3	11	15	
4	8	21	
5	3	12	15
6	4	4	
Meadows Elem. (San Jose)			
2	43	35	
3	39	33	
4	35	29	
5	55	76	57
6	51	70	
Santee Elem. (San Jose)			
2	16	56	
3	9	17	
4	4	4	
5	5	10	6
6	14	8	
Seven Trees Elem. (San Jose)			
2	9	11	
3	13	18	
4	11	16	
5	22	25	41
6	20	13	
Shirakawa Elem. (San Jose)			
2	43	42	
3	36	31	
4	25	20	
5	23	42	29
6	60	52	
7	55	71	
8	49		
Stonegate Elem. (San Jose)			
2	60	49	
3	51	68	
4	53	49	
5	32	30	27
6	55	48	
Sylvandale Jr. High (San Jose)			
7	50	57	
8	36		
Windmill Springs Elem. (San Jose)			
2	76	88	
3	35	52	
4	30	37	
5	50	79	83
6	50	73	
7	28	34	
8	36		

Fremont Union High School Dist.

Grade	Eng	Ma	Sci
Cupertino High			
9	91		
10	91		
11	91		
Fremont High (Sunnyvale)			
9	62		
10	66		
11	68		

Scores range from 1-99. A school scoring 75 has done better than 75 percent of other public schools in California.
Key: Eng (English), Ma (Math), Sci (Science).

Grade	Eng	Ma	Sci
Homestead High (Cupertino)			
9	96		
10	95		
11	89		
Lynbrook High (San Jose)			
9	98		
10	98		
11	99		
Monta Vista High (Cupertino)			
9	99		
10	99		
11	98		
Gilroy Unified School Dist.			
Aprea Elem.			
2	84	70	
3	89	85	
4	76	76	
5	77	82	66
Brownell Middle			
6	50	39	
7	55	46	
8	55		
Del Buono Elem.			
2	62	53	
3	65	40	
4	60	47	
5	50	37	39
El Roble Elem.			
2	58	61	
3	32	31	
4	29	38	
5	32	22	16
Eliot Elem.			
2	33	40	
3	27	47	
4	26	36	
5	17	6	9
Gilroy Comm. Day			
8	3		
Gilroy High			
9	66		
10	69		
11	67		
Glen View Elem.			
2	19	15	
3	48	72	
4	25	33	
5	36	42	24
Kelley Rod Elem.			
2	35	31	
3	43	58	
4	52	35	
5	49	39	28
Las Animas Elem.			
2	38	47	
3	48	58	
4	18	19	
5	39	7	24

Grade	Eng	Ma	Sci
MACSA El Portal			
9	18		
10	26		
Mt. Madonna High (Cont.)			
10	40		
11	30		
Rucker Elem.			
2	28	32	
3	44	36	
4	50	43	
5	56	43	60
Solorsano Middle			
6	61	44	
7	73	61	
South Valley Middle			
6	40	23	
7	38	32	
8	39		
Lakeside Joint Elem. School Dist.			
Lakeside Elem. (Los Gatos)			
2	84	96	
3	89	95	
4	97	95	
5	99	99	97
Loma Prieta Joint Union Elem. Sch. Dist.			
English Middle (Los Gatos)			
6	95	87	
7	97	92	
8	99		
Loma Prieta Elem. (Los Gatos)			
2	75	86	
3	82	75	
4	89	88	
5	95	97	98
Los Altos Elem. School Dist.			
Almond Elem.			
2	99	98	
3	99	99	
4	99	98	
5	99	98	98
6	99	99	
Blach Int.			
7	99	98	
8	99		
Covington Elem.			
2	95	98	
3	98	99	
4	99	99	
5	99	98	98
6	99	99	
Egan Int.			
7	99	99	
8	99		

Scores range from 1-99. A school scoring 75 has done better than 75 percent of other public schools in California.
Key: Eng (English), Ma (Math), Sci (Science).

Loyola Elem.

Grade	Eng	Ma	Sci
2	99	99	
3	99	98	
4	98	96	
5	99	99	98
6	99	99	

Oak Ave. Elem.

Grade	Eng	Ma	Sci
2	99	98	
3	99	97	
4	99	99	
5	99	99	99
6	99	99	

Santa Rita Elem.

Grade	Eng	Ma	Sci
2	98	98	
3	99	99	
4	99	98	
5	99	99	99
6	99	99	

Springer Elem. (Mountain View)

Grade	Eng	Ma	Sci
2	97	97	
3	98	95	
4	99	99	
5	99	98	99
6	99	98	

Los Gatos Union Elem. School Dist.

Blossom Hill Elem. (Los Altos)

Grade	Eng	Ma	Sci
2	97	95	
3	93	88	
4	96	88	
5	97	96	98

Daves Ave. Elem. (Los Altos)

Grade	Eng	Ma	Sci
2	93	84	
3	98	90	
4	95	87	
5	97	82	97

Fisher Middle (Los Altos)

Grade	Eng	Ma	Sci
6	95	93	
7	96	95	
8	97		

Lexington Elem. (Los Altos)

Grade	Eng	Ma	Sci
2	91	86	
3	93	86	
4	94	91	
5	96	98	98

Louise Van Meter Elem. (Los Altos)

Grade	Eng	Ma	Sci
2	94	79	
3	94	88	
4	93	85	
5	90	81	90

Los Gatos-Saratoga High Sch. Dist.

Los Gatos High (Los Gatos)

Grade	Eng	Ma	Sci
9	97		
10	98		
11	97		

Saratoga High (Saratoga)

Grade	Eng	Ma	Sci
9	99		
10	99		
11	99		

Luther Burbank Elem. School Dist.

Luther Burbank Elem. (San Jose)

Grade	Eng	Ma	Sci
2	30	23	
3	38	43	
4	31	80	
5	16	44	27
6	26	22	
7	23	33	
8	14		

Milpitas Unified School Dist.

Burnett Elem.

Grade	Eng	Ma	Sci
2	74	82	
3	63	74	
4	60	64	
5	70	87	64
6	45	63	

Calaveras Hills Cont. High

Grade	Eng	Ma	Sci
10	41		
11	28		

Curtner Elem.

Grade	Eng	Ma	Sci
2	83	82	
3	86	86	
4	87	88	
5	81	87	70
6	93	96	

Milpitas Comm. Day

Grade	Eng	Ma	Sci
12	1		

Milpitas High

Grade	Eng	Ma	Sci
9	80		
10	82		
11	85		

Pomeroy Elem.

Grade	Eng	Ma	Sci
2	81	81	
3	84	88	
4	81	83	
5	92	95	93
6	82	90	

Rancho Milpitas Jr. High

Grade	Eng	Ma	Sci
7	63	76	
8	74		

Randall Elem.

Grade	Eng	Ma	Sci
2	14	11	
3	42	55	
4	40	36	
5	41	28	42
6	52	55	

Rose Elem.

Grade	Eng	Ma	Sci
2	16	41	
3	50	54	
4	47	47	
5	59	49	89
6	60	49	

Russell Jr. High

Grade	Eng	Ma	Sci
7	79	89	
8	83		

Scores range from 1-99. A school scoring 75 has done better than 75 percent of other public schools in California.
Key: Eng (English), Ma (Math), Sci (Science).

Grade	Eng	Ma	Sci
Sinnott Elem.			
2	71	78	
3	80	90	
4	82	84	
5	80	82	85
6	85	85	
Spangler Elem.			
2	48	42	
3	79	78	
4	61	40	
5	80	71	70
6	68	77	
Weller Elem.			
2	42	53	
3	79	71	
4	81	86	
5	64	76	61
6	57	69	
Zanker Elem.			
2	81	83	
3	58	66	
4	71	76	
5	78	68	73
6	82	74	

Moreland Elem. School Dist. (San Jose)

Grade	Eng	Ma	Sci
Anderson Elem.			
2	8	4	
3	20	28	
4	32	11	
5	16	19	17
Baker Elem.			
2	90	90	
3	93	78	
4	91	95	
5	88	88	88
Castro Middle			
6	84	85	
7	76	85	
8	85		
Country Lane Elem.			
2	95	95	
3	98	94	
4	98	98	
5	95	84	95
Easterbrook Discovery Elem.			
2	86	90	
3	87	90	
4	89	80	
5	86	81	89
Latimer Elem.			
2	84	66	
3	90	95	
4	90	93	
5	87	93	90
Payne Elem.			
2	95	92	
3	89	81	
4	85	82	
5	81	72	84

Grade	Eng	Ma	Sci
Rogers Middle			
6	71	71	
7	73	89	
8	79		

Morgan Hill Unified School Dist.

Grade	Eng	Ma	Sci
Advent Academy			
11	3		
Ann Sobrato High			
9	79		
10	75		
Barrett Elem.			
2	62	53	
3	45	38	
4	48	8	
5	72	68	66
6	65	61	
Britton Middle			
7	65	77	
8	63		
Burnett Elem.			
2	22	33	
3	47	47	
4	24	13	
5	30	10	18
6	41	58	
Central High (Cont.)			
10	5		
11	28		
Char. School of Morgan Hill			
2	90	92	
3	85	75	
4	96	86	
5	71	35	60
6	69	54	
7	78	65	
8	79		
El Toro Elem.			
2	61	41	
3	49	26	
4	67	35	
5	64	28	56
6	74	70	
Jackson Elem.			
2	61	38	
3	75	69	
4	75	58	
5	57	45	67
6	76	64	
Live Oak High			
9	72		
10	83		
11	82		
Los Paseos Elem. (San Jose)			
2	74	71	
3	74	78	
4	58	27	
5	73	63	71
6	67	53	

Scores range from 1-99. A school scoring 75 has done better than 75 percent of other public schools in California.
Key: Eng (English), Ma (Math), Sci (Science).

Grade	Eng	Ma	Sci
Murphy Middle (San Jose)			
7	79	75	
8	71		
Nordstrom Elem.			
2	77	76	
3	80	82	
4	88	80	
5	89	89	86
6	94	89	
Paradise Valley/Machado Elem.			
2	74	72	
3	73	52	
4	70	35	
5	85	68	89
6	83	74	
San Martin/Gwinn Elem. (San Martin)			
2	15	16	
3	33	26	
4	49	44	
5	57	68	67
6	28	19	
Walsh Elem.			
2	48	25	
3	39	27	
4	48	41	
5	49	28	44
6	50	61	

Mountain View-Los Altos High Sch. Dist.

Alta Vista High (Cont.) (Mountain View)

Grade	Eng	Ma	Sci
10	38		
11	37		
Los Altos High (Mountain View)			
9	93		
10	93		
11	95		
Mountain View High (Mountain View)			
9	95		
10	97		
11	93		

Mountain View-Whisman Elem. Sch. Dist. (Mountain View)

Grade	Eng	Ma	Sci
Bubb Elem.			
2	86	87	
3	89	89	
4	91	95	
5	86	85	90
Castro Elem.			
2	4	10	
3	9	14	
4	17	32	
5	31	50	53
Crittenden Middle			
6	45	45	
7	69	60	
8	58		

Grade	Eng	Ma	Sci
Graham Middle			
6	61	58	
7	72	82	
8	77		
Huff Elem.			
2	99	99	
3	98	99	
4	96	97	
5	98	99	99
Landels Elem.			
2	60	55	
3	80	81	
4	85	92	
5	79	78	78
Monta Loma			
2	84	86	
3	58	42	
4	60	40	
5	64	56	78
Slater Elem.			
2	41	58	
3	77	59	
4	59	39	
5	43	30	61
Theuerkauf Elem.			
2	64	52	
3	45	30	
4	54	55	
5	30	20	43

Mt. Pleasant Elem. School Dist. (San Jose)

Grade	Eng	Ma	Sci
Boeger Jr. High			
7	44	45	
8	48		
Jew Int.			
4	40	34	
5	48	47	56
6	44	44	
Mt. Pleasant Elem.			
2	33	33	
3	57	55	
Sanders Elem.			
2	25	30	
3	31	39	
Valle Vista Elem.			
2	98	99	
3	49	52	

Oak Grove Elem. School Dist. (San Jose)

Grade	Eng	Ma	Sci
Anderson Elem.			
2	68	48	
3	63	77	
4	54	49	
5	56	50	56
6	65	57	

Scores range from 1-99. A school scoring 75 has done better than 75 percent of other public schools in California.
Key: Eng (English), Ma (Math), Sci (Science).

Grade	Eng	Ma	Sci
Baldwin Elem.			
2	72	78	
3	56	68	
4	65	47	
5	58	32	39
6	69	54	
Bernal Int.			
7	66	75	
8	74		
Christopher Elem.			
2	9	15	
3	14	18	
4	22	15	
5	31	41	39
6	35	26	
Davis Elem.			
7	56	73	
8	63		
Del Roble Elem.			
2	54	39	
3	40	56	
4	46	38	
5	52	43	44
6	45	37	
Edenvale Elem.			
2	37	53	
3	38	55	
4	33	70	
5	21	47	47
6	37	39	
Frost Elem.			
2	73	68	
3	76	38	
4	37	15	
5	41	14	48
6	51	30	
Glider Elem.			
2	79	76	
3	78	80	
4	67	69	
5	75	58	55
6	70	73	
Hayes Elem.			
2	73	89	
3	56	48	
4	61	39	
5	62	25	59
6	55	35	
Herman Int.			
7	67	78	
8	68		
Ledesma Elem.			
2	65	71	
3	75	89	
4	52	71	
5	77	78	63
6	63	73	

Grade	Eng	Ma	Sci
Miner Elem.			
2	63	82	
3	57	65	
4	51	53	
5	34	31	26
6	32	24	
Oak Ridge Elem.			
2	80	78	
3	84	84	
4	69	70	
5	83	90	66
6	83	84	
Parkview Elem.			
2	89	86	
3	72	73	
4	60	69	
5	72	71	56
6	59	61	
Sakamoto Elem.			
2	79	80	
3	94	91	
4	93	94	
5	83	81	72
6	94	88	
Santa Teresa Elem.			
2	63	45	
3	66	70	
4	77	75	
5	68	56	70
6	77	77	
Stipe Elem.			
2	34	62	
3	32	41	
4	39	59	
5	45	44	14
6	31	34	
Taylor (Bertha) Elem.			
2	93	95	
3	75	81	
4	79	80	
5	74	71	76
6	78	68	
The Academy			
8	7		

Orchard Elem. School Dist.
Orchard Elem. (San Jose)

Grade	Eng	Ma	Sci
2	52	56	
3	51	45	
4	55	38	
5	62	65	60
6	62	53	
7	47	34	
8	53		

Scores range from 1-99. A school scoring 75 has done better than 75 percent of other public schools in California.
Key: Eng (English), Ma (Math), Sci (Science).

Palo Alto Unified School Dist.

Grade	Eng	Ma	Sci
Addison Elem.			
2	93	91	
3	98	92	
4	98	99	
5	97	96	92
Barron Park Elem.			
2	81	83	
3	78	73	
4	87	74	
5	93	82	94
Briones Elem.			
2	90	85	
3	84	81	
4	92	98	
5	95	94	93
Duveneck Elem.			
2	95	96	
3	99	99	
4	99	98	
5	99	97	99
El Carmelo Elem.			
2	82	87	
3	99	96	
4	93	88	
5	97	98	97
Escondido Elem. (Stanford)			
2	82	97	
3	94	92	
4	98	99	
5	99	99	99
Fairmeadow Elem.			
2	93	99	
3	97	93	
4	97	96	
5	94	89	95
Gunn High			
9	99		
10	98		
11	97		
Hays Elem.			
2	99	99	
3	99	97	
4	96	93	
5	98	96	96
Hoover Elem.			
2	95	97	
3	99	99	
4	99	97	
5	99	99	99
Jordan Middle			
6	97	97	
7	97	96	
8	98		
Nixon Elem.			
2	88	89	
3	96	91	
4	99	99	
5	99	99	98

Grade	Eng	Ma	Sci
Ohlone Elem.			
2	88	89	
3	96	86	
4	97	93	
5	97	91	98
Palo Alto High			
9	99		
10	99		
11	98		
Palo Verde Elem.			
2	97	96	
3	96	93	
4	91	89	
5	97	95	94
Stanford Middle			
6	90	87	
7	96	98	
8	98		
Terman Middle			
6	99	99	
7	98	98	
8	98		

San Jose Unified School Dist. (San Jose)

Grade	Eng	Ma	Sci
Allen Elem.			
2	23	45	
3	59	53	
4	38	24	
5	34	12	35
Almaden Elem.			
2	17	55	
3	19	41	
4	23	34	
5	35	30	45
Bachrodt Elem.			
2	19	34	
3	3	7	
4	7	27	
5	9	21	13
Booksin Elem.			
2	93	89	
3	85	92	
4	94	94	
5	86	87	82
Broadway High (Cont.)			
10	7		
11	9		
Burnett Middle			
6	11	12	
7	15	15	
8	21		
Canoas Elem.			
2	56	70	
3	57	76	
4	36	26	
5	28	16	35

Scores range from 1-99. A school scoring 75 has done better than 75 percent of other public schools in California.
Key: Eng (English), Ma (Math), Sci (Science).

Carson Elem.

Grade	Eng	Ma	Sci
2	64	62	
3	67	78	
4	63	59	
5	62	64	60

Castillero Middle

Grade	Eng	Ma	Sci
6	78	67	
7	85	80	
8	83		

Comm. Career Academy

Grade	Eng	Ma	Sci
11	16		

Cory Elem.

Grade	Eng	Ma	Sci
2	32	34	

Darling Elem.

Grade	Eng	Ma	Sci
2	43	64	
3	11	15	
4	7	11	
5	17	17	22

Downtown College Prep.

Grade	Eng	Ma	Sci
9	40		
10	49		
11	73		

Empire Gardens Elem.

Grade	Eng	Ma	Sci
2	5	5	
3	4	10	
4	27	46	
5	10	14	14

Galarza (Ernesto) Elem.

Grade	Eng	Ma	Sci
2	25	32	
3	18	25	
4	26	18	
5	23	8	36

Gardner Elem.

Grade	Eng	Ma	Sci
2	4	8	
3	3	7	
4	6	15	
5	3	5	4

Grant Elem.

Grade	Eng	Ma	Sci
2	28	49	
3	30	49	
4	31	22	
5	35	41	41

Graystone Elem.

Grade	Eng	Ma	Sci
2	96	95	
3	92	92	
4	98	97	
5	97	96	98

Gunderson High

Grade	Eng	Ma	Sci
9	40		
10	58		
11	58		

Gunderson Plus (Cont.)

Grade	Eng	Ma	Sci
11	28		

Hacienda Magnet

Grade	Eng	Ma	Sci
2	76	77	
3	88	69	
4	87	77	
5	78	51	86

Hammer Montessori at Galarza

Grade	Eng	Ma	Sci
2	75	68	
3	66	46	
4	59	26	
5	79	58	88

Harte Middle

Grade	Eng	Ma	Sci
6	97	96	
7	96	98	
8	95		

Hoover Middle

Grade	Eng	Ma	Sci
6	25	22	
7	30	29	
8	34		

Leland High

Grade	Eng	Ma	Sci
9	97		
10	97		
11	98		

Leland Plus (Cont.)

Grade	Eng	Ma	Sci
11	54		

Liberty High (Alt.)

Grade	Eng	Ma	Sci
8	12		
9	45		
10	40		
11	23		

Lincoln High

Grade	Eng	Ma	Sci
9	63		
10	76		
11	69		

Lincoln Plus High

Grade	Eng	Ma	Sci
11	26		

Los Alamitos Elem.

Grade	Eng	Ma	Sci
2	95	89	
3	98	88	
4	98	95	
5	97	91	95

Lowell Elem.

Grade	Eng	Ma	Sci
2	13	36	
3	12	21	
4	20	31	
5	33	20	19

Mann Elem.

Grade	Eng	Ma	Sci
2	9	36	
3	27	28	
4	24	41	
5	28	57	32

Middle College High

Grade	Eng	Ma	Sci
11	64		

Muir Middle

Grade	Eng	Ma	Sci
6	60	51	
7	60	57	
8	60		

Olinder Elem.

Grade	Eng	Ma	Sci
2	3	4	
3	7	9	
4	7	4	
5	16	7	21

Scores range from 1-99. A school scoring 75 has done better than 75 percent of other public schools in California.
Key: Eng (English), Ma (Math), Sci (Science).

Grade	Eng	Ma	Sci
Pioneer High			
9	86		
10	88		
11	90		
Pioneer Plus (Cont.)			
11	34		
Randol Elem.			
2	82	79	
3	85	82	
4	85	83	
5	87	87	85
Reed Elem.			
2	74	70	
3	78	64	
4	67	52	
5	81	60	83
River Glen Elem.			
2	60	59	
3	47	33	
4	66	63	
5	67	50	51
6	47	25	
7	80	80	
8	83		
San Jose Comm. High			
9	8		
10	7		
11	16		
San Jose Comm. Middle			
8	1		
San Jose High Acad. Plus			
11	36		
San Jose High Academy			
9	51		
10	54		
11	59		
Schallenberger Elem.			
2	56	68	
3	66	79	
4	63	74	
5	69	69	70
Simonds Elem.			
2	97	96	
3	95	93	
4	92	90	
5	94	85	91
Steinbeck Middle			
6	27	20	
7	24	18	
8	30		
Terrell Elem.			
2	69	70	
3	38	33	
4	53	44	
5	71	57	57
Trace Elem.			
3	49	54	
4	50	59	
5	41	53	45

Grade	Eng	Ma	Sci
Washington Elem.			
2	6	36	
3	4	6	
4	6	35	
5	9	19	6
Williams Elem.			
2	99	99	
3	98	99	
4	98	97	
5	98	98	99
Willow Glen Elem.			
2	48	68	
3	56	36	
4	52	42	
5	47	42	42
Willow Glen High			
9	48		
10	53		
11	60		
Willow Glen Middle			
6	33	18	
7	38	29	
8	42		
Willow Glen Plus (Cont.)			
11	23		

Santa Clara Unified School Dist.

Grade	Eng	Ma	Sci
Bowers Elem.			
2	41	44	
3	51	66	
4	60	62	
5	51	47	82
Bracher Elem.			
2	77	78	
3	73	85	
4	78	82	
5	54	64	44
Braly Elem.			
2	56	59	
3	66	50	
4	65	61	
5	67	59	64
Briarwood Elem.			
2	58	43	
3	42	25	
4	67	86	
5	57	31	63
Buchser Middle			
6	58	48	
7	48	41	
8	49		
Cabrillo Middle			
6	52	40	
7	47	47	
8	44		
Haman Elem.			
2	37	30	
3	25	18	
4	54	50	
5	56	21	43

Scores range from 1-99. A school scoring 75 has done better than 75 percent of other public schools in California.
Key: Eng (English), Ma (Math), Sci (Science).

Grade	Eng	Ma	Sci	Grade	Eng	Ma	Sci
Hughes Elem.				**Washington Elem.**			
2	51	36		2	76	85	
3	46	40		3	84	60	
4	47	29		4	81	72	
5	50	40	48	5	90	75	96
Laurelwood Elem.				**Westwood Elem.**			
2	79	82		2	35	29	
3	91	88		3	44	24	
4	88	89		4	53	17	
5	85	77	93	5	60	20	67
Mayne Elem.				**Wilcox High**			
2	41	42		9	50		
3	62	82		10	73		
4	49	43		11	72		
5	40	28	55	**Wilson Alt.**			
Millikin Elem.				9	68		
2	99	99		10	50		
3	99	99		11	29		
4	99	99					
5	99	99	99	**Saratoga Union Elem. School Dist.**			
Montague Elem.				**Argonaut Elem.**			
2	57	71		2	99	98	
3	41	29		3	96	97	
4	49	38		4	95	98	
5	37	39	51	5	99	99	99
New Valley Cont. High				**Foothill Elem.**			
9	16			2	96	98	
10	21			3	98	96	
11	15			4	98	98	
Peterson Middle				5	99	99	98
6	72	70		**Redwood Middle**			
7	72	79		6	99	98	
8	75			7	99	98	
Pomeroy Elem.				8	99		
2	46	38		**Saratoga Elem.**			
3	60	57		2	98	98	
4	61	60		3	98	98	
5	58	29	60	4	99	99	
Ponderosa Elem.				5	99	97	99
2	79	76					
3	71	71		**Sunnyvale Elem. School Dist.**			
4	76	73		**Bishop Elem.**			
5	82	64	75	2	37	28	
Santa Clara High				3	57	58	
9	65			4	55	33	
10	70			5	56	57	56
11	77			**Cherry Chase Elem.**			
Scott Lane Elem.				2	98	96	
2	50	57		3	95	96	
3	52	51		4	96	90	
4	32	40		5	91	93	91
5	24	35	37	**Columbia Middle**			
Sutter Elem.				6	55	47	
2	72	68		7	50	53	
3	85	79		8	51		
4	81	75		**Cumberland Elem.**			
5	65	27	65	2	94	93	
				3	95	97	
				4	82	78	
				5	79	86	84

Scores range from 1-99. A school scoring 75 has done better than 75 percent of other public schools in California.
Key: Eng (English), Ma (Math), Sci (Science).

Grade	Eng	Ma	Sci
	Ellis Elem.		
2	68	38	
3	49	30	
4	70	71	
5	76	82	55
	Fairwood Elem.		
2	61	45	
3	48	53	
4	70	78	
5	62	69	66
	Lakewood Elem.		
2	61	47	
3	54	64	
4	59	44	
5	54	20	45
	San Miguel Elem.		
2	34	22	
3	64	51	
4	51	43	
5	65	69	56
	Sunnyvale Middle		
6	75	76	
7	81	86	
8	80		
	Vargas Elem.		
2	42	21	
3	31	18	
4	66	46	
5	72	53	70

Grade	Eng	Ma	Sci
	Union Elem. School Dist.		
	Alta Vista Elem. (Los Gatos)		
2	77	81	
3	83	83	
4	92	88	
5	91	81	93
	Carlton Elem. (San Jose)		
2	78	86	
3	82	83	
4	87	83	
5	86	81	89
	Dartmouth Middle (San Jose)		
6	83	78	
7	82	81	
8	84		
	Guadalupe Elem. (San Jose)		
2	96	88	
3	97	92	
4	91	90	
5	97	90	94
	Lietz Elem. (San Jose)		
2	59	50	
3	75	69	
4	80	74	
5	73	40	68
	Noddin Elem. (San Jose)		
2	85	85	
3	91	96	
4	94	94	
5	84	77	85
	Oster Elem. (San Jose)		
2	70	53	
3	79	72	
4	80	84	
5	89	91	87
	Union Middle (San Jose)		
6	85	82	
7	89	87	
8	83		

Chapter **2b**

State 1 to 10 Rankings

FOR EASE OF COMPREHENSION, the California Department of Education has worked out a system to rank schools by their test scores.

This system takes several forms, the simplest of which is a ranking of 1 to 10.

One is the lowest score, ten is the highest.

This chapter lists the rankings for just about every school in the county.

Keep in mind that this is a crude representation of how the schools are scoring. If you combine this data with the rankings in Chapter 2a and the SAT scores and other data in Chapter 7, you will have a more rounded picture of the scores at each school.

Nonetheless, the scores can still mislead. Almost every school, even those at the bottom, will graduate students who score at the top.

Almost every school with scores at the top will graduate kids who score at the bottom and the middle.

For a general discussion of scores and what they mean, read the chapter on How Public Schools Work.

School	District	City/Town	Rank
Arbuckle Elem.	Alum Rock Union Elem.	San Jose	4
Cassell Elem.	Alum Rock Union Elem.	San Jose	5
Chavez Elem.	Alum Rock Union Elem.	San Jose	2
Cureton Elem.	Alum Rock Union Elem.	San Jose	4
Dorsa Elem.	Alum Rock Union Elem.	San Jose	1
Goss Elem.	Alum Rock Union Elem.	San Jose	1
Hubbard Elem.	Alum Rock Union Elem.	San Jose	2
Linda Vista Elem.	Alum Rock Union Elem.	San Jose	5
Lyndale Elem.	Alum Rock Union Elem.	San Jose	4
McCollam Elem.	Alum Rock Union Elem.	San Jose	8
Meyer Elem.	Alum Rock Union Elem.	San Jose	3
Painter Elem.	Alum Rock Union Elem.	San Jose	6
Rogers Elem.	Alum Rock Union Elem.	San Jose	2
Ryan Elem.	Alum Rock Union Elem.	San Jose	4
San Antonio Elem.	Alum Rock Union Elem.	San Jose	4
Shields Elem.	Alum Rock Union Elem.	San Jose	2
Slonaker Elem.	Alum Rock Union Elem.	San Jose	1
Fischer Middle	Alum Rock Union Elem.	San Jose	2
George Middle	Alum Rock Union Elem.	San Jose	3
Mathson Middle	Alum Rock Union Elem.	San Jose	2
Ocala Middle	Alum Rock Union Elem.	San Jose	4
Pala Middle	Alum Rock Union Elem.	San Jose	2
Sheppard Middle	Alum Rock Union Elem.	San Jose	3
Brooktree Elem.	Berryessa Union Elem.	San Jose	8
Cherrywood Elem.	Berryessa Union Elem.	San Jose	7
Laneview Elem.	Berryessa Union Elem.	San Jose	7
Majestic Way Elem.	Berryessa Union Elem.	San Jose	7
Noble Elem.	Berryessa Union Elem.	San Jose	8
Northwood Elem.	Berryessa Union Elem.	San Jose	7
Ruskin Elem.	Berryessa Union Elem.	San Jose	9
Summerdale Elem.	Berryessa Union Elem.	San Jose	6
Toyon Elem.	Berryessa Union Elem.	San Jose	4
Vinci Park Elem.	Berryessa Union Elem.	San Jose	6
Morrill Middle	Berryessa Union Elem.	San Jose	8
Piedmont Middle	Berryessa Union Elem.	San Jose	7
Sierramont Middle	Berryessa Union Elem.	San Jose	9
Bagby Elem.	Cambrian Elem.	San Jose	10
Fammatre Elem.	Cambrian Elem.	San Jose	9

School	District	City/Town	Rank
Farnham Charter	Cambrian Elem.	San Jose	8
Sartorette Charter	Cambrian Elem.	San Jose	9
Price Charter Mid.	Cambrian Elem.	San Jose	9
Blackford Elem.	Campbell Union Elem.	San Jose	4
Capri Elem.	Campbell Union Elem.	Campbell	9
Castlemont Elem.	Campbell Union Elem.	Campbell	8
Forest Hill Elem.	Campbell Union Elem.	San Jose	9
Hazelwood Elem.	Campbell Union Elem.	Campbell	6
Lynhaven Elem.	Campbell Union Elem.	San Jose	7
Marshall Ln. Elem.	Campbell Union Elem.	Saratoga	10
Rosemary Elem.	Campbell Union Elem.	Campbell	3
Sherman Oaks Elem.	Campbell Union Elem.	San Jose	2
Campbell Middle	Campbell Union Elem.	Campbell	4
Monroe Middle	Campbell Union Elem.	San Jose	7
Rolling Hills Middle	Campbell Union Elem.	Los Gatos	9
Branham High	Campbell Union High	San Jose	8
Leigh High	Campbell Union High	San Jose	9
Prospect High	Campbell Union High	San Jose	6
Westmont High	Campbell Union High	Campbell	7
Blue Hills Elem.	Cupertino Union School	Saratoga	10
Collins Elem.	Cupertino Union School	Cupertino	10
De Vargas Elem.	Cupertino Union School	San Jose	9
Dilworth Elem.	Cupertino Union School	San Jose	10
Eaton Elem.	Cupertino Union School	Cupertino	10
Eisenhower Elem.	Cupertino Union School	Santa Clara	10
Faria Elem.	Cupertino Union School	Cupertino	10
Garden Gate Elem.	Cupertino Union School	Cupertino	10
Lincoln Elem.	Cupertino Union School	Cupertino	10
Meyerholz Elem.	Cupertino Union School	San Jose	10
Montclaire Elem.	Cupertino Union School	Los Altos	10
Muir Elem.	Cupertino Union School	San Jose	10
Murdock-Portal Elem.	Cupertino Union School	Cupertino	10
Nimitz Elem.	Cupertino Union School	Sunnyvale	8
Regnart Elem.	Cupertino Union School	Cupertino	10
Sedgwick Elem.	Cupertino Union School	Cupertino	9
Stevens Creek Elem.	Cupertino Union School	Sunnyvale	10
Stocklmeir Elem.	Cupertino Union School	Sunnyvale	10
West Valley Elem.	Cupertino Union School	Sunnyvale	10

School	District	City/Town	Rank
Cupertino Middle	Cupertino Union School	Sunnyvale	10
Hyde Middle	Cupertino Union School	Cupertino	9
Kennedy Middle	Cupertino Union School	Cupertino	10
Miller Middle	Cupertino Union School	San Jose	10
Escuela Popular	East Side Union High	San Jose	1
Evergreen Valley High	East Side Union High	San Jose	9
Hill High	East Side Union High	San Jose	4
Independence High	East Side Union High	San Jose	6
Latino Coll. Prep.	East Side Union High	San Jose	1
Lick High	East Side Union High	San Jose	2
MACSA Academia	East Side Union High	San Jose	2
Mt. Pleasant High	East Side Union High	San Jose	4
Oak Grove High	East Side Union High	San Jose	6
Overfelt High	East Side Union High	San Jose	3
Piedmont Hills High	East Side Union High	San Jose	9
Santa Teresa High	East Side Union High	San Jose	8
Silver Creek High	East Side Union High	San Jose	6
Yerba Buena High	East Side Union High	San Jose	3
Cadwallader Elem.	Evergreen Elem.	San Jose	8
Cedar Grove Elem.	Evergreen Elem.	San Jose	7
Dove Hill Elem.	Evergreen Elem.	San Jose	6
Evergreen Elem.	Evergreen Elem.	San Jose	10
Holly Oak Elem.	Evergreen Elem.	San Jose	7
Laurelwood Elem.	Evergreen Elem.	San Jose	8
Matsumoto Elem.	Evergreen Elem.	San Jose	10
Millbrook Elem.	Evergreen Elem.	San Jose	9
Montgomery Elem.	Evergreen Elem.	San Jose	7
Norwood Creek Elem.	Evergreen Elem.	San Jose	9
Silver Oak Elem.	Evergreen Elem.	San Jose	10
Smith (J.F.) Elem.	Evergreen Elem.	San Jose	10
Smith (K.R.) Elem.	Evergreen Elem.	San Jose	7
Whaley Elem.	Evergreen Elem.	San Jose	7
Chaboya Middle	Evergreen Elem.	San Jose	9
Levya Intermediate	Evergreen Elem.	San Jose	7
Quimby Oak Intermediate	Evergreen Elem.	San Jose	8
Captain Dahl Elem.	Franklin-McKinley Elem.	San Jose	3
Franklin Elem.	Franklin-McKinley Elem.	San Jose	4
Hellyer Elem.	Franklin-McKinley Elem.	San Jose	6

School	District	City/Town	Rank
Kennedy Elem.	Franklin-McKinley Elem.	San Jose	4
Los Arboles Elem.	Franklin-McKinley Elem.	San Jose	2
McKinley Elem.	Franklin-McKinley Elem.	San Jose	1
Meadows Elem.	Franklin-McKinley Elem.	San Jose	5
Santee Elem.	Franklin-McKinley Elem.	San Jose	1
Seven Trees Elem.	Franklin-McKinley Elem.	San Jose	2
Shirakawa Elem.	Franklin-McKinley Elem.	San Jose	4
Stonegate Elem.	Franklin-McKinley Elem.	San Jose	6
Windmill Springs Elem.	Franklin-McKinley Elem.	San Jose	5
Fair Jr. High	Franklin-McKinley Elem.	San Jose	4
Sylvandale Jr. High	Franklin-McKinley Elem.	San Jose	3
Cupertino High	Fremont Union High	Cupertino	10
Fremont High	Fremont Union High	Sunnyvale	6
Homestead High	Fremont Union High	Cupertino	10
Lynbrook High	Fremont Union High	San Jose	10
Monta Vista High	Fremont Union High	Cupertino	10
Aprea Elem.	Gilroy Unified	Gilroy	9
Ascencion Solorsano Mid.	Gilroy Unified	Gilroy	5
Del Buono Elem.	Gilroy Unified	Gilroy	6
El Roble Elem.	Gilroy Unified	Gilroy	4
Eliot Elem.	Gilroy Unified	Gilroy	3
Glen View Elem.	Gilroy Unified	Gilroy	3
Kelley Rod Elem.	Gilroy Unified	Gilroy	5
Las Animas Elem.	Gilroy Unified	Gilroy	2
Rucker Elem.	Gilroy Unified	Gilroy	5
Brownell Middle	Gilroy Unified	Gilroy	6
South Valley Middle	Gilroy Unified	Gilroy	4
Gilroy High	Gilroy Unified	Gilroy	5
MACSA El Portal	Gilroy Unified	Gilroy	1
Loma Prieta Elem.	Loma Prieta Jt. Union Elem.	Los Gatos	10
English Middle	Loma Prieta Jt. Union Elem.	Los Gatos	10
Almond Elem.	Los Altos Elem.	Los Altos	10
Covington Elem.	Los Altos Elem.	Los Altos	10
Loyola Elem.	Los Altos Elem.	Los Altos	10
Oak Ave. Elem.	Los Altos Elem.	Los Altos	10
Santa Rita Elem.	Los Altos Elem.	Los Altos	10
Springer Elem.	Los Altos Elem.	Mountain View	10
Blach Intermediate	Los Altos Elem.	Los Altos	10

School	District	City/Town	Rank
Egan Intermediate	Los Altos Elem.	Los Altos	10
Blossom Hill Elem.	Los Gatos Union Elem.	Los Altos	10
Daves Ave. Elem.	Los Gatos Union Elem.	Los Altos	10
Van Meter Elem.	Los Gatos Union Elem.	Los Altos	10
Fisher Middle	Los Gatos Union Elem.	Los Altos	10
Los Gatos High	Los Gatos-Saratoga Jt. Un.	Los Gatos	10
Saratoga High	Los Gatos-Saratoga Jt. Un.	Saratoga	10
Luther Burbank Elem.	Luther Burbank Elem.	San Jose	3
Burnett Elem.	Milpitas Unified	Milpitas	7
Curtner Elem.	Milpitas Unified	Milpitas	9
Pomeroy Elem.	Milpitas Unified	Milpitas	9
Randall Elem.	Milpitas Unified	Milpitas	5
Rose Elem.	Milpitas Unified	Milpitas	6
Sinnott Elem.	Milpitas Unified	Milpitas	9
Spangler Elem.	Milpitas Unified	Milpitas	8
Weller Elem.	Milpitas Unified	Milpitas	8
Zanker Elem.	Milpitas Unified	Milpitas	8
Rancho Milpitas Jr. High	Milpitas Unified	Milpitas	8
Russell Jr. High	Milpitas Unified	Milpitas	9
Milpitas High	Milpitas Unified	Milpitas	8
Anderson Elem.	Moreland Elem.	San Jose	2
Baker Elem.	Moreland Elem.	San Jose	9
Country Ln. Elem.	Moreland Elem.	San Jose	10
Easterbrook Elem.	Moreland Elem.	San Jose	8
Latimer Elem.	Moreland Elem.	San Jose	8
Moreland Disc. Elem.	Moreland Elem.	San Jose	10
Payne Elem.	Moreland Elem.	San Jose	8
Castro Middle	Moreland Elem.	San Jose	9
Rogers Middle	Moreland Elem.	San Jose	8
Barrett Elem.	Morgan Hill Unified	Morgan Hill	5
Burnett Elem.	Morgan Hill Unified	Morgan Hill	4
Charter Sch. Of Morgan Hill	Morgan Hill Unified	Morgan Hill	8
El Toro Elem.	Morgan Hill Unified	Morgan Hill	7
Jackson Elem.	Morgan Hill Unified	Morgan Hill	7
Los Paseos Elem.	Morgan Hill Unified	San Jose	8
Nordstrom Elem.	Morgan Hill Unified	Morgan Hill	9
Paradise Val./Machado Elem.	Morgan Hill Unified	Morgan Hill	8
San Martin/Gwinn Elem.	Morgan Hill Unified	San Martin	4

School	District	City/Town	Rank
Walsh Elem.	Morgan Hill Unified	Morgan Hill	5
Britton Middle	Morgan Hill Unified	Morgan Hill	6
Murphy Middle	Morgan Hill Unified	San Jose	7
Live Oak High	Morgan Hill Unified	Morgan Hill	8
Los Altos High	Mtn. View-Los Altos Union	Mountain View	10
Mountain View High	Mtn. View-Los Altos Union	Mountain View	10
Bubb Elem.	Mtn. View-Whisman Elem.	Mountain View	9
Castro Elem.	Mtn. View-Whisman Elem.	Mountain View	2
Huff Elem.	Mtn. View-Whisman Elem.	Mountain View	10
Landels Elem.	Mtn. View-Whisman Elem.	Mountain View	8
Monta Loma Elem.	Mtn. View-Whisman Elem.	Mountain View	7
Slater Elem.	Mtn. View-Whisman Elem.	Mountain View	5
Theuerkauf Elem.	Mtn. View-Whisman Elem.	Mountain View	5
Crittenden Middle	Mtn. View-Whisman Elem.	Mountain View	7
Graham Middle	Mtn. View-Whisman Elem.	Mountain View	8
Foothill Intermediate	Mt. Pleasant Elem.	San Jose	5
Mt. Pleasant Elem.	Mt. Pleasant Elem.	San Jose	5
Sanders Elem.	Mt. Pleasant Elem.	San Jose	4
Valle Vista Elem.	Mt. Pleasant Elem.	San Jose	8
Boeger Jr. High	Mt. Pleasant Elem.	San Jose	5
Anderson Elem.	Oak Grove Elem.	San Jose	6
Baldwin Elem.	Oak Grove Elem.	San Jose	7
Christopher Elem.	Oak Grove Elem.	San Jose	4
Del Roble Elem.	Oak Grove Elem.	San Jose	5
Edenvale Elem.	Oak Grove Elem.	San Jose	4
Frost Elem.	Oak Grove Elem.	San Jose	6
Glider Elem.	Oak Grove Elem.	San Jose	8
Hayes Elem.	Oak Grove Elem.	San Jose	6
Ledesma Elem.	Oak Grove Elem.	San Jose	7
Miner Elem.	Oak Grove Elem.	San Jose	5
Oak Ridge Elem.	Oak Grove Elem.	San Jose	9
Parkview Elem.	Oak Grove Elem.	San Jose	8
Sakamoto Elem.	Oak Grove Elem.	San Jose	10
Santa Teresa Elem.	Oak Grove Elem.	San Jose	8
Stipe Elem.	Oak Grove Elem.	San Jose	4
Taylor Elem.	Oak Grove Elem.	San Jose	8
Bernal Intermediate	Oak Grove Elem.	San Jose	8
Davis Elem.	Oak Grove Elem.	San Jose	6

School	District	City/Town	Rank
Herman Intermediate	Oak Grove Elem.	San Jose	7
Orchard Elem.	Orchard Elem.	San Jose	4
Addison Elem.	Palo Alto Unified	Palo Alto	10
Barron Park Elem.	Palo Alto Unified	Palo Alto	9
Briones Elem.	Palo Alto Unified	Palo Alto	9
Duveneck Elem.	Palo Alto Unified	Palo Alto	10
El Carmelo Elem.	Palo Alto Unified	Palo Alto	10
Escondido Elem.	Palo Alto Unified	Palo Alto	10
Fairmeadow Elem.	Palo Alto Unified	Palo Alto	10
Hays Elem.	Palo Alto Unified	Palo Alto	10
Hoover Elem.	Palo Alto Unified	Palo Alto	10
Nixon Elem.	Palo Alto Unified	Palo Alto	10
Ohlone Elem.	Palo Alto Unified	Palo Alto	10
Palo Verde Elem.	Palo Alto Unified	Palo Alto	10
Jordan Middle	Palo Alto Unified	Palo Alto	10
Stanford Middle	Palo Alto Unified	Palo Alto	10
Terman Middle	Palo Alto Unified	Palo Alto	10
Gunn High	Palo Alto Unified	Palo Alto	10
Palo Alto High	Palo Alto Unified	Palo Alto	10
Allen Elem.	San Jose Unified	San Jose	5
Almaden Elem.	San Jose Unified	San Jose	2
Bachrodt Elem.	San Jose Unified	San Jose	2
Booksin Elem.	San Jose Unified	San Jose	9
Canoas Elem.	San Jose Unified	San Jose	6
Carson Elem.	San Jose Unified	San Jose	6
Cory Elem.	San Jose Unified	San Jose	4
Darling Elem.	San Jose Unified	San Jose	1
Empire Gardens Elem.	San Jose Unified	San Jose	2
Erikson Elem.	San Jose Unified	San Jose	4
Galarza Elem.	San Jose Unified	San Jose	2
Gardner Elem.	San Jose Unified	San Jose	1
Grant Elem.	San Jose Unified	San Jose	2
Graystone Elem.	San Jose Unified	San Jose	10
Hacienda Science/Env.	San Jose Unified	San Jose	9
Hammer Elem.	San Jose Unified	San Jose	6
Hester Elem.	San Jose Unified	San Jose	3
Los Alamitos Elem.	San Jose Unified	San Jose	10
Lowell Elem.	San Jose Unified	San Jose	3

School	District	City/Town	Rank
Mann Elem.	San Jose Unified	San Jose	1
Olinder Elem.	San Jose Unified	San Jose	1
Randol Elem.	San Jose Unified	San Jose	9
Reed Elem.	San Jose Unified	San Jose	8
River Glen Elem.	San Jose Unified	San Jose	6
Schallenberger Elem.	San Jose Unified	San Jose	7
Simonds Elem.	San Jose Unified	San Jose	10
Terrell Elem.	San Jose Unified	San Jose	6
Trace Elem.	San Jose Unified	San Jose	3
Washington Elem.	San Jose Unified	San Jose	1
Williams Elem.	San Jose Unified	San Jose	10
Willow Glen Elem.	San Jose Unified	San Jose	4
Burnett Middle	San Jose Unified	San Jose	3
Castillero Middle	San Jose Unified	San Jose	8
Harte Middle	San Jose Unified	San Jose	10
Hoover Middle	San Jose Unified	San Jose	3
Muir Middle	San Jose Unified	San Jose	6
Steinbeck Middle	San Jose Unified	San Jose	3
Willow Glen Middle	San Jose Unified	San Jose	5
Downtown Coll. Prep.	San Jose Unified	San Jose	4
Gunderson High	San Jose Unified	San Jose	4
Leland High	San Jose Unified	San Jose	10
Lincoln High	San Jose Unified	San Jose	6
Pioneer High	San Jose Unified	San Jose	8
San Jose High Acad.	San Jose Unified	San Jose	3
Willow Glen High	San Jose Unified	San Jose	5
Bowers Elem.	Santa Clara Unified	Santa Clara	6
Bracher Elem.	Santa Clara Unified	Santa Clara	6
Braly Elem.	Santa Clara Unified	Sunnyvale	7
Briarwood Elem.	Santa Clara Unified	Santa Clara	6
Haman Elem.	Santa Clara Unified	Santa Clara	5
Hughes Elem.	Santa Clara Unified	Santa Clara	5
Laurelwood Elem.	Santa Clara Unified	Santa Clara	9
Mayne Elem.	Santa Clara Unified	Alviso	5
Millikin Elem.	Santa Clara Unified	Santa Clara	10
Montague Elem.	Santa Clara Unified	Santa Clara	5
Pomeroy Elem.	Santa Clara Unified	Santa Clara	5
Ponderosa Elem.	Santa Clara Unified	Sunnyvale	9

School	District	City/Town	Rank
Scott Ln. Elem.	Santa Clara Unified	Santa Clara	4
Sutter Elem.	Santa Clara Unified	Santa Clara	8
Washington Elem.	Santa Clara Unified	Santa Clara	9
Westwood Elem.	Santa Clara Unified	Santa Clara	6
Buchser Middle	Santa Clara Unified	Santa Clara	6
Cabrillo Middle	Santa Clara Unified	Santa Clara	6
Peterson Middle	Santa Clara Unified	Sunnyvale	8
Santa Clara High	Santa Clara Unified	Santa Clara	8
Wilcox High	Santa Clara Unified	Santa Clara	8
Argonaut Elem.	Saratoga Union Elem.	Saratoga	10
Foothill Elem.	Saratoga Union Elem.	Saratoga	10
Saratoga Elem.	Saratoga Union Elem.	Saratoga	10
Redwood Middle	Saratoga Union Elem.	Saratoga	10
Bishop Elem.	Sunnyvale Elem.	Sunnyvale	6
Cherry Chase Elem.	Sunnyvale Elem.	Sunnyvale	10
Cumberland Elem.	Sunnyvale Elem.	Sunnyvale	9
Ellis Elem.	Sunnyvale Elem.	Sunnyvale	7
Fairwood Elem.	Sunnyvale Elem.	Sunnyvale	8
Lakewood Elem.	Sunnyvale Elem.	Sunnyvale	6
San Miguel Elem.	Sunnyvale Elem.	Sunnyvale	6
Vargas Elem.	Sunnyvale Elem.	Sunnyvale	6
Columbia Middle	Sunnyvale Elem.	Sunnyvale	5
Sunnyvale Middle	Sunnyvale Elem.	Sunnyvale	9
Alta Vista Elem.	Union Elem.	Los Gatos	10
Athenour Elem.	Union Elem.	San Jose	8
Carlton Elem.	Union Elem.	San Jose	9
Guadalupe Elem.	Union Elem.	San Jose	10
Lietz Elem.	Union Elem.	San Jose	7
Lone Hill Elem.	Union Elem.	San Jose	9
Noddin Elem.	Union Elem.	San Jose	10
Oster Elem.	Union Elem.	San Jose	9
Dartmouth Middle	Union Elem.	San Jose	9
Union Middle	Union Elem.	San Jose	9

Chapter 3

City & Town Profiles

COMMUNITIES HERE COME in all sizes, shapes and life-styles— rich and poor, rural and urban. Where do you want to live? What can you afford? What are the choices? The following profiles of Santa Clara County cities and towns may help.

INDEX TO SANTA CLARA PROFILES

CAMPBELL

BEDROOM COMMUNITY, population 38,415, that in 2005 greatly improved its commute with the opening of a light-rail line connecting Campbell with most of Silicon Valley. From downtown Campbell to downtown San Jose, about 16 minutes.

Built for the middle class and now pretty much built out, Campbell has polishing itself for decades and adding amenities that make the town all the more attractive. Crime is low, school scores generally high, the commute, for many, short. The main criticism: surrounded by other communities, Campbell gets an inordinate amount of drive-through traffic. City Hall has upgraded lights to keep cars and trucks moving.

Campbell was famous for its prunes and apricots. The name "Sunsweet" was first used in reference to a local plant that processed dried fruit. Orchards all went in the building boom that started in the 1940s. Campbell remembers its past in diverse ways, among them The PruneYard, a picturesque shopping mall and an annual Prune Festival.

Residential units in 2005 numbered 16,459 of which 6,999 were single homes, 2,006 single attached, 7,197 multiples, 257 mobile homes. In the 1940s, the town built about 1,100 residential units; in the 1950s, about 3,100 homes and apartments, in the 1960s about 4,100 units, in the 1970s about 4,000 and in the 1980s about 2,600 units. In the 1990s, as buildable lots became fewer, Campbell erected about 700 units.

To summarize: About three-fourths of the housing was built between 1940 and 1980, and one-fourth in the last 25 years — an old-new suburb. With light-rail, Campbell, like many other communities, is looking to intensify development around the stations and favoring designs that mix stores with apartments or condos.

In appearance, Campbell falls into the category of typical suburban but the neighborhoods differ. The homes east of Bascom Avenue are slightly older and more upscale and have more trees and foliage than the homes west of Bascom. Most of the single homes will have three bedrooms but possibly because home values have soared many homes have been remodeled and expanded. Well-cared-for town. Residents mow the lawns, apply the paint and generally do a good job of keeping up appearances. Many of the apartments are located along Campbell Avenue, one of the main thoroughfares.

Campbell is bisected by two freeways and one expressway and close to another expressway. The light-rail line, which has three stations in Campbell, glides to downtown San Jose then branches off to Mountain View, Almaden Valley (south San Jose), and East San Jose, with stops in cities along the way. Campbell is within 5-10 miles of Cupertino, Santa Clara and Sunnyvale, major job centers. If you work in the tall office buildings near downtown Campbell and in its few high-tech businesses, the commute is all the easier.

Civic leaders hope the light rail will attract more shoppers to Campbell's downtown, on which the town has lavished money and care. Many of the historic buildings were saved and refitted for modern retail and a variety of restaurants and coffee houses. In 2004, the town opened a performing arts center in the auditorium of the old downtown high school. Among recent headliners or shows: Lou Rawls, Best of Broadway, Duke Ellington Orchestra.

The downtown ends at a park and linear trail and Highway 17. On the other side of the freeway is The PruneYard Mall: restaurants, Barnes and Noble Bookstore, Trader Joe's, movie complex. Other stores include Whole Foods, Staples, Home Depot, Fry's Electronics. On the way, Kohl's department store.

Education by Moreland and Campbell elementary districts and Campbell High School District, which also serves kids in other towns. All districts have passed bonds to renovate their facilities and wire and equip them for high-tech. In 2004, because of declining enrollment, Hazelwood Elementary was closed and the buildings leased to a private school. When the high school district in 2004 said that it might have to eliminate the seventh period, parents and community raised the necessary funds to keep the period for another year and then passed a parcel tax to make the salvation permanent. In 2005, Campbell elem. district won a grant of $518,000 to improve technology instruction.

One homicide in 2004, zero between 2003 and 2000, three in 1999. Zero between 1998 and 1993, one each in 1992 and 1991, zero in 1990 and 1989.

Campbell recreation listings runs over 50 pages, everything from ice skating, to pilates, to rock climbing to dance, tennis, club sports, etc. Activities for children, adults and elderly. High school, a 30-acre site, was converted into a community center (gyms, auditorium, track, tennis). University classes. Year-round pool. Eight parks. City museum. Bike-jogging trail along creek. You can pedal to Los Gatos or, if your job is close by, to work. One park features giant plastic tubes with water spigots. Exercise courses. Summer day camps. Fly-casting ponds. Scottish Highland games, Prune Festival, Bunnies and Bonnets Parade, Easter Egg Hunt, Christmas Crafts Faire, Oktoberfest. Summer concerts. Gaslight Theater stages melodramas and vaudeville and hosts jazz nights and comedians and presents other events. New off-leash park for dogs. Private cooking school opened in 2005.

Politicians know residents want to retain small-town atmosphere and try to build consensus for anything major. Chamber of commerce (408) 378-6252.

CUPERTINO

SILICON VALLEY town, population 53,452, famous for the quality of its schools, some of which score among the tops in the nation.

In housing, Cupertino seems to rebuilding itself, home by home. Many of the first homes were built for the middle class — two- and three-bedrooms, often small, modest and now over 50 years old. These homes are being replaced by larger homes, built to modern standards with modern touches — walk-in closets, high-tech wiring, open kitchens, etc. Some of these homes are mansions; the majority fall into the category of four and five bedrooms, two story, ample but not overwhelming.

The west side of town contains the newest neighborhoods — generally two-story Mediterranean homes, three-car garages, 4-6 bedrooms. Some hill sections jump up into custom homes.

Cupertino has several hidden neighborhoods, squeezed in near railroad tracks and freeways or hidden in the hills or down in arroyos. For an affluent town, it offers a good variety of housing but even small and old and decrepit will go for a pretty penny. Because of its schools, its location (close to many jobs) and its amenities, Cupertino is very popular with home buyers.

In recent years, Cupertino has gone in for "smart" growth, building condos and apartments in its downtown. This pumps money into the downtown and cuts the commute for residents. But worried about the pace of construction, some residents forced a vote in 2005 on development. Residents rejected the anti-growth measures.

Being almost in the heart of Silicon Valley, many Cupertino residents have a short but sometimes sluggish commute. Town is served by Highway 85, Interstate 289, Foothill Expressway and on the east side by the Lawrence Expressway. Local streets lead to the job centers. Shuttle bus to Caltrain, which travels up the Peninsula to San Francisco. Buses.

Crime low. Zero homicides in 2004, one in 2003, zero in 2002. One each in 2001 and 2000, zero from 1994 to 1999. In 2005, sheriff opened substation in town.

Heart of town is De Anza Community College, lovely campus that includes a planetarium and Flint Center for Performing Arts, which presents top talents — recently, Colin Powell, David Sedaris, San Francisco Symphony — and touring Broadway shows. The college has an Advanced Technology Center to train students in math, physics, computers, programming.

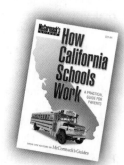

Served mainly by Cupertino elementary district and Fremont high school district. Both districts also educate students in adjoining towns. In 1995, voters in the elementary district passed a $71 million bond to improve schools and upgrade their wiring and technology. In 1999, the high school district won approval of a $144 million bond for renovations, equipment and improvements to labs and facilities. In 2004, Cupertino High opened a new swimming pool. In 2001, yet another bond was passed, $80 million, to build a fifth middle school (opened in 2005), renovate two elementary schools, and make general improvements at the other schools. In 2005, another elementary was opened, replacing a demolished school.

With the state budget crisis, schools are being squeezed for operational funds (electives, programs, salaries). This has put the burden on local districts and many have responded by attempting parcel tax elections, which require two-thirds approval. In 2004, Cupertino elementary district went for a parcel tax but to the surprise of many lost by less than 1 percent. In the meantime, parents are being asked to step up donations to the school foundations to keep programs. On the other hand, in 2004 the Fremont high school district, by less than 1 percent, passed a parcel tax to maintain programs and electives. Many schools have won state and national recognition for academic excellence. Every year only about two dozen high schools in the state break the 600 mark in the math SAT. In 2005, as they usually do, the local high schools, Cupertino, Homestead and Monta Vista, all broke the 600 mark and Monta Vista, again, placed among the top three schools in the state.

Cupertino elementary district gives parents choices in how they want their kids educated: in one approach, students are grouped by age and stay with same team of teachers for up to three years; the second method follows a traditional structure; the third requires parent participation, working in schools as aides and other positions, the fourth, offers English-Mandarin immersion. Of the remaining schools, some accept children from any address in the district, space permitting, some restrict to immediate neighborhood. Admission to some schools is determined by lottery. Five high schools in or near Cupertino are offering classes in Chinese. Private groups offer instruction in various foreign languages.

The city rec department runs after-school programs that include classes in foreign languages, science, violin-cello, flute, debating and public speaking, theater, Indian culture and cartooning. In 2005, survey of music teachers put the Cupertino music program into top 100 in U.S.

Cupertino is the headquarters city for Apple and Symantec, and has about 50 high-tech firms. Many businesses have gotten behind the schools and work with the kids to make them computer sharp. Town is jammed with high-tech parents, who strongly support academics. When selling homes in Cupertino, Realtors almost invariably emphasize school quality.

De Anza College offers "College for Kids" in summer and runs a high-school program during the regular school year. NASA, the space agency, is located nearby at Moffett Field. Its scientists occasionally pitch in on projects with the school kids. A special tax was renewed in 2005 to allow libraries to stay open seven days a week.

A farm village for most of its life, Cupertino started 1950 with about 2,500 residents. Over the next three decades, it added about 32,000 people and built thousands of three-bedroom homes, the most popular tract model of that era. In the 1980s, the town constructed 2,300 residential units, a sharp drop from previous decades, and in the 1990s, about 2,600 housing units, the majority of them single homes. Sensitive about growth. Anything big will find opponents.

In 2005, the state tallied 19,724 housing units: single homes 12,148, single attached 2,028, multiples 5,539, mobile homes 9.

Town shows a lot of care but there are some transition blocks that mix the old and rundown with the replacement new. Country flavor on some streets — mature trees, no sidewalks, utility lines overhead, and usually several homes being remodeled or rebuilt. As homes are improved, the city may require sidewalks. Move a few blocks to the west, especially beyond Highway 85, and middle-plus and affluent tracts with sidewalks and buried utility lines will present themselves. The median strips on the thoroughfares have been planted with flowers, shrubs and small trees.

Vallco Fashion Park, 180 shops and restaurants. Anchored by Sears, Penneys. Adding a movie complex. Other stores in town: Mervyns, Home Depot, Good Earth. In choices of Asian and East Asian restaurants, one of the best cities in the Bay Area. New 10-story hotel and apartment complex in the downtown. Whole Foods is replacing its store with what is billed as the largest Whole Foods in the U.S.

Baseball, gymnastics, girls softball. City rec department offers hundreds of activities or classes every quarter — belly dancing, computers, aerobics, swimming, gymnastics, bowling, etc. Soccer draws over 1,000 kids. Thirteen parks, nature preserve, a winery, a racquet club. Loads of classes, events at De Anza, which has an art gallery. Two golf courses, seniors center, movies, community center, sports center, bowling alley, ice skating rink, YMCA, city museum, arts and wine festival, De Anza Days, Heritage parade, Oktoberfest, Dickens Faire, Cherry Blossom Festival. Shakespeare Festival. University of California extension classes. City has spent millions on bike paths, which extend into other towns. New library and community hall (2004). Chamber of commerce (408) 252-7054.

- Signs of the times. The new middle school has a rock-climbing wall.

- City has web site that accesses educational programs for kids and adults.

- Get rid of it! Every fall Cupertino throws a city-wide garage sale.

GILROY, SAN MARTIN

THE SOUTHERN-MOST TOWN in Santa Clara County, Gilroy, population 47,671, is a bedroom community with farming on the outskirts. In the last decade, town increased its population by about 30 percent and now limits the amount of homes that can be built in any year.

San Martin, population about 4,500, is a small hamlet north of Gilroy near Highway 101. For as long as anyone can remember, the village has cultivated the grape and puttered around farming. But in recent years, it has attracted up-market housing — wine estates that sell for well over $1 million. This and more stores are dramatically changing the reputation and appearance of San Martin.

San Martin is unincorporated, meaning it has no fixed boundaries. Morgan Hill, on the north, and Gilroy are legal cities with powers to annex and grow. And that's what they have been doing. Both are nearing San Martin and nibbling away and it's possible that in a few years San Martin will annex to one or the other.

San Martin has a train station, freeway access, park-and-ride lot. Small airport near the freeway. Part of the Morgan Hill Unified School District. One elementary in San Martin; scores in the 40th percentile but with the demographics changing, these numbers should rise.

Old town Gilroy, situated west of Highway 101, has been spruced up with brick sidewalks and trees. The train station and the city hall have been restored and the latter pressed into service for classrooms for college courses. Monterey Street, the main boulevard, is lined with restaurants, antique shops and a variety of small stores. To bring more life to the area, the city is replacing closed food plants with housing. Live music weekends.

Gilroy has one of the most successful outlet malls in the state and another large mall called Gilroy Crossing. Located near Highway 101, these malls and other stores, including a Home Depot and a Costco, draw millions of shoppers, some coming on tour buses. All raise revenue for the city and fund city programs. Several car dealerships sweeten the tax pot. New additions include a Target, a Barnes and Noble bookstore and a Kohl's department store. In 2005, Wal-Mart opened one of its giant stores.

Despite the suburban boom, miles of open space around the town give it a strong feeling of country. The town is famous for its Garlic Festival. If you have never savored garlic-flavored ice cream or beer, well, what are you waiting for?

Although old by California standards — incorporated in 1870 — Gilroy will strike many as modern.

Removed from Silicon Valley, it was ignored in the first waves of suburbia that swept over Santa Clara County between 1940 and 1970. It lacked an infrastructure — notably sewage treatment — to support rapid growth and Highway 101 in the south county was no more than a two-lane country road that frequently jammed.

Gradually Highway 101 was improved and in the 1970s Gilroy came into play as a suburban address. By this time, urban planners had learned a lot about what worked and what didn't in suburbia and Gilroy probably benefitted from this knowledge. Also the flawed infrastructure and town sentiment forced the town's leaders to proceed slowly.

The result: a community that's intelligently planned. The major stores and St. Louise Regional Hospital were placed east of the freeway, the housing west of the freeway. The oldest housing, cottages and bungalows, borders the downtown businesses and as you move west and south, the housing gets newer and often bigger. Gilroy built initially for the middle class and in recent years moved a little up the scale; it has some variety. As the newcomers settled in, shops, supermarkets and stores were opened to meet their needs.

The old town gives Gilroy some historical and emotional continuity; this is not just a bunch of tracts plunked down in the middle of nowhere. Gilroy has a memory and a sense of coherence.

Neat streets, many tree-lined. Attractive suburban, three- and four-bedroom homes, lawns mowed, shrubs trimmed. In 1994, a sewage treatment plant for Morgan Hill and Gilroy was opened. In 2005, Gilroy tallied 14,054 residential units — 9,384 single homes, 756 single attached, 3,483 multiples, 431 mobiles.

The west side also has a community college, Gavilan, that's been there for decades and in many ways nurtures academics and job training.

Educationally, Gilroy straddles two demographic groups: low-income farm (the region) and middle-class white collar and professional. In recent years, the Gilroy district has been revamping its programs to meet the needs of both, and not surprisingly, getting into the arguments.

Until 2002, the school district used magnet schools to blend kids. Magnet schools use enriched programs to draw students away from their neighborhoods, thereby breaking down segregation based on housing patterns.

But the program required the busing of kids out of their neighborhood schools, which some parents didn't like.

In 2002, the district abandoned the magnet approach and assigned students to neighborhood schools. The district also gave up year-round schools; all schools now run the traditional September to June. Finally, separate classes for advanced students, in place at the elementary and middle schools, were introduced into the high school. This prompted the resignation of the principal and two assistant principals. They said they were worried that the honors program would segregate students by their ethnicity. In 2003, the honors program was revamped to admit more students.

In the 1990s, the school district spent $4 million to renovate elementary schools and junior highs, the money coming from a bond passed in 1993. Several schools have been built in recent years. In 2002, after failing once, the district passed a $69 million bond to build and renovate facilities. Schools score low to middling, a few high, a reflection of the town's demographics. Gilroy is a good town for playmates. In the 2000 census, 33 percent of the residents came in under age 18, unusually high.

Bookstores, historical museum, two golf courses, kid sports, youth center, swimming, softball, bingo, dancing, roller-skating, athletic clubs, bowling, 10 parks, regional parks nearby, ice cream and yogurt parlors, poker parlor, movies, community theater, delis, restaurants — for a small town, Gilroy does all right in amusements. County park, four miles west of town, honors and calls attention to culture of Ohlone Indians.

Gilroy is trying to tap the tourist trade. Wineries and redwoods a short distance off. Hilton Hotel, 140 rooms, on the south side, near Highway 101. Opened in 2001, Bonfante Gardens, a horticultural theme park, 167 acres off Highway 152, on the southwest side of town. The county and conservationists have purchased for open space about 16,000 acres in the hills. For information about activities, call the visitors bureau at (408) 842-6436.

Annual Garlic Festival (last full weekend in July) draws about 120,000 who consume about 5,000 pounds of garlic. Gilroy also throws a Hispanic Cultural Festival, dancing, singing, cultural events, eating (food booths). Mexican Independence Day in September. Antique and Micro-Breweries Fest. Farmers market, called El Mercado, good for fresh vegetables. In the spring, flowers, grown commercially, brighten up the countryside. Voters in 2004 renewed a tax to support libraries.

Commute is better than it has been in years but still pretty bad. It's a long haul to Silicon Valley and this is the main drawback to Gilroy. Highway 101 has been and is being improved and widened but it often gets overwhelmed by traffic. Even on Saturdays and Sundays, Highway 101 clogs at points but the main bottleneck, between Morgan Hill and San Jose, has been widened.

Home Price Sampler from Classified Ads

Almaden Valley (San Jose)
- 3BR/2BA, $875,000
- 5BR/3BA, $1.1 mil.

Blossom Valley (San Jose)
- 4BR/2BA, $668,000
- 2BR/1BA, condo, $425,000

Cambrian (San Jose)
- 3BR/2BA, $739,000
- 4BR/2BA, $699,000

Campbell
- 3BR/2BA, $769,000
- 3BR/2.5BA, townhouse, $595,000

Cupertino
- 3BR/2BA, fixer, $650,000
- 3BR/2BA, $979,000

Evergreen (San Jose)
- 4BR/3BA, $888,000
- 2BR/2BA, townhouse, $530,000

Gilroy
- 3BR/2BA, $699,000
- 4BR/2BA, $749,000

Los Altos
- 3BR/2.5BA, $1.9 mil.
- 3BR/1BA, $1.3 mil.

Los Gatos
- 3BR/2.5BA, $1.2 mil.
- 3BR/2.5BA, $1.1 mil.

Milpitas
- 3BR/2BA, $595,000
- 4BR/2BA, $725,000

Morgan Hill
- 3BR/2BA, $675,000
- 2BR/2BA, condo, $469,000

Mountain View
- 3BR/2.5BA, $789,000
- 1BR/1BA, $410,000

Palo Alto
- 3BR/1BA, $699,000
- 4BR/2BA, $899,000
- 2BR/2BA, $1.3 mil.

Rose Garden (San Jose)
- 2BR/2BA, fixer, $585,000
- 3BR/1.5BA, $689,000

San Jose (Central)
- 3BR/1BA, $640,000
- 2BR/2.5BA, townhouse, $579,000

San Jose (South)
- 4BR/2BA, $690,000
- 2BR/2BA, condo, $450,000

San Jose (West)
- 3BR/2BA, $789,000
- 1BR/1BA, condo, $460,000

Santa Clara
- 3BR/2.5BA, $725,000
- 1BR/1BA, condo, $325,000

Saratoga
- 3BR/2BA, $870,000
- 2BR/2BA, condo, $500,000

Sunnyvale
- 4BR/2BA, $648,000
- 2BR/2BA, townhouse, $668,000
- 4BR/2BA, $675,000

Willow Glen (San Jose)
- 5BR/3BA, $849,000
- 2BR/2BA, townhouse, $429,000

Caltrain runs commuter trains from Gilroy to San Jose to San Francisco with stops at Silicon Valley cities. Another alternative: buses and carpooling.

Zero homicides in 2004, one in 2003, zero in 2002, three in 2001. Six in 2000, zero in 1999, three in 1998 and 1997, one in 1996, two in 1995, zero in 1994, two in 1993, one each in 1992, 1991 and 1990, two in 1989, two in 1988, and none the three preceding years, reports FBI. Chamber of commerce (408) 842-6437.

• Kaiser has clinic-offices in town.

• In 2004, bond was passed to renovate Gavilan College and upgrade its tech facilities.

LOS ALTOS

PRESTIGE TOWN. School rankings are right at top in the state. Home prices high, crime low. Many homes have been remodeled into something bigger and better or torn down and replaced with larger homes.

Quaint downtown. Streets lined with tall redwoods, pines and other trees. Woodsy. Police station and civic center hide behind apricot trees. A demographer in 2005 pronounced Los Altos as the best family town in the Bay Area.

Sibling city to Los Altos Hills, the "top drawer" among the county's cities. They share school districts, shops and some civic projects. Community foundation raises money for worthwhile projects in both towns.

One of the lowest crime ratings in the state. Zero homicides between 2004 and 1993, one in 1992, three in 1991, zero in 1990 and in 1989.

Only drawback: traffic congests on commercial streets and if you work in San Jose or up the peninsula, you will get caught in delays — the price of working in or near Silicon Valley.

Los Altos started 1990 with 26,303 residents and finished the decade with 27,693, an increase of 1,390. In its annual guess, the state in 2005 put the population at 27,614. By the year 2010, predict regional planners, Los Altos should have 29,100 — essentially built out.

Home to managers, administrators and professionals and, increasingly, retirees. Median age of residents is 44. About 32 percent are over age 55, about 24 percent are under age 18, reported 2000 census.

Several shopping centers. Downtown has attracted first-class restaurants, bakeries, coffee shops, sidewalk cafes, boutiques and art galleries. Statues spotted here and there. At the corner of Main and State streets is a spic-and-span plaza decorated with bricks and stones and a large four-faced clock that looks like it stepped out of London. Town started as a summer vacation spot. When railroad arrived, Los Altos took off as second home of San Francisco wealthy, then as home for upper-middle class.

One problem: 44 restaurants and 41 salons. In an effort to diversify the town's businesses, the city council in 2004 said no more salons on two popular streets in the downtown and may invite in a luxury hotel and larger stores.

Single homes account for 89 percent of housing stock. Great majority built on about quarter-acre lots. In 2005, the state counted 10,731 residential

units — 9,151 single homes, 364 single-family attached, 1,200 multiples, 16 mobile homes. Many of the streets go without sidewalks, part of the country atmosphere that residents seem to love. Despite the name, Los Altos has few hills but it does slope gently toward the Bay.

All schools in the Los Altos Elementary District have been designated "distinguished," meaning the state thinks they are well run. Junior high and high schools received similar honors. Day care at elementary schools. In 1998, voters passed a $95 million bond to renovate all the schools in the elementary district and to build facilities. Voters also have passed and renewed and increased a parcel tax to maintain the quality of electives and academic programs. This tax is hard to pass because it requires a two-thirds vote; construction tax requires 55 percent approval. Older students attend the schools of the Mountain View-Los Altos High School District. In 1995, the district passed a $58 million bond. The money was used to remodel and add class-rooms, repair heating and plumbing, and add security lighting. Other funds are paying for more improvements. Tax passed in 1994 and renewed in 2005 to keep libraries in Los Altos and Los Altos Hills open longer.

Montclair Elementary is in Los Altos but served by Cupertino School District, which has passed several bonds. Eight private schools are located either in Los Altos Hills or Los Altos. Public charter school opened in 2004 (see Los Altos Hills).

Commute pretty good. Foothill Expressway runs through town. Interstate 280 and Highway 101 are close by. Other freeways, Silicon Valley industries, within a short drive. Nearby train station with service to San Francisco and San Jose. Traffic often creeps along the business streets.

Community Center, skateboard playground, 10 parks, including one with a redwood grove, adult education and recreation programs at the schools. Little theater. Art and wine festival, antique fairs, a lot to do. Baseball, soccer, drama, dance, many clubs. Seniors center. In planning and arguments, a community swimming complex. Youth center. Library expanded. Farmers market. Festival of Lights Parade draws 20,000-30,000. Annual pet parade. In 1900, a few progressives started the Sempervirens Fund to buy or conserve forests in Santa Clara and Santa Cruz counties, The fund, still rolling, is based in Los Altos. It has purchased over 21,000 acres. Many people hike the trails on these lands.

Los Altos Morning Forum secures pundits and celebrities for its talks. Nearby Foothill College attracts big-name speakers at its forums: George Bush (the elder), Jimmy Carter and Colin Powell, to name a few. For many people, a drive of 10 minutes brings them all that Palo Alto and Stanford offer. No gas-powered leaf blowers; only battery and electric. (But a local reporter, relying on her ears, concluded the ban was often ignored.)

Immigrants used gather on El Camino Real in Los Altos looking for jobs. In 2005, City passed an ordinance that effectively moved them over the border into Mountain View. Chamber of commerce (650) 948-1455.

How **much** is your **house worth?**

Go to www.dataquick.com to find the latest sale prices in your neighborhood. DataQuick products provide sale price and trend information, comparable sales and local crime reports in minutes from your computer.

Instant Access to **Property Information**

Complete property ownership information on every parcel in California and most properties across the U.S.

Perfect for lenders, appraisers, insurance providers, Realtors®, investors and investigators.

Available via the Internet, CD-ROM, list and dial-up network.

DataQuick is the nation's leading provider of real estate information products combining timely, in-depth real estate, consumer and business information with over 20 years of experience in product and technological innovation.

Call us today at 888.604.DATA
3 2 8 2
or visit www.dataquick.com

a MacDonald Dettwiler Company

LOS ALTOS HILLS

●Palo Alto
Los Altos Hills
San Jose
Gilroy

MOST PRESTIGIOUS CITY in Santa Clara County. Home to many of Silicon Valley's bosses and bigwigs. Small and essentially built-out. Located in hills and valleys above Silicon Valley. One of the lowest crime rates in state. Many mansions and custom homes. No business (except for private schools), no commercial. Town started off as a place for wealthy San Franciscans to escape summer fog.

Several years ago, the Associated Press analyzed STAR scores of fourth- and eighth-graders throughout the state. Los Altos Elementary District was first in reading in both grades, and first in math at the eighth grade, and second in math for the fourth grade. High schools also score very high. Bonds passed to improve and rebuild schools; parcel tax passed to keep up instructional quality and retain electives.

Some streets are located in the Palo Alto Unified School District, which also has some of the highest-scoring schools in the state. Check with Realtors or call school districts for attendance boundaries.

In 2003, the elementary district closed the last public school in Los Altos Hills, an action that did not sit well with many residents, even those who did not have children in the school. The school was sort of a community center for Los Altos Hills.

Opponents countered by starting a charter school, now located in Los Altos, but with hopes that it will be relocated to Los Altos Hills. Lawyers were called in, arguments persisted, and belatedly some of the district staff hinted that if they knew the closing was going to be so divisive, they would have kept the school open. In late 2005, with a new superintendent, the district is thinking about reopening the school.

One news story said that about 40 percent of Los Altos Hills kids attend private schools. Two private schools in Los Altos Hills, about six in Los Altos.

Minimum one-acre lots. Valley views. Trees overhang roads, creating tunnels of leaves and branches. Some mansions hide behind walls and shrubs.

Los Altos Hills faces two directions. Homes on the east side look toward the Bay and Stanford University. Homes on the west look toward the coastal mountains, heavily wooded. In its terrain, from east to west, the city goes up, then down and up again and in some areas down again. Along first valley, near the freeway, you'll find corrals and riding stables.

In the 1980s, the city increased its population by 93 people and in the 1990s by about 400. The 2000 census counted 7,902 inhabitants and in 2005 the state estimated the population at 8,452. How that's for slow growth! Large unincorporated neighborhood to south of town. Also upscale. Managed by residents through homeowner association.

City has issued handbook spelling out what Los Altos Hills would like to see — homes that fit in, heed neighbors' wishes, etc. Down through the years, newcomers and old-timers have clashed on tearing down older homes and replacing them with larger homes. It might seem that the old guard has the edge on this argument; many of the older homes are nicely done. But a fair number are modest in size and ordinary in design, usually ranchers. The new homes favor more windows and natural light, modern wiring, living and family rooms designed around entertainment centers, walk-in closets, and bathrooms-showers that you never want to leave. Both sides favor the tasteful (but taste can be defined in a number of ways). Housing units in 2005 numbered 3,035, of which 2,971 were single homes, 32 single attached, 26 multiples, 6 mobile. Many homes go for millions. Not a town for the faint of wallet.

Many homes have pools and tennis courts, some have horses grazing out back. About 63 miles of paths — used for walking and jogging, horses and bikes — wander through the town and irritate a few who think the routes step on their privacy. The town has a map of the paths; check it out.

Ride-a-thons to save open space on ridges. Law protects redwoods, oaks, large trees. Fremont Hills Country Club: pool, 10 tennis courts, riding facility, golf. Two other golf courses nearby. Foothill Community College adds life to cultural scenes and runs a speakers program, attracting top names, Tom Wolfe, Colin Powell, Bill Moyers. Palo Alto borders Los Altos Hills. Short drive to movies, plays, delights of Stanford. Interstate 280, which bisects the town, soothes the nerves, a scenic freeway.

Zero homicides between 1994 and 2004. In 2005, just outside city limits, a landscape worker who apparently had become embroiled in an argument partially bit off the ear of a co-worker and gashed his arms with a machete and struck an 80-year old woman with the butt of the machete. Confronted by a deputy, the man lunged and was shot twice. All appear to be recovering.

An intimate town. Stable. Residents know one another. Highest percentage (79) of married households in the county.

Getting older. Median age 47. Those over 55 make up 33 percent of the town, those under 18 account for 24 percent.

New town hall opened in 2005, a "green" building with solar panels and shrubs requiring little water. Chamber of commerce shared with Los Altos (650) 948-1455.

Before you move ... buy

$13⁹⁵
SINGLE COPY
VOLUME DISCOUNTS

McCormack's Guides are published for:

- ALAMEDA-CENTRAL VALLEY • CONTRA COSTA-SOLANO
- SANTA CLARA-SANTA CRUZ-SILICON VALLEY
- SAN FRANCISCO-SAN MATEO-MARIN-SONOMA
- SAN DIEGO • ORANGE COUNTY • GREATER SACRAMENTO

Available in e-book format at www.mccormacks.com:

LOS ANGELES • RIVERSIDE • SANTA BARBARA • SAN BERNARDINO • VENTURA

Also from McCormack's Guides:
How California Schools Work

www.mccormacks.com
1•800•222•3602

LOS GATOS

PRETTY, PRESTIGIOUS, LOVELY HOMES, charming old town. Crime low. School scores high. Population 28,976. Great job of revamping its downtown into an inviting place to shop, stroll, dine and peruse. The price of success: shortage of parking and complaints about street traffic.

Flat or gently sloping land rising to wooded hills and open hills. Many trees. Good views. For cat lovers, the name translates into "The Cats." First city in county to adopt ordinance preserving historic buildings, and Los Gatos has reputation for being hypersensitive about development and quality of life. Trader Joe's and Whole Foods. Fall foliage; maples throughout the downtown. Also redwoods, magnolias, palms. Short drive to Santa Cruz and Pacific.

Between 1980 and 1990, Los Gatos added about 1,100 residential units, about three-fourths of them single homes or single attached. Many of the new homes jump up the scale but a good deal of the housing runs to well-done suburban with a high level of maintenance.

In the 1990s, Los Gatos built about 800 units, about half of them single homes, and increased its population by 1,235. Town is essentially built out but the market is rewarding owners who tear down the old and small and replace it with something bigger. Or remodelings that add rooms. Many people are remodeling just to spruce up and to install modern kitchens, bathrooms and wiring. Housing units in 2005 numbered 12,579, of which 7,126 were single homes, 1,837 single attached, 3,493 multiples, 123 mobile homes. Rentals in the downtown, which also has the older homes.

Median age of residents is 41. Those under age 18 make up 21 percent of the town's residents, those over 55 make up 27 percent. Demographic translation: not that many kids, more grey heads.

The commute, historically awful, got better in 1994 with the opening of Highway 85 to Cupertino and Saratoga and other Silicon Valley cities. One of these years, light rail will connect Los Gatos to San Jose.

Los Gatos suffered major damage in 1989 quake, mostly to old structures, although chimneys and walls were cracked in newer homes. No one killed but many emotionally shaken. Building codes were revised to make reconstructed buildings better able to withstand earthquakes. Town recovered quickly.

One homicide each in 2004 and 2003, zero between 2002 and 1998, one in 1997, zero in 1996, one in 1995, zero between 1991 and 1994, one in 1990,

two in 1989, zero in 1988, two in 1987, and one in 1986. In 2005, a firefighter was killed at a home blaze when he stepped on a live power line.

Schools among the tops in the state. Los Gatos High and Fisher School have received national honors for their programs. Computer labs, music, art at elementary. Foreign languages at junior high. Teen center next to high school.

Los Gatos Union School District voters in 1990 approved a $180-a-year parcel tax. Money is used to keep class sizes down, services up, repair buildings and buy books and supplies. The tax was to have expired in 1994 but residents voted to renew it and in 2002 renewed it again. Parents also fund elementary school programs through a foundation. Steve Wozniak, a.k.a. "the Woz," co-founder of Apple, is a Los Gatos resident. He helped set up computer lab-arcade at Fisher school and trained many of the teachers. Also chipped in for a math lab at high school. High school district in 1998 passed a $79 million bond. Some of the money was used to add more classrooms and a science wing to the high school. Located in the downtown, the high school, with its fields, swimming pool, gym and rooms, is used by residents and community groups for a variety of activities. Volunteers plant flowers at the high school.

Oak Meadows-Vasona Park, one of the nicest in the county (reservoir, miniature trains, playgrounds), is full on weekends with parents cooing over kiddies. Fifteen parks total, eight playgrounds, over 400 acres of open space, miles of trails for hiking and biking. Golf course on the northwest side. Tennis, softball, soccer, rowing club, baseball, activities, classes. Concerts. Movie house. YMCA. Jewish Community Center with pool. High-school pool is used to teach children and adults to swim. Racquet and swim club. Banquet hall. Creek trail. Fitness clubs. Farmers market. Bocce courts. Skate park in planning.

Summer concerts. Two historical museums. Library open seven days a week. Art galleries. Fiesta de Artes. Cats Festival. Quaint Old Town Shopping Plaza. Top-notch and diverse restaurants, bookstores, delis, furniture and antique stores. Picky about what's allowed. In 2004, after much debate, the city council gave the go-ahead to a Cold Stone Creamery, a chain (shudder) store. Community Foundation throws parties to raise money for parks, service groups and such endeavors as the high school band. Many small towns can't or won't support a local newspaper. Los Gatos is an exception.

Among those who call or have called Los Gatos home: Peggy Fleming, Olympic ice skater; writer John Steinbeck; and Yehudi Menuhin, violinist. Fleming and her husband are wine enthusiasts and run a small winery.

At Christmas, residents gather in old town for tree lighting, caroling and kids' parade. Stores go all out for holidays with lights and displays. Chamber of commerce (408) 354-9300.

• Quarry in east hills, near Aztec Ridge Drive. Complaints about noise.

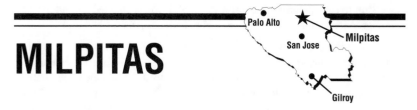

MILPITAS

FAMILY, HI-TECH TOWN RISING UP THE SCALE as more professionals move in. Increased its population by 29 percent in the last decade and now claims 64,998 residents. School rankings middling to high with over half the schools scoring in the top 30 percent of the state. Low crime. In 2004, commuters got a break when light-rail line was extended to Milpitas and beyond. The line runs to downtown San Jose and many job centers of Silicon Valley and as of 2005, to Campbell.

Although the commute gets slammed for delays, compared to other towns it has to be viewed as acceptable. Milpitas is crossed by two freeways, Interstates 680 and 880, both running north-south. Highway 267 splits these freeways and shoots east through North San Jose and the City of Santa Clara and ends in Mountain View.

Santa Clara and Mountain View are two of the founding cities of Silicon Valley. North San Jose is also loaded with high-tech. Many Milpitas residents work in these towns. In the 1990s, Highway 237, pretty much ignored in the past, became the hot corridor for new firms. Inevitably traffic problems arose. In recent years, money was secured and improvements made to Highway 237 and its connectors and several of the main roads in Milpitas. More improvements are coming and the light rail should help a lot.

Milpitas is a short drive to San Jose Airport and about 20 minutes from Oakland airport. BART (commute rail) station located in nearby Fremont; trains to Oakland and San Francisco. With the extension of the half-cent sales tax, the BART line, one of these distant years, will be extended from Fremont to San Jose with at least one stop in Milpitas.

Milpitas started out as an industrial community, home to a giant Ford auto plant, but switched gears in the 1980s when it wooed high-tech firms and moved within the elastic boundaries of "Silicon Valley." Business parks are scattered throughout the flatlands. The city began the 1960s with 6,572 residents. In that decade, it added about 20,000 and in the 1970s about 11,000. The 1980s saw another jump, 13,000 people, and in the 1990s Milpitas added about 14,500 residents.

Because of this rapid growth, a great deal of Milpitas is new or fairly new. South and middle Milpitas mix single homes (some upscale — two stories, three-car garages), townhouses and a few apartments. More apartments can be found east of Interstate 680, along with new tracts. Sound walls buffer the newer subdivisions from traffic noise. Arterial traffic is shunted around many neighborhoods and this makes the residential streets safer.

As you drive north, you encounter the old neighborhood, generally small single homes, somewhat faded, but many showing signs of care and attention. Here and there new tracts will be found. Further north, more new tracts. In the northeast hills, a gated golf-course subdivision.

Good housing mix, 18,095 residential units — 10,929 single homes, 2,225 single attached, 4,355 multiples, 586 mobile homes (2005 count). The 2000 census found 25 percent of residents under age 18, only 15 percent above 55. The industrial section near Interstate 880 has a county jail with about 3,000 inmates. City has established "urban boundary limit" to discourage housing in hills but the hills still get homes, usually posh.

On state comparisons, just about every school in the Milpitas district is scoring at or above the 50th percentile and over half the schools are hitting the 70th to 90th percentile, which indicates strong support for education. As the demographics of the town change — more professionals — the scores keep rising. In 2002, Milpitas High opened an Academy of Engineering and Technology. In 1996, the district passed a $65 million bond to build and renovate schools.

Zero homicides in 2004, three in 2003, zero in 2002 and 2001, one each in 2000 and 1999, zero in 1998, two in 1997, 1996 and 1995, three in 1994.

Lots of family activities. Twenty-one parks, 11 playgrounds. Community center and library. Aquatics center (four pools). Soccer, tennis, baseball, Little League, racquetball, waterslides, two golf courses in foothills, basketball, softball, volleyball, hang gliding, day camp, movies, bowling, roller skating, billiard parlor. On the unusual side, a teen choir and kids' theater. Many fast-food and middling restaurants. Art and Wine Festival.

The old Ford assembly plant was converted into "The Great Mall," specializing in outlet stores. A big plus for Milpitas, providing not only tax revenues but many entry-level and part-time jobs for local residents. Milpitas has also landed a Wal-Mart, a Home Depot and a Borders bookstore. Movie complex, 20 screens, at the Great Mall.

When Milpitas boomed, its old Main Street, the downtown, got lost in the shuffle. City hall and the library were relocated to a new mall on Calaveras Boulevard (Highway 237). Main Street is making a comeback. Large apartment complexes have opened on the street, bringing in customers for the stores. Also opened, a striking marble edifice, the Jain Center of Northern California. Marble imported from India. The city plans to build parks and trails in the downtown and bring in more stores and housing.

Home prices high but lower than those on opposite side of Silicon Valley. Many immigrants and first-generation families. Milpitas promotes harmony among its groups. Chamber of commerce (408) 262-2613.

MONTE SERENO

● Palo Alto

★ San Jose

Monte Sereno

Gilroy

SMALL CITY between Los Gatos and Saratoga, famous in a minor way for saying no to growth. Many custom homes on large lots. Built over gentle hills. Country feeling. Prestige address. Population 3,505.

In the 1980s, Monte Sereno saw its population decrease by 147. In the 1990s, the town roared back by adding 196 residents. Median age is 43. Those under 18 make up 28 percent of the population, those over 55 also make up 28 percent. These figures suggest a rounded town, many elderly but also many children.

When development galloped toward Monte Sereno in the 1950s, the town's leaders said, hell, no. They incorporated the hamlet as a city to keep planning under the control of the locals (through the city council), and since then have pretty much kept new construction down. State tally (2005) showed 1,249 residences, of which 1,145 were single homes (many of them custom jobs), 13 single attached, 91 apartments, zero mobile homes.

Every few years Monte Sereno or some of its residents manage to sue or get sued, usually over aesthetics or something to do with home designs or lot layouts.

Many kids attend Los Gatos schools. Scores very high. High school has added a science wing and made other improvements. Lot of attention paid to schools. Los Gatos police are paid to patrol the town. Monte Sereno has one of the lowest crime rates in the state. Zero homicides between 1996 and 2004.

Commute improved in 1994 with the opening of Highway 85, which runs from South San Jose up to Mountain View (Silicon Valley). Another popular freeway: Highway 17. Several four-lane arterials help move traffic along.

Golf course to north. Community college (many classes-activities) in adjoining Saratoga along with concerts and other events. Many parks and trails in region. One big plus for the town: it's right next to Los Gatos, which has probably the most charming downtown of the region, restaurants, delis, coffee shops, bookstores, galleries, boutiques, etc. Every year, the two towns sponsor a large garage sale. Another plus: Saratoga, restaurants, shops, charm.

Locals call town "Monte Snoreno" but residents want it that way, quiet. Without Los Gatos and Saratoga, however, Monte Sereno would be a duller place. John Steinbeck, while living in Monte Sereno, wrote "Of Mice and Men." Steinbeck wrote about poor Americans trying to survive the Depression. Homes in Monte Sereno are selling for millions. The ironies of history.

MORGAN HILL

SOUTH COUNTY TOWN, a mixture of country and suburbia. If San Jose epitomized the building spirit of 50 years ago, Morgan Hill captures the different mood of modern Santa Clara County.

San Jose said, "let 'er rip," and cheered as developers marched their tracts down the Santa Clara Valley.

A half century later, in the late 1990s, when Silicon Valley was booming and in desperate need of housing, it looked south to Morgan Hill and South San Jose. This time, the word was, nice and slow. Let's plan. Morgan Hills vows not to repeat the mistakes of yore and is searching for the right blend of elements to buy and sustain the amenities of modern life.

This includes a mix of housing and local jobs. Morgan Hill has landed a number of high-tech firms and would love more. Another addition, a large hotel on the north side.

The town takes its name not from a striking hill, called El Toro, to the west but from Hiram Morgan Hill who married into a pioneer family. Stately oaks grace a few lawns and trees planted around the city soften the housing lines. Hills to east and west. Most of town built on valley floor. Pretty town. Population 36,423. In the 1990s, the city added about 9,600 residents and 2,300 housing units, the great majority single or single-attached homes.

Served by Morgan Hill Unified School District. About 12 years ago, Morgan Hill, at that time still fairly rural, was scoring in the 50th and 60th percentiles. Now many of the scores are landing in the 60th to 90th percentile, a reflection of the changing demographics of the town, more professionals, more high-tech people.

Renovation bond was passed in 1991. In 1999, another bond was passed, $73 million, to renovate Live Oak High School and upgrade its technology and build another high school and an elementary school. The new high school, called Sobrato, opened in 2004 with freshman and sophomore classes and just now is getting a senior class. The elementary school has been opened.

Crime low. Zero homicides in 2004 and 2003, one in 2002, zero in 2001, 2000, and 1999, one each in 1998 and 1997, zero in 1996 and 1995, the FBI reports. The counts for the previous years are 1, 1, 1, 0, 0, 0, 1, 1, 0.

Morgan Hill depends on Highway 101 to move its motoring commuters. For years, this road was a nightmare because it narrowed between South San

Santa Clara County Single Home Resale Prices

City	Sales	Lowest	Median	Highest	Average
Alviso	6	$ 350,000	$ 665,000	$696,000	$574,500
Campbell	147	58,500	645,000	1,361,500	633,575
Cupertino	179	65,000	885,000	1,900,000	892,576
Gilroy	239	50,000	555,000	2,500,000	593,884
Los Altos	137	42,500	1,350,000	3,850,000	1,425,086
Los Gatos	210	40,500	1,000,000	6,850,000	1,170,854
Milpitas	244	31,500	540,000	1,350,000	535,335
Morgan Hill	194	26,000	645,000	2,300,000	668,675
Mountain View	132	166,000	758,000	1,550,000	768,654
Palo Alto	189	62,500	700,000	2,400,000	774,098
San Jose	3,535	25,000	560,000	2,516,000	581,863
San Martin	22	177,000	795,000	1,450,000	789,842
Santa Clara	283	57,500	579,000	1,000,000	577,506
Saratoga	114	30,000	1,260,000	4,125,000	1,380,481
Sunnyvale	329	66,000	660,000	1,112,500	644,341

Source: DataQuick Information Systems, LaJolla: Single Family residence sales from May 2004 through July 31, 2004. Median means halfway. In 100 homes, the 50th is the median.

Jose and Morgan Hill. The good news: In 2003, the highway was widened by an extra lane in each direction. Big difference but the road still congests; more traffic. For an alternative: Monterey Road, four-lanes; it parallels the freeway.

Another alternative: Caltrain, which runs commute trains to San Jose and to other Silicon Valley cities, finishing in San Francisco. Expanded parking at the train station. New bullet trains. See commute chapter.

In the early 1990s, Morgan Hill ran into money woes and scrapped its recreation department (public works maintained the parks). Parent groups, the school district, the YMCA and private firms either stepped into the breech or had their own programs in place. Soccer, football, the typical kids' sports, swimming, dance, ballet — all there. Skate park opened. In 1998, the city brought back its recreation program with instructions to work with the local gyms and recreation, dance, sports groups etc. to help them publicize and coordinate their activities. The city is also offering its own activities, especially for the small children. Contact city hall for a calendar of activities. Morgan Hill recently opened a community center with a playhouse and offices for the recreation department. In 2004, the town opened an aquatics center with two pools and slides. Under construction in 2005: a new library.

Large regional park and lake (reservoir) to east of town. Boating on lake. The county and private groups have purchased for open space about 16,000 acres in the hills around Gilroy and Morgan Hill.

Morgan Hill used to a be shopper's nightmare — very few stores. Different picture now: several large supermarkets, T.J. Maxx, Target, Ross. Big time shopping in Gilroy to the south.

To listen to many people, what San Jose did in the 1950s was a horror. It allowed (gasp!) developers to run free. So did thousands of cities across the country. America was coming out of a world war and the Depression. Freeways were built, the car came into full flower and the great exodus was on, from city to suburbs. Governments imposed few controls not only because they wanted the growth but because they didn't know what controls to impose.

Morgan Hill missed this era. Until the 1980s, it was a hick hamlet in the middle of fields and orchards. When its time came to develop, planners were in place, they had a much better idea of what worked and what didn't, the public was aware of environmental concerns, protecting open space was accepted — a different ball game. If you buy into Morgan Hill, you are very much buying into a planned, controlled-growth community. And a community moving up the scale. The 1980s and most of the 1990s housing coincided with a period of prosperity in the South Bay. The same holds for the housing going up now. This said, much of the town's housing serves the farm workers.

Morgan Hill traces the fortunes of the county: small and modest, bungalows and cottages, in the old town. Three-bedroom, two-car-garage homes in the next ring and on the outer ring, two-story, four- to six-bedroom homes built in the modern style, creamy stucco and red-tile roofs, plenty of light, California Mediterranean. In the east hills, many of the homes were custom built along tract designs and positioned to command views of the valley or Lake Anderson. State in 2005 counted 12,092 residential units — 7,572 single detached homes, 1,713 single attached, 1,895 multiples, 912 mobile homes.

San Jose has approved the construction of office and research buildings and about 25,000 homes on thousands of acres in Coyote Valley, near Morgan Hill. Morgan Hill opposes this project and is trying to limit its size.

Morgan Hill honors the mushroom with a festival. The town also has a few wineries. The winter holidays are welcomed with a crafts fair, caroling and the lighting of a Christmas tree. Downtown Morgan Hill, spruced up with trees and brick sidewalks and crosswalks, has attracted coffee shops, brew pubs and restaurants. Chamber of commerce (408) 779-9444. Miscellaneous:

• Tiny airport in San Martin to the south. Check tolerance for noise; also noise from trains.

• Job center opened in 2005 to help laborers secure day jobs.

• In 2005, Morgan Hill won a $2.6 million grant to fix up the streets near the train station. Among improvements: a statue of Hiram Morgan Hill and his wife and daughter.

• Two more parks. In 2005, the county purchased Bear Ranch, 2,968 acres, and Mendoza Ranch, 711 acres, in the hills east of Morgan Hill. When more money is available, some recreational facilities will be built. For now, the ranches are open for hiking, biking and horsing.

MOUNTAIN VIEW

ONE OF ONLY TWO CITIES in Santa Clara County where apartments outnumber single homes. Attracts many of the young and newcomers to the county. Some of best night-life of county. Population 72,033.

Key city of Silicon Valley. Home to about 200 high-tech and manufacturing firms, and a space operation at an old airfield. Among major players: Google, Silicon Graphics, Alza pharmaceuticals, Verizon, Intuit, PayPal and Microsoft. Mountain View borders Palo Alto and Stanford University.

In recent years, Mountain View has been favoring apartments and mixed residential-retail in its downtown, especially near its light-rail stations.

Crime low. School rankings fairly high. Voters have approved higher taxes to rebuild schools. With enrollments dropping, some schools have been closed.

A city that's doing a lot of hand wringing over what could be one of the region's biggest assets: Moffett Field, which borders Mountain View on land controlled by the county government. The Navy in 1994 said good-bye to its air base in Moffett, a landmark because of its tall hangars that used to house dirigibles. NASA Ames Research Center, which employs about 2,600, took over Moffett, about 2,000 choice acres. NASA is researching computer systems for space exploration and hopes to find private partners for its projects. Many people want to save the hangars. The military employs about 1,300 at the base to run a variety of operations, many having to do with the reserves. In 2005, Google and NASA announced they would collaborate on some research.

In an advisory vote in 1996, Mountain View voters said no to opening Moffett to air cargo flights but many power people in Silicon Valley would like to keep this option open. The county's two other airports, San Jose and Reid-Hillview, are crowded, and many business leaders see air cargo from Moffett as important to the county's prosperity. Check with city hall for more information.

Apartments outnumber single homes two to one. Total housing units 33,148: single homes 9,211, single attached 3,889, multiple units 18,817 and 1,231 mobile homes (2005 count).

Apartments are not everyone's cup of tea but for the many people starting out in the high-tech business, they are quite acceptable.

Most of the single homes can be found west of El Camino Real; most of the apartments east of El Camino Real but this section also has many single homes. New homes and townhouses were opened recently on Whisman Road, near the Central Expressway and light-rail line. Innovative designs.

Many Mountain View homes sell as much as $250,000 to $300,000 above what you would pay for similar homes in other parts of the Bay Area. Signs of the times: BMWs, Volvos, SUVs parked in front of small, old homes.

Many homes were built in the Fifties and Sixties and in size and design reflect what people wanted in those decades, generally three-bedroom units. In other Bay Area cities, older neighborhoods serve as way stations for people going up the scale or just marking time. Some homes are well kept, some neglected. In Mountain View, high prices are encouraging residents to remodel and expand or tear down and build something bigger.

Lawns are well tended, streets lined with trees. Older, smaller (two-bedroom) homes can be found south of City Hall.

In the 1980s, Mountain View added 8,800 residents and 4,000 residential units. In the 1990s, it added about 3,300 people and 2,900 units, not including new condo towers.

The 2000 census put the median age at 35. About 18 percent of the residents are under age 18, which is low. Mountain View is more a singles town than a family town. About 18 percent of the residents are over age 55 — also low.

Downtown overhauled: brick sidewalks, kiosks, pedestrian lighting, more trees. Choice of about 70 restaurants (Asian cuisine popular). Nice place to stroll. Bookstore, free parking, monthly festivals, art. Ballet school. City hall and Performing Arts Center (plays, musicals, dance, recitals). Community School of Music and Arts. Annual art and wine festival draws 200,000. Obon (Buddhist) Festival. City hall encourages public art. New library opened in 1997. In 2002, in a town vote, residents said no to a Home Depot at the site of a closed department store. The land was turned to use as medical clinic.

Many activities. Tennis, swimming, boating, movies, theater, art and wine festival, sports — the typical offerings of well-managed town with some money in its pocket. City and school districts have gone partners on play-grounds used by kids and community.

Big park on Bay shore with golf course. Swim Center. Movie complex. Palo Alto and Stanford, and all they offer, are just up the road. Shopping centers off of El Camino Real on north side of town. They include Costco, Wal-mart, Sears, Mervyns and two In-N-Out Burgers. Among stores added recently: Best Buy and REI. Also a beauty salon for men; upon entering, the customer is offered a free beer.

Shoreline Theater, managed by Bill Graham organization, draws top performers in U.S.

One homicide each in 2004, 2003, 2002 and 2001, two in 2000, zero in 1999, 1998, one in 1997, zero in 1996, one in 1995, five in 1994, two in 1993 and 1992, zero in 1991, four in 1990, three in 1989 and 1988, and one in 1987 and 1986.

Academic rankings, in statewide comparisons, land mostly in the 70th to 90th percentile, which reflects well on parents and schools. Mountain View High School and many of the elementary schools have won awards for academic excellence.

In 1995, a $58 million bond measure passed. The money was used to remodel high-school classrooms in the Mountain View-Los Altos High School District, repair heating and plumbing and add security lights. In other jobs, high-speed wiring was installed at Mountain View High and a theater-cafeteria added.

Whisman elementary district, which served part of Mountain View, passed a $34 million bond in 1996 to replace portable buildings with permanent and upgrade wiring, plumbing and heating. Mountain View Elementary District in 1998 won a $36 million bond to renovate all schools. In 2000, voters approved merging the two elementary districts.

Faced with cuts from the state, the Mountain View-Whisman district in 2004 passed a parcel tax that supported electives and the curriculum. Nonetheless, because of declining enrollments, the district in 2005 voted to close Slater Elementary School.

Freeways crisscross town. In 1994, Highway 85 was opened, another connection with San Jose. Highway 24-Interstate 101 interchange is being improved. The whole job should be finished by 2006.

Day laborers congregate along El Camino Real near Los Altos looking for work. Merchants and the cities, unhappy with the situation, have tried several ways to move the workers into hiring halls. Has not worked. If you are interested in hiring, try $12-$15 an hour.

Being in the heart of Silicon Valley, Mountain View does much better in the commuting department than many other cities in the county. Bullet trains to San Francisco, San Jose and other cities. The light-rail line recently was extended to Campbell. See commuting. Chamber of commerce (650) 968-8378.

PALO ALTO

ONE OF THE MOST DESIRABLE ADDRESSES in the nation and one of the most expensive. Many homes go for well over $1 million.

Cultural center of Silicon Valley. Prestigious. Sophisticated. A financial powerhouse. What Wall Street is to New York, Sand Hill Road (which Palo Alto shares with Menlo Park) is to venture capital. Some of the sand has gone out of Sand Hill but approaching 2006 some people think that ever so slightly the innovative engines are revving up.

Well-to-do, highly educated, cosmopolitan, squeezing in units but almost built out. Between 1960 and 1990, the town's population bounced between 55,000 and 56,000. In 2005, the state estimated the population at 61,674.

"Home" of Stanford University, birthplace of Silicon Valley. The university is actually located just west of Palo Alto city limits.

Stanford has its own community, 13,315 residents, according to the 2000 census. A few are families with children, a few are university employees and faculty, a few are people who just reside in the neighborhood. About 70 percent are students.

In 1995, the Palo Alto Unified School District, which also takes in part of Los Altos Hills, passed at that time one the largest school-renovation bonds in the history of California, $143 million. A great boost for local schools. All the schools have been renovated or rebuilt and equipped with modern technology. In 1998, the district opened another elementary school.

In 2001, voters continued a parcel tax to raise money for salaries and programs and in 2005 renewed the parcel tax.

School district, under a court agreement, accepts minority students from East Palo Alto. It also gets many requests from parents who live in other towns but want their children to attend Palo Alto schools.

In recent years, enrollments have risen at the public schools, to the point where some are short of space and have waiting lists. For information, phone (650) 329-3707.

Every year, the town's two high schools score among the highest in the state in the math SAT. The graduation rates at Gunn and Palo Alto High schools are hitting almost 100 percent and the schools advance students to the most prestigious universities in the country. Schools offer instruction in French,

German, Spanish and Japanese. In 2005, Gunn High, again, was named one of the top 100 public schools in U.S. by Newsweek magazine.

Parents are not just interested in the schools; they are, as some concede, obsessive about them. The town is full of academics and high-tech boffins and the unwritten rule is that you don't screw around with or compromise on education. The other rule is that it is OK and expected to argue ad infinitum and sometimes ad nauseam about how schools should be improved.

Tree-lined streets. Walls of ivy. Lovely campus. Excellent restaurants and coffee shops. Bookstores. First-run and foreign films near campus. Many cultural events on campus, theater, classical to rock music. Stanford movie house shows classics. Big-time college football and basketball (men and women).

One of every four acres in parks, 4,233 acres total, 30 parks in all, including one, 1,400 acres in the Santa Cruz Mountains solely for Palo Alto residents. Swimming, libraries, community centers, farmers' market, play-grounds, bike and pedestrian trails, first children's theater in U.S., junior museum and zoo, teen center, ice-skating rink, skateboard bowl, golf, soccer, baseball, many fitness and seniors classes. Children's library. Summer concerts. Several years ago, the Stanford Shopping Center added the only Bloomingdales in the Bay Area (San Francisco is opening one.)

Some recent samplings from the city recreation program: T'ai Chi, Strollerrobics (parents and babies), lawn bowling, table tennis, chess, circuit training, drawing and painting (about dozen classes), bead making, photography, ceramics.

Also, indoor soccer, gym for boys and girls, rock climbing, skateboarding (several levels), Tae Kwon Do, tennis, tumbling, dance (including preschool ballet) and piano for kids, library readings, kinder science.

Dance including classes in clog, country, folk, Lindy, line, tap, salsa, swing and jitterbug, ballet, belly, Brazilian, Carribean, flamenco, jazz and tango. Other groups run soccer, baseball, football and basketball leagues.

Children's hospital opened in 1991. State-of-the-art. Named for Lucille Salter Packard, late philanthropist and wife of David Packard, high-tech tycoon.

Berkeley is the considered the liberal campus in the Bay Area, Stanford, with its Hoover Institute, the conservative. But in social matters Stanford and Palo Alto have moved to the left, pro-choice, pro-gay, anti-discrimination. In recent years, Stanford has gotten into heated arguments with local residents over developing its property on Sand Hill Road and over preserving open space land. In Berkeley, the anti-growths would win; in Palo Alto, Stanford won. Stanford draws on a deep reservoir of good will and people are more willing to let market demand influence decisions but there is a town-gown division that surfaces over development.

Stanford has built thousands of apartments or dorm or family units for students and faculty and hopes to build more. The university's housing office helps students and faculty find rental homes and apartments in Palo Alto and other communities.

Housing units within city limits number 27,522 — 15,592 single homes, 976 single-family attached, 10,790 multiples, 164 mobile homes (2005 state figures).

For a rough guide on housing choices, 16 percent of Palo Alto's housing units were built before 1940, about 42 percent between 1940 and 1960 and 28 percent between 1960 and 1980 — or about 86 percent of everything (2000 census).

Palo Alto has many lovely neighborhoods and homes as well as interesting homes and it has many tract homes, three bedrooms, built in the postwar years for veterans coming into the housing market. The tract homes include about 3,000 Eichlers, an unusual but appealing design with flat roofs, atriums and many windows, the better to let in natural light.

Trees line many streets. Level of care is generally quite high — a handsome collegiate town. Barriers have been erected on many residential streets to slow the cars and nudge them and onto the arterials. Cozy restaurants and small shops have moved out to the neighborhoods, adding to their charm.

In the late 1980s, homeowners were tearing down small homes and replacing them with often very big homes. Other people protested over aesthetics and some restrictions were imposed. Many people have remodeled and modernized their homes and added a bedroom or two.

A lot of shaking during the 1989 quake but almost no damage to the town. The university, however, took a bad hit: damage well over $100 million. Cuts and bruises, no major injuries. Stanford library rebuilt; opened in 1999.

Two homicides each in 2004 and 2003, one in 2002, two in 2001, one in 2000, zero in 1999, three in 1998, one in 1997, one in 1996, zero in 1995, one in 1994, zero in 1993, one in 1992 and 1991, zero in 1990 and 1989, one in 1988, zero in 1987, and two in 1986, reports FBI.

Commute generally good, because of location. Two freeways to other Silicon Valley towns, several wide arterials, Caltrain up to San Francisco or down to San Jose, with stops along the way. Not too far from San Francisco International Airport. Buses to East Bay. Free shuttle bus service around town. New bullet train to San Francisco and Silicon Valley. See commute chapter.

A sizeable portion of Silicon Valley is located in Palo Alto — Hewlett-Packard, Varian, Syntex, Ford Aerospace. Historic tour shows the garage where Bill Hewlett and David Packard started out.

- On some occasions having to do with cloud cover, the music from the Shoreline Theater in Mountain View bounces into Palo Alto and irritates some residents. Mountain View made some adjustments and then stopped paying attention to the complaints.

- When people complained about noise from planes from San Francisco International Airport, the approach height was raised 1,000 feet, from 4,000 to 5,000. This seems to have done the job.

- Stanford is reducing the size of its stadium from 85,000 seats to 50,000 and practically rebuilding the place from the ground up.

- A few streets on the south side, near Mountain View, have been placed within the Mountain View-Whisman elementary school districts.

- It used to be that every Parents-Teachers Association in the Palo Alto district did its own fund-raising but this led to bad feelings because the rich neighborhoods raised more than the merely affluent and the middle income. In 2002, the district decided to pool the funds and distribute them according to a school's enrollment.

- In 2004, community foundation raised $1.7 million for Palo Alto schools — an unusually large amount and indicative of strong support for education. One reason why Palo Alto schools come out on top.

- Construction scheduled to start in 2006 on a "Jewish Town Square," a 12-acre complex of seniors housing, child care and fitness facilities, starter homes and offices for Jewish community agencies. Also Jewish Community Center. Many buildings will be situated around a central square with a promenade. In 2005, Jewish high school moved from San Jose to Palo Alto. Town hosts annual Jewish festival.

- If you want to meet the town's shakers and movers and activists and dance and dine the night away, then the annual Black and White Ball, held in summer, is just the ticket. The event raises money for good causes.

- Stanford and city government worked out a deal that allows university to build 250 housing units in exchange for providing land for two soccer fields and a practice field. The fields opened in 2005.

- New housing angle: Building deep — basements that go down two stories and are used for hobbies and home theaters.

- Four Seasons Hotel opened in 2005 in East Palo Alto but will also burnish reputation of Palo Alto. The hotel, with 200 rooms, is being called the most luxurious in Silicon Valley. Prices range from $375 a night to $2,500. Free shoe shine. Spa extra.

- Small private airport near the Bay.

Chamber of commerce (650) 324-3121.

CITY OF
San Jose

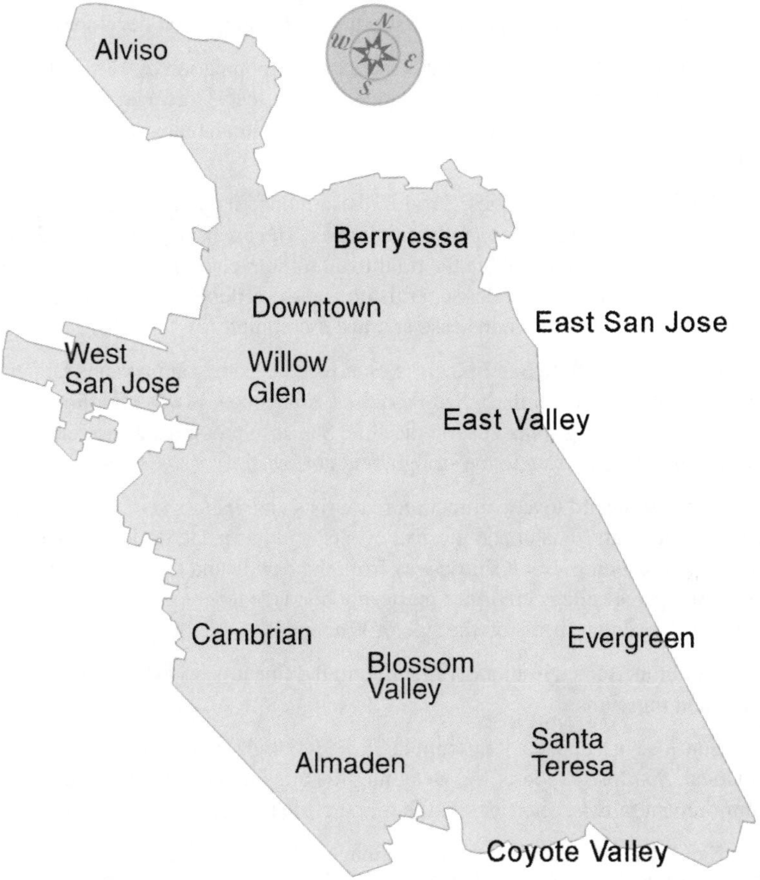

Alviso

Berryessa

Downtown

East San Jose

West
San Jose

Willow
Glen

East Valley

Cambrian

Evergreen

Blossom
Valley

Santa
Teresa

Almaden

Coyote Valley

SAN JOSE

LARGEST CITY IN SANTA CLARA COUNTY and Northern California. Population 944,857. One of the high-tech giants. School scores a mix but many high. Crime low. Suburban in nature but it's muscling up its downtown, expanding its airport and opening its south side to commercial development.

Santa Clara County in the 1990s increased its population by 185,000. Of this number, 112,700, or 61 percent, landed in San Jose. Others talk the talk; San Jose does the lifting when it comes to housing. In planning, over 50,000 housing units.

Unlike many major cities, San Jose has retained its middle class. It has its poor and its rich but it is not a city of extremes. The great majority of residents land in the middle and practice the traditional middle-class habits of keeping appearances up, the kids under supervision and the schools focused on basics. The town likes jobs, common sense and faster commutes.

Often compared to San Francisco, San Jose lacks the zaniness and venality of its neighbor to the north. In San Francisco, someone is always fiddling with the budget or cutting some deal on the side. San Jose pressures its politicians to run a tighter ship, to stay to the straight and narrow.

San Jose would love to attract more tourists and visitors and, with clubs, shops, restaurants, theater and musical events, and has made its downtown much more enticing. But it shies away from the bawdy and the bizarre. San Francisco gives college credit for mastering bondage techniques and in matters of sex comes down firmly on the side of Whoopee!

San Francisco pays a lot of attention to the fine arts, to exhibits, dance, plays and museums.

San Jose has opened a museum dedicated to high-tech ... interesting but practical. San Jose supports and welcomes the arts but its patronage and money commitment falls far short of what San Francisco musters.

San Francisco has the lowest percentage of children of any county in the Bay Area, about 14 percent of all residents. San Jose runs to about 26 percent. It is much more of a family town. Just about every school district in the city has passed a renovation bond and in 2002, San Jose Unified, the largest district, passed a renovation-construction bond for $429 million (and this is after passing a similar bond for $165 million in 1997). Lot of money; good support for schools.

For a large city (over 400,000) San Jose has one of the lowest crime rates in the U.S. The FBI reported 24 homicides in 2004. The counts for the previous years are 29, 26, 22,19, 29, 29, 43, 40, 38, 33, 41, 43, 53, 35, 39, 37, 24, 39. Curfew for kids: 15 and under, 10 p.m. to 5 a.m.; older kids, in by 11:30 p.m.

In appearance, suburban, and some critics call the town bland. Among homes, the tract look dominates. Many people put their creative energies into landscaping and gardening and interior decorating. San Jose has hills but much of the city is built on flat land. Outside of the downtown, very few buildings rise over three stories.

San Jose is not an "old" city with cosmopolitan traditions. Well into the 20th century, it was no more than the largest town in an agricultural region. The city's population in 1950 was only 95,000. When it grew, it grew rapidly, adding subdivision after subdivision, annexing almost everything in its path. In large measure, this explains the traffic jams in Silicon Valley. As fast as freeways are erected and light rail extended, they are overtaken by more people.

Ethnically diverse, many Hispanics, Southeast Asians and Asians. Town, schools, churches and civic leaders work hard at helping people get along.

School situation is confusing because San Jose is served by 19 separate school districts. The city grew up around established school districts, some of which serve other communities besides San Jose. If you have children, check with the local district to find out where your child will be attending school. Ask about hours and times of attendance. Some schools will offer buses, some will start later than others, some have year-round schedules with vacations in October. Some districts are losing enrollments and closing schools; this will change attendance boundaries.

The San Jose Arena opened in 1993, part of the effort to equip San Jose with the trappings of a big-time city. The Arena came with a professional hockey team, the Sharks, who have won San Jose's fancy and support.

Since about 1980, the city has been overhauling and improving its downtown. The jobs included a light-rail system, a convention center, the Fairmont Hotel, the Children's Discovery Museum, Tech Museum of Innovation, a retail mall, a highway and the arena. In recent years, it has built several office towers and another major hotel. In 2005, San Jose opened a large (18 stories) and striking city hall.

The downtown also offers the cultural and recreational ornaments of metropolitan life: an opera, light opera, ballet, a repertory theater, a jazz festival, two museums, film festival. San Jose is a frequent stop when big-name singers, rock bands and opera stars tour the country. San Jose State University, one of the largest in the state, is located in the downtown. Besides the state university, San Jose City College and Evergreen Valley College enhance the educational offerings of the town. In 2004, an old ornate movie palace was reopened, refurbished for plays, musicals and other events. More improvements have been made, including a river park that promises to delight strollers and joggers.

But as much as the city tries to pump up its downtown, the results often fall short of hopes — for one big reason. San Jose has three giant malls, all on the west side, ValleyFair, Westgate and going up next to Westgate what promises be the mother of all malls, Santana Row. They vacuum in the retail dollars and leave the downtown gasping for shoppers.

To be fair to the city's efforts, we're not talking a ghost town here. The downtown has is fans and its night life and its shoppers — just not as many as wanted. And it may be only a matter of time.

The international airport, located near the downtown, is renovating and expanding its facilities, adding parking and improving access roads. Runways are to be extended, a central terminal constructed and a "people mover" installed to get people over to a light-rail station. Among recent jobs: new facilities for international passengers.

Although many residents suffer a long commute, many others live close to their jobs. In recent years, the opening of two freeway stretches —Highways 85 and 87— has improved matters. Light rail was extended to east San Jose and to Campbell.

In family and neighborhood activities, Little League, soccer, all the usual sports, youth service organizations, libraries, museums, many nice parks, water slide. Cinco de Mayo parade draws 100,000.

The real strength of the city is in its neighborhoods, all sustained by their own shops, movies, restaurants, video outlets, churches and social organizations and activities, many of them organized around schools. The great majority of residents take their pleasures in the back yard or local park. City council members are elected by district, which gives the neighborhoods more clout in local politics.

Good choice of housing; a lot of the new, the great majority of it suburban tract, although some streets seem straight out of New England or the Midwest. San Jose in the 1980s added about 41,500 residential units, far more than any other city in the Bay Area. In the 1990s, it added about 35,000 units. Prices bounce all over. Even within the category of suburban tract, variety is plentiful, housing styles having changed frequently over the past 50 years. Residential units in 2005 numbered 298,901, of which 165,818 were single homes, 27,822 single attached, 94,233 multiples, 11,028 mobile homes.

San Jose's Neighborhoods

San Jose is spread over 178 square miles of Santa Clara Valley floor and hillside — about 3.5 times the size of San Francisco. In some instances, the neighborhoods are distinct: they might contain housing from a certain era, or have a "look" that sets them apart, or contain many members of a particular ethnic group. But in many places market forces have placed new subdivisions next to old. A good deal of the older housing has been carefully maintained or restored while other housing has received little attention. San Jose neighborhoods do not have clearly marked boundaries. Some neighborhoods — such as the downtown — have natural or man-made borders, usually the freeways. Others just flow into one another without any dividers. Many of the hill homes on the east side are outside city limits.

As a rough guide, San Jose was built out from its downtown. As you move south, you can trace the designs of modern suburbia: two-bedroom homes move up to three, then to four; lot sizes shrink, garages get bigger. In the newer neighborhoods, utility lines have been buried. Store mixes are changing. Just about every neighborhood has its Starbucks or equivalents. The big bookstores, such as Barnes and Noble, have moved into neighborhood plazas. Fast-food and chain stores — the Rite Aids, the McDonalds, the Safeways — the neighborhoods have in abundance but especially in the upper-income areas they are attracting the cuisine restaurants and the newer shops, Bed, Bath and Beyond, Jamba Juice, Sweet Tomato, Trader Joes and so on. Here are some of the major neighborhoods and their locations. As a point of reference, we have included the approximate distance from each neighborhood to the City of Santa Clara, near the heart of Silicon Valley.

- Santa Teresa. Southeast section of the city. About 40 years ago farm country. Now divided into housing, high tech, schools and stores. Borders large county park with golf course. Another golf course to south. Some homes built in '50s and '60s. Most homes built in the '70s. Well-maintained. Stucco and wood shingles. Many two-story homes. After the first wave of construction, developers came back years later and filled in some lots with large upscale homes.

  End of the line for one spur of the light-rail trolleys to downtown San Jose and Silicon Valley. Parking lot at station. To southeast of Santa Teresa is Coyote Valley, which city has zoned for major development (25,000 homes on 7,000 acres, maybe 75,000 people). In 2006, the city may decide specifics of how Coyote area is to be developed. From 10-14 miles to Santa Clara.

- Evergreen. Southeast San Jose, slightly above and to the east of Santa Teresa neighborhood. Rolling hills. Subdivisions, three-bedroom, built over 12-20 years ago and earlier. Apartments. Newer subs feature four bedrooms. Many new homes, with a fair number jumping way up the scale. Three country club subdivisions. Evergreen Elementary District is using bond money to build new schools, renovate and improve others. Local schools have won national blue ribbons for meeting high academic standards. YMCA with swimming pool. Evergreen Community College. Community center expanded. From 10-14 miles to Santa Clara.

About 4,000 to 5,000 more residential units are planned the hills; for info, check with city hall.

- East Valley. Also known as "Eastside." Above Evergreen. Typical home is over 25 years old but many new homes mixed in. Diverse cultures and choices among restaurants. Many apartments. Some custom homes in hills. Note Reid-Hillview Airport, near Eastridge Mall (Macys, Penneys, 150 outlets, movies, restaurants). Every once in a while a plane crashes taking off or landing. Some want to close airport but it will probably be around for a long time. Large park with water slides and pools, Raging Waters. From 10-14 miles to Santa Clara.

- Berryessa. Also known as North Valley. Above East Valley. Also above a large unincorporated (governed by county) neighborhood called East San Jose. Middle to upper income. Many four-bedroom, two-story homes. Also townhouses and condos. Some apartments. Bedroom community. Many homes in this area were built in the 1950s to 1970s. Berryessa Art and Wine Festival, an annual event. Section includes San Jose Flea Market, which claims to be largest in U.S. (4 million visitors a year). Alum Rock and Penitencia Creek Parks, large. From 8-12 miles to Santa Clara. Split by Interstate 680, a fast shot to downtown San Jose. In 2004, commute got much better with the extension of the light rail down from Great Mall of Milpitas down to Alum Rock Road. Youth center at Morrill Middle School. In planning, a Costco. In 2005, expanded library opened.

East San Jose recently opened a Mexican Cultural Heritage Center and Plaza. Facility includes theater, art gallery, rooms for workshops. Teen center opened near James Lick High School.

- Alviso-North San Jose. Just north and south of Highway 237. Alviso is tiny, low-income neighborhood north of the highway. Used to be seaport. History of flooding. Little housing turnover but homes are cheaper than elsewhere. Small marina. Favorite town of local writers when they want to bewail the loss of the old, bucolic San Jose. Change is coming. New housing complex on edge of hamlet. Coffee-deli in town. With some planning and money, city might be able to preserve portion of town and buffer residents from the new. North San Jose is bustling with high-tech and new housing, mostly apartments. Smart growth — build housing next to jobs. Borders Santa Clara. Overhauled park will add launch for canoes and small boats.

- Central San Jose. Offices, government buildings, hotels, restaurants — and a lot of housing. Great variety, from apartments to bungalows to mansions. Queen Annes, Tudors. Condos coming in strong. San Jose State University generates much foot traffic. Rose Garden adds nice touch to its neighborhood. River park gives strollers and runners a pleasant course. Light rail. Well-kept neighborhoods. Note the location of San Jose International Airport; possible noise problems for some sections. Close to many ornaments of city life: restaurants, arena, museums, night life. Farmers' market. University puts thousands of students into the downtown and gives it, somewhat, a collegiate air . From 2-5 miles to Santa Clara.

- Willow Glen. Located south and slightly west of downtown. Older neighborhood. Many streets worthy of the adjective "lovely." Well-kept, leafy, quaint. Many custom homes built in '30s, basements, hardwood floors, brick, large gardens. Midwest-New England look, expensive. Restaurants, cafes, shops along Lincoln Avenue, also praised for ambiance. Light-rail station. Caltrain station. Park-and-ride lots. Willow Glen and the Rose Garden present some of the finest "old" housing in San Jose. Library to be renovated and expanded.

Close to Highway 17 and Interstate 280 but near enough to downtown San Jose to drive by street. Many residents are within walking distance of light-rail station. From 7-11 miles to Santa Clara.

- South San Jose. Blurry neighborhood. Some people consider South San Jose to be the south section of the city, near Coyote Valley, others mix it in with Blossom Valley. For McCormack's Guides, we are placing it south of downtown, east of Willow Glen. Homes and apartment complexes built just before and after World War II, mixed in with new apartment complexes. Older housing means lower rents and prices. Mobile homes. Light rail accessible. Close to several freeways, Caltrain station. Park-and-ride lots. County fairgrounds. Bisected by the linear Kelley-Stonegate Park, one of the largest in San Jose. Park has a tea garden and a zoo. From 8-12 miles to Santa Clara. Under construction, 4,000 homes and apartments on hills near Oak Hill cemetery.

- Blossom Valley. South of South San Jose, north of Santa Teresa. Identifying street: Blossom Hill Road.

Didn't start developing until '60s. Typical home is three-bedroom, two-bath, 1,400 sq. feet. Many single homes and condos. Got its name from blossoming fruit trees. Middle America. Oakridge Mall — Sears, Macys — added movie complex. Many small parks in area. Trails around Almaden Lake.

Light-rail station. Highways 85 and 87. Straight ride to downtown San Jose. From 10-14 miles to Santa Clara.

- Almaden Valley. South, southwest of Blossom Valley. Mix of housing, some old, some from 60s, many new, custom, upscale. Scenic views from hill homes. Country feeling to the point where some residents complain about the coyotes. Almaden Quicksilver Park. Almaden Country Club. Light-rail station at Coleman Street, on north border.

Large mound-hill divides Almaden from Santa Teresa neighborhood and helps define Almaden as a neighborhood. From 12-16 miles to Santa Clara. Oakridge Mall added movies and restaurants.

- Cambrian. Borders Los Gatos and Campbell. Northwest of Almaden. Tract homes, many ranch style, built over last 10 to 30 years. Big trees. Stable. Many original owners. Some remodelings. Some townhouses, condos, duplexes. Considered middle, upper-middle class. Terrain starts level and rises into hills as it nears Los Gatos. In 2001, voters in the Cambrian school district passed a parcel tax to improve instruction. New library to open in 2006.

Commute made easier with the opening of Highway 85. Short drive to light-rail station. From 9-13 miles to Santa Clara.

- West San Jose. From about Highway 17 west to Cupertino. Parts of neighborhood are bordered on the south by Saratoga and Campbell and on the north by Cupertino and Santa Clara. Real mix of housing. Many streets in the older section, on the east side, were developed just before and after World War II. As you move west, the housing becomes newer. Most of the homes and apartments were built in the 1960s and 1970s. San Jose City College, many activities, is located on the east side, a big plus. Lynbrook High, which draws students from part of this neighborhood, is one of highest scoring in the state. Archbishop Mitty, one of the largest Catholic high schools in the country. Three malls within a drive of a few miles: ValleyFair, Westmont and the dazzling new, Santana Row, which also includes apartments and condos. At least two libraries, about a dozen parks. Highways 17, 280 and 85. Several expressways. Park-and-ride lots. Usual congestion at peak hours but this neighborhood has to be considered a good commute because it is close to major job centers.

San Jose Chamber of Commerce (408) 291-5250. Convention and Visitors Bureau (408) 295-9600.

- San Jose is slogging forward on two giant projects: Coyote Valley and North San Jose. The first, located on the southern border, near Morgan Hill, envisions 25,000 homes on 7,000 acres and 75,000 people. The North San Jose job sees 24,700 units being built north of the airport on 5,000 acres — and 20 million square feet of offices, research buildings and manufacturing plants. Both projects have opponents inside and outside San Jose but it's a safe bet that the projects, probably with fewer units, will go forward.

- Power plant, a source of many arguments, was opened in 2005. It is located off Monterey Road on the south side of San Jose

- International airport forbids takeoff of large planes after 11 p.m. Over the next few years, the runways are to be expanded. Neighbors complain of airport noises. Airport has soundproofed 1,400 homes; more to be done. Some plane owners, who say their crafts are quiet, want the airport to revise its curfew. The airport handles 13 million passengers annually and hopes to boost this to 17 million. In planning for airport area, office buildings, hotels, condos and apartments.

- Palmy days. City has all but adopted the palm. It's tall, graceful, easy to maintain, doesn't block signs or the vision of motorists.

- In 2005, the city opened seven libraries for Sunday reading and made up the time by reducing Monday hours at these libraries.

- Among major in-filling projects: 3,500 apartments and townhouses near Cottle Road near intersection of Highway 85. Light rail and Caltrain stations closeby.

- Declining enrollments forced the closing of Cory, Randal, Erikson, Hammer and Hester Elementary schools in the San Jose District and Athenour and Lone Hill elementaries in the Union School District. The Oak Grove and Moreland districts have closed schools.

- Up and away. New to San Jose Airport, Jet Blue.

- In stages, San Jose is building a bike-hiking trail from downtown to airport to Alviso and Bay.

- In 2005, San Jose hosted its first Grand Prix car race. Event drew 153,000 fans over three days.

- The county government wants to build a concert hall at the county fairgrounds on the north side. The City of San Jose wants to build a concert hall in the downtown. One concert hall may succeed; two, unlikely. The arguments continue.

- Major library built several years ago in the downtown. Two-story, atriums, computer rooms, energy efficient, located next to a park and a swim center.

- BART. One of these years — the gods of funding willing — BART will be extended from Fremont to downtown San Jose. The price, about $4 billion, seems astronomical but this is one job the county seems committed to finish — if not in your lifetime, perhaps your grandchild's. Another sales tax increase for transit projects may be attempted in 2006.

- Tail wagger. In 2004, San Jose opened one of the largest animal shelters in the West.

SANTA CLARA

THIRD-MOST POPULOUS city in the county. One of the high-tech heavy-weights: many industries. An unusual mix of fun, commerce and education. Population 109,106. The city borders the job centers of Sunnyvale and San Jose.

With its Rivermark development, a good idea of how Santa Clara County is changing and mixing the new with the old. Rivermark includes about 3,000 homes, apartments and condos, a shopping center, a library, a hotel, a school (under construction in 2005), a park and a police substation.

In 2000, Sun Microsystems, in what was formerly a part of Agnews State Hospital, opened a large complex. To win community approval, Sun agreed to set aside and maintain 14 acres for a public park, to retain 450 trees, to make the director's mansion from the Agnews days available for community events. The building has a large auditorium, which Sun will also use to showcase new products. Sun also helped fund a homeless shelter, a child-care facility and housing for the homeless. In exchange, Sun got one of the last best parcels in the original Silicon Valley.

The Sun campus and Rivermark sit side by side north of the Montague Expressway, along Lafayette Street. More homes and apartment complexes have erected nearby. If you want new housing and modern layouts and designs, look here. Rivermark encourages local shopping and getting around on foot.

Most students attend the schools of the Santa Clara Unified School District, which in 1997 passed $145 million renovation bond. Compared to other public schools in the state, Santa Clara's score generally in the top 25 percent and a few in the top 10 percent. Some students attend Eisenhower Elementary School, part of the Cupertino School District. About 15 private schools complement the public schools.

Home to Santa Clara University, Jesuit institution. A pretty campus and the site of Mission Santa Clara De Asis. Also Mission College, a campus of West Valley Community College. Among other ornaments, the Triton Museum of Art, a large convention center, popular for high-tech shows, and Great America, an amusement park.

Santa Clara dates back to 1777 when the original mission was erected. For almost 170 years, the town lived as a farming village. By 1940, the population had reached 6,650 residents, the great majority living in 1,400 cottages, bungalows and apartments in the downtown, around the university.

Came World War II and Santa Clara County blossomed as a military-industrial center. In the 1940s, the city more than doubled its housing units. Then came the real boom, fueled by veterans returning to sun-kissed California and an economy that sought to contain the Soviet Union (the Cold War).

In 1950s and 1960s, the city built about 21,000 homes and apartments and in the 1970s, about 8,000 more. In 2005, the state tallied in Santa Clara 42,454 residential units, of which 18,422 were single homes, 3,712 single attached, 20,211 multiples, 109 mobile homes.

Almost most seven of every ten homes and apartments in Santa Clara were built between 1950 and 1980. This was the era of the G.I. Bill and the tract home, usually one story, three bedrooms, with a garage for one big fat car. And with the exception the new housing at or near Rivermark and older housing in the downtown, this is essentially Santa Clara — a city of thousands of three-bedroom tract homes.

The neighborhoods differ but usually in variations off the tract model: some homes will be slightly bigger, some slightly smaller, some will have many shrubs and flowers, some few. Well-kept town: lawns mowed, houses painted, streets clean, apartment complexes maintained. Some homes will front right on the arterials, which planners today avoid. Most are built on quiet residential streets.

Almost all cities say they want business but few aggressively pursue it. Santa Clara went after and got a lot of high-tech, and made itself into one of the silicon cities. Its industries include: Intel, Applied Materials, Cisco, 3Com, Nortel and Synoptics.

The payoff for a strong business sector comes in parks and recreation, and in ability to fill potholes, keep up appearances and perform dozens of jobs cities are supposed to do but often don't. When you look at a map of Santa Clara, you see parks positioned all around town.

About 30 parks and playgrounds. One city-owned golf course, plus private course. Tennis, baseball, basketball, adult classes, community theater and ballet, loads of activities. International Swim Center, famous for training Olympic winners. Restaurants, major hotels, bowling greens, seniors center, college basketball, movie complex, youth center, ample shopping, and on and on. During football season, Forty Niners train at facility near Great America, on Centennial Boulevard. Great America: rides, musicals, water slides and wave pools. Annual camellia festival, one of the most popular in the West. Bike trail along San Tomas Expressway.

Large library opened 2004 — 200,000 books, 16 internet workstations, art gallery, cafe, more. Nice plus for Santa Clara. New police headquarters.

Santa Clara has to be rated fairly good in commuting because of its central location. Freeways or parkways traverse the city. Caltrain up the shore to San

Francisco with stops on the way or down to San Jose. Light rail starts in South San Jose, runs through the San Jose downtown, then through Santa Clara, Sunnyvale and Mountain View. The light rail was extended in 2004 to take in Milpitas and east San Jose, and in 2005, to include Campbell.

Close to San Jose International Airport. Takeoffs and landings are away from most of Santa Clara's residential sections but check out noise for yourself. San Jose is improving the access roads to the airport and expanding the airport. The airport has paid to sound proof some homes.

Two homicides in 2004, seven in 2003, four in 2002. Zero in 2001 and 2000, two in 1999, one each in 1998 and 1997, zero in 1996. The counts for previous years, 3, 2, 3, 4, 3, 9, 6, 5, 3.

Chamber of commerce (408) 244-8244.

• In 2005, the Santa Clara school district appealed to parents and the public to sponsor a school child with a $100 donation to an education fund. The appeal reflected the concerns statewide that many schools are not adequately funded.

• Good idea but .... To dampen plane noises at a condo complex, the airport paid for storm doors with thick glass. The result: noise down only a little and when sunlight hit some of the doors, it heated the glass, by one measure, to 185 degrees. Other solutions being tested.

• Another source of noise: the trains. Some people find the whistles and rumblings haunting and soothing; others can't stand them.

• Carmelite Monastery in the downtown. The surrounding streets get a lot of tender loving care, nice neighborhood.

• Santa Clara has its run-down sections, remnants of the farm housing and quick-build tracts of the 1940s. In some places, they sit close to brand new tracts. The downside: not too pretty, although many homes are fussed over; the upside, cheap or cheaper housing, something in short supply in Silicon Valley.

SARATOGA

UPSCALE TOWN ON EDGE OF SILICON VALLEY. Population 30,850. Flatlands and hills and valleys. Some of the finest housing you will see in Santa Clara County, especially in the hills where high-tech moguls have built estate homes with vineyards.

The flatland homes favor ranchers, one story, wood shingles, four and five bedrooms, large front yards professionally landscaped, variety of trees, many tall and full, meadering streets without sidewalks. To the west, mountains, heavily wooded. Strong feeling of country. On many streets, at high noon, deer will be found grazing along the ditches, indifferent to passing cars. Like ... this is our land, not yours. The newer housing rises into two stories and if the homes are really new, even if in a small tract, they will look like something out of a glossy magazine.

Saratoga is famous — or notorious — for being picky about development and protecting its charms. Large tracts ... forget it! The town is in-filling but its days of rapid growth are long over.

Downtown small and intimate. Restaurants, delis, coffee houses and sidewalk cafes, wine shop, markets, barbers, lawyers, art galleries, spas, nail parlors, small hotels. Nothing big. Many of the stores have gutted and modernized their insides and retained and brightened their old facades. Ornamental street lights. Farmers market. Not quite something out of Thomas Kincaid but working in this direction. Proposals to add more stores (or parking) almost always run into town's wish to remain low-key and rustic. City restricts use of portable signs, streamers, banners, balloons in commercial district.

On the downside, lacking many stores and therefore having a weak tax base, Saratoga often struggles to fund city services but if the shoe really starts pinching, residents have ample resources to relieve the pain. City is home to entrepreneurs, judges, doctors, computer chiefs, plus many middle and upper managers.

Academic scores very high. Residents in 1998 passed a bond to add a library and science building to the high school. With other funds, the high school built a performance and lecture center.

Served by six school districts, among which the most popular are Saratoga Elementary and the Los Gatos-Saratoga High School District. Overall rankings for Saratoga High and the Saratoga elementary schools are in the high 90s, among the tops in the state. Almost every year Saratoga High on the math SAT lands in the top five high schools in the state. Three private schools, located in or near the town: Harker, St. Andrew's, Sacred Heart.

To renovate and upgrade schools, the Saratoga Elementary district passed a $40 million bond in 1997 and $20 million bond in 2002.

Another recent addition: a town library, twice the size of the old one. The city, after much argument, purchased a church for a community center with gardens.

Crime very low. Zero homicides in 2004, 2003, 2002 and 2001. One homicide in 2000. Between 1999 and 1985, Saratoga had zero homicides.

The Saratoga commute falls into the category of "not that bad." The city borders or is close to the job centers of Cupertino, Sunnyvale, San Jose and Santa Clara. In 1996, Highway 85, which bites off a corner of Saratoga, was completed. This ties the town into the freeway network serving Santa Clara County. Walls muffle sounds from Highway 85. Buses from Santa Clara Valley Transportation Authority. Caltrain to downtown San Francisco or San Jose can be picked up in Santa Clara.

Lovely town, one reason why its homes cost so much. Much attention to preserving old town. Streets clean. Homes well-maintained. City codes restrict repairing cars in driveway or street, allowing junk to accumulate in yards, leaving cars parked on public street for more than three days.

Recreation, cultural ornaments, unusually bountiful. Concerts, art exhibits at Villa Montalvo, a mansion that was turned into an artists' residence and art museum. Jazz and pop concerts at the Mountain Winery. City hall runs recreation programs for kids and adults. About nine parks. Community theater. Hakone Gardens, created by a gardener who worked for the Emperor of Japan. Shakespeare festival. Just west, over the hills, lies the redwood country of Santa Cruz County. If you play an instrument, the town has its own band. Old-fashioned night club with dancing. Horse trails and stables in the hills.

In the middle of town sits West Valley, a community college, a cornucopia of facilities and activities, cheaply priced, all open to local residents. West Valley has a library, a theater, a gym and workout rooms, a track and playing fields, plus many classes on arts, literature, computers and business subjects. Annual Mustard Walk. Theatricals and light operas. Golf course-country club on the west side.

First a lumber town, Saratoga in last century evolved into a resort-farming community that attracted people of money who liked the mild climate, the mountain setting and possibly the mineral springs in the hills. In one version of how Saratoga got its name, civic leaders lifted it from Saratoga, New York, a wealthy town that also has mineral springs.

Among the early residents was James Phelan, a U.S. senator who built a palatial home (Villa Montalvo) in the Mediterranean style. Phelan was a patron of the arts and helped set the artistic tone of the town. The home was later deeded to the county for the benefit of artists. By 1940, the census counted about 350 homes. The war decade, when Santa Clara County developed its electronic muscles, saw the number of Saratoga homes more than double and in the 1950s, home construction boomed, 2,884 units. In 1956, Saratoga incorporated as a legal city. This took planning and zoning away from the county government, which was pro-growth, and placed them in the hands of local residents. In the 1960s, Saratoga built 3,200 units, in the next decade, 2,200 units and in the 1980s, 900 units.

In the 1990s, Saratoga built about 650 residential units and added about 1,800 residents. The state in 2005 counted 11,009 units, of which 9,644 were single homes, 560 single attached, 798 multiples and 7 mobile homes. About one-third of the single homes have three bedrooms, about 40 percent have four bedrooms and 16 percent have five or more bedrooms (census data). In recent years, the trend has been to build larger homes. For the most part, the four-bedroom homes run to software engineer upscale: two-story structures built along enticing tract designs. The custom homes, many opulent, can be found west of city hall, around Villa Montalvo and in the hills off of Big Basin Way. If you have ever wondered where the wealth of Silicon Valley is invested, take a spin up Pierce Road. Saratoga in its oldest sections has a few grand monsters that might have sheltered the Great Gatsby. The new homes can be viewed from the roads; the old often hide behind tall hedges. Although considered part of Silicon Valley, Saratoga is not home to computer industries.

Saratoga has a formal government, the city council, and an informal one, the Good Government Group, a sort of watchdog, particularly sensitive to growth and aesthetics. If you like to argue about art, beauty and quality of life, this is the burg for you.

Local lasses who made good: the daughters of Lillian Fontaine, who ran a theater workshop and staged plays. Her daughters: Joan Fontaine ("The Women") and Olivia de Haviland ("Gone with the Wind").

Another star: the Hakone Gardens. They were used as background for the movie, "Memoirs of a Geisha."

Chamber of commerce (408) 867-0753.

• Not a hiking town — few sidewalks outside the downtown — but crude paths have been carved along the main roads. City is looking to improve old rail right-of-way and use it for a trail.

• Tempest in a coffee pot. City council met in special session to rule on a request from Starbucks to open a second shop in the downtown. Verdict 4-0 in favor of coffee chain. Council said Starbucks would bring in more shoppers.

• Congrats to Marshall Lane Elementary. In 2005, it won a national Blue Ribbon for academic excellence.

SUNNYVALE

Palo Alto

San Jose

Sunnyvale

Gilroy

HIGH-TECH BEDROOM CITY located in center of the original Silicon Valley. Bordered by Mountain View, Cupertino and Santa Clara, and on north side, San Francisco Bay and a wildlife refuge of marshes and salt ponds and trails.

A city with a genuine old town and on Murphy Avenue a popular restaurant row with sidewalk cafes. And a city that regrets that it bulldozed other streets in its old town to make way for a mall that never caught on. In 2005, Sunnyvale was revamping the mall to restore the old-town look and bring back more grid streets. The mall will retain its Macys and Target. Also in the works for this section, a movie complex and more offices and stores.

For many residents, a great commute because the jobs are so close. Second-most populous city in Santa Clara County, 133,086 residents, and still adding homes and apartments but at a slower pace. Although some housing can be found the north side, most residents live south of Highway 101.

Housing units in 2005 totaled 54,476 and included 21,178 single homes, 4,047 single attached, 25,155 apartments and 4,096 mobile homes.

From 1950 to 1960, Sunnyvale built about 11,000 residential units; the following decade, about 13,000; the next decade, another 13,000. In the 1980s, construction dropped to 6,300 units. In the 1990s, the census reported, about 6,600 units were built.

When Sunnyvale boomed, the three-bedroom home was the rage and not too far behind was the two-bedroom home. In later years, the four-bedroom home became popular. With new housing these days, lots are small and homes large, almost filling their lots. Many Sunnyvale homes have large front lawns, streets lined with tall trees, roofs shingled with wood. The look of the town is more suburban traditional but there are surprises. Some neighborhoods favor an A-frame design with big windows.

Many of the homes have been renovated or remodeled. Level of care generally high.

Good mix of housing — cottages in the old town, small homes with one-car garages, several large mobile home parks, sprawling one-story ranchers from the 1950s. The newer homes favor two stories and four-plus bedrooms. On the north side, near the light-rail stations, are large condo and apartment complexes built in the last 10 years.

With the exception of San Jose, Sunnyvale has the most mobile homes of any city in the county, the great majority of them located in parks on the east side, north of Highway 101. Some mobile parks have been demolished to make way for apartments.

The neighborhood malls and shops have been improved and updated. The supermarket will have a natural foods section, the deli will carry prosciutto and a variety of cheeses. Trader Joe's and Starbucks. And an occasional throwback, such as a smoke shop. Great variety of restaurants.

Sunnyvale is home to hundreds of high-tech firms — semiconductors, software, telecommunications, global positioning equipment. Sunnyvale has a large Lockheed Martin complex and its the headquarters city for several firms, including Yahoo and Advanced Micro Devices.

The National Aeronautics and Aerospace Administration (NASA) took over Moffett Field, on the Sunnyvale border, from the Navy and is creating a research and development campus. Among partners, Google. If moving to Sunnyvale, take a look how the runways line up at Moffett, which still has a fair number of flights, and check out the noise.

For a fairly large city, Sunnyvale has a low crime rate. Two homicides each in 2004, 2003 and 2002, zero in 2001. The counts for previous years, 1, 1, 2, 0, 0, 3, 2, 3, 2, 3, 2, 2.

In summer, cops patrol parks on bicycles. Cops work with schools and counselors to keep kids straight. Neighborhood Watch discourages crime. Police and firefighters are one and the same, public safety officers.

Served by Sunnyvale, Cupertino and Santa Clara School districts and, at high school, by Santa Clara and Fremont School districts, for the latter, mainly Homestead and Fremont High schools. Rankings on a statewide comparison for all come in well above the 50th percentile, some in the 80s and 90s, an indication of high parental interest in education. Many of the schools have won state and national awards for academic excellence or for being well run.

Voters in Sunnyvale Elementary District in 1996 passed a renovation bond. In 1998, Fremont Union High School District passed a renovation-construction bond for $144 million. Fremont High School has opened a science center. In 2004, the Fremont district passed a tax to maintain its programs.

The Cupertino district gets high marks for its instructional programs. See profile on Cupertino.

About 20 parks, tennis center with 13 courts, another 55 courts at other locations, two theater groups, 200-seat theater, dance company. Community center. Senior center. City has contracted with school district to make school facilities open to public: gyms, swimming pools, playing fields. Baseball, soccer, two golf courses (9 and 18 holes). Twin Creeks Softball Complex (privately operated) has 10 fields. Bowling alley, lawn bowling. Youth Family Center-sports complex at Columbia Middle School. Gymnastic center. Skate park. Several town events, including, Holi, a Hindu carnival. Just up the road, the Shoreline Amphitheater, which books big-name performers and bands.

Baylands Park, 70 acres, opened in 1993. Trails to Bay, picnic grounds, playground, next to a 100-acre wildlife preserve. One trail is part of an effort to run 400-mile trail around Bay Area.

Four freeways, two expressways. Highway 237 at north end had its traffic lights removed, which speeded up traffic. Caltrain up the shore to San Francisco or down to San Jose, with stops at major cities. In 2005, Caltrain made Sunnyvale a stop for its bullet trains to downtown San Francisco. Buses. San Jose Airport, when traffic moves, is within a drive of 10-15 minutes.

Light-rail line, which runs from Campbell to San Jose to Mountain View and other cities, has six stops in Sunnyvale: three in Moffett Industrial Park, three along Tasman Drive.

In the early Thirties, when Sunnyvale was orchard country, an employee of Libby, McNeil & Libby, the canner, scooped up leftover chunks of pears, pineapples, peaches and cherries to bring home to his children. Presto! The first fruit cocktail. Water tank at company was painted to resemble a fruit cocktail can. When the company closed the plant, the tank was retained and declared an historic monument.

Another Sunnyvale first: Rooster T. Feathers, a comedy club, was the first place to install a video game — 1972. For the ooh-la-la side of life, Sunnyvale has at least one topless club tucked away in the industrial side of town.

In 2002, the Sunnyvale said goodbye to one of its last orchards, replaced by a retail center and 300 apartments. Chamber of commerce (408) 736-4971.

• Sputnik kaputnik! Built to track the satellites of the Soviet empire, the Onizuka Air Base — which had no planes — at Sunnyvale at one time employed over 3,500. When the Evil Empire went belly up, the base was whittled to 278 people and in 2005 was ordered closed. Many of the jobs were transferred to Vandenberg base in Santa Barbara County.

• Work began in 2005 on a pedestrian-bike bridge over Highway 280 connecting Sunnyvale with Cupertino and linking segments of a bike trail popular with the public. Bike riding, and bike commuting are catching on in Silicon Valley, which has about 75 miles of bike lanes.

• Sunnyvale is encouraging its neighborhoods to form associations to advise the city what to fund, what to encourage and what to avoid.

SANTA CRUZ COUNTY

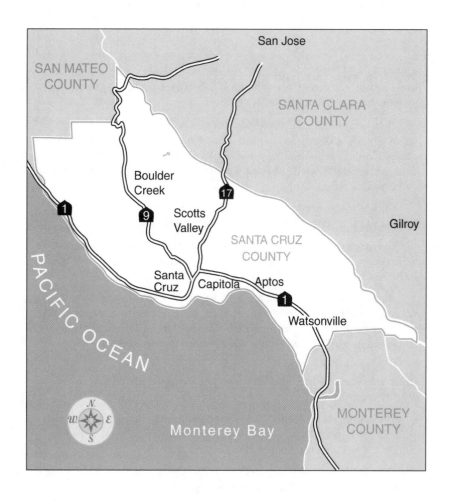

Chapter 4

County at A Glance

BORDERING SILICON VALLEY, situated on the Pacific, Santa Cruz is a lovely and rugged county that is home to 260,240 residents, the great majority of whom live close to the ocean.

There are two Santa Cruzes —the county and the City of Santa Cruz, the largest city in the county and the seat of the county government. Santa Cruz (Sacred Cross) was named by Spanish-Mexican explorers who founded a mission near downtown Santa Cruz. The original mission fell to ruin; a replica has been constructed.

The county covers 441 square miles, about nine times the size of San Francisco County, about the same size as the City of Los Angeles.

The Santa Cruz Mountains, divided by steep ravines, dominate almost the entire county. Mt. McPherson, located on the northeast side of the county, is the highest peak, 3,231 feet.

As the mountains near the coast, they descend to gentle hills, terraces, mesas and flatlands. Upon them, most of the homes, cottages and apartments have been built. Much of the remaining housing is located in narrow valleys along streams and small rivers that wind through the mountains.

Besides the City of Santa Cruz, there are three other cities, Capitola, Scotts Valley and Watsonville. In population, the legal cities are home to 127,547 residents.

The majority of residents, 132,693 people, live in unincorporated towns, neighborhoods, tracts or on country lots. The major unincorporated towns include Aptos, Live Oak, Soquel, Ben Lomond and Felton.

The median age of county residents is 35. About 24 percent of all residents are under age 18, about 18 percent are over age 55.

Neither town nor city, the University of California at Santa Cruz is almost a municipality unto itself. It enrolls about 15,000 students, many of whom live on campus or in the City of Santa Cruz.

In a bit of whimsy, students, for a school mascot, chose the banana slug.

Long famous as a tourist-vacation center, the county has attracted a small number of high-tech businesses but Silicon Valley it is not.

High-tech is tempting — local jobs, more money for shops, more revenue for amenities, such as parks. But many residents believe that the county should stop or tightly limit development. Make that, passionately believe.

According to state estimates and the 2000 census, the county increased its population by about 25,868 or 11 percent in the 1990s and erected about 10,000 residential units, the majority of them single homes, This may seem like a lot but it's peanuts compared to the numbers that would pour in if market restraints were loosened.

On its southwest side, near Watsonville, Santa Cruz is still devoted to farming. Apple trees grow row on row and the fields are furrowed for brussels sprouts, strawberries and other crops and flowers.

In 2005, the state counted within the county 102,872 housing units, of which 64,802 were single homes, 8,847 single-attached, 21,970 apartments, condos or dorm units and 7,253 mobile homes.

Crime and Weather

The crime is low. In 2004, the county recorded 5 homicides. The counts for previous years: 13, 6, 13, 9, 4.

The weather balmy but it has its foggy bite. Much of the county is open to the fogs of the Pacific, perfect for redwoods. In its hills and mountains, Santa Cruz is covered, in many places, with forests of firs and redwoods, the latter mainly second growth but some giant virgins still stand.

At its coastal center, the county curves into Monterey Bay, a shelter that protects the shore communities from the biting winds that whistle down and into the coast. But even with this protection, the winds can blow mighty cold in the spring and winter.

Many storms move in from the south and as they squeeze into the valley created by the San Lorenzo River and rise against the mountains, they yield more water.

In one recent year, the City of Santa Cruz received 30 inches of rain but Ben Lomond splashed in at 41 inches.

Schools and Education

Scores range from single digits to the high 90s. In its demographics, Santa Cruz is divided between high-income suburban and low-income farm. The former posts high scores, the latter low. As for the middle, it's there but thin.

The University of California and Cabrillo Community College in Aptos, with a branch campus in Watsonville, wave the flag for higher education and in

Santa Cruz County Population

City or Area	1990	2000	2005*
Aptos	9,061	9,396	NA
Ben Lomond	7,884	2,364	NA
Boulder Creek	6,725	4,081	NA
Capitola	10,171	10,033	9,924
Felton	5,350	1,051	NA
Santa Cruz	49,040	54,593	56,451
Scotts Valley	8,615	11,385	11,571
Soquel	9,188	5,081	NA
Watsonville	31,099	44,265	49,601
Countywide	229,734	255,602	260,240

Source: 1990 Census, 2000 Census. *California Dept. of Finance, 2005.

many ways enrich the cultural and intellectual life of the county. Both offer many classes and activities open to the public.

Santa Cruz County has 9 school districts, of which four — Bonny Doon, Happy Valley, Mountain and Pacific — enroll fewer than 175 students. These are all elementary districts, kindergarten through sixth grade. All graduate their students into the high schools of the Santa Cruz Unified School District.

Of the remaining, Live Oak Elementary District enrolls 2,100, and Soquel, 2,000 students, cover kindergarten through eighth grade, and advance their students to the high schools of the Santa Cruz district. A few Soquel students attend Aptos High in the Pajaro district.

Pajaro Valley Unified District, kindergarten through 12th, enrolls 19,000 and covers Aptos and Watsonville (and a small part of Monterey County.)

San Lorenzo Unified, enrollment 4,200, kindergarten through 12th grade, educates the mountain communities, including Ben Lomond and Boulder Creek.

With the exception of Watsonville and the university, Santa Cruz County is building very little housing. This fact and the high cost of homes has priced housing generally beyond the reach of young families. With enrollments dropping, several school districts have closed schools and more closings may be unavoidable. When enrolling their children, parents should ask about chances of schools closing.

The Santa Cruz Elementary District and the Santa Cruz High district were legally separate but run by same people. In 2004, the legal fiction was dropped and the two became one with and have a combined enrollment of 7,600.

Scotts Valley Unified, kindergarten through 12th grade, enrolls 2,600 students. This district recently built a high school.

Finally, the county superintendent of schools runs a charter school, grades 7-12, in the City of Santa Cruz, Pacific Collegiate, enrollment about 400, that specializes in academics and has the highest scores in the county. See profile on City of Santa Cruz for more on this school.

As these numbers suggest, education in Santa Cruz County is an intimate affair. There are only seven regular high schools and at many elementary schools, the grade levels count fewer than 100 children. This adds to the ....

Charm of the County

Woodsy, peaceful, scenic, friendly, neighborly, small townish, yet private (all those trees). The Pacific roars up on 29 miles of rugged and tame coastline. Public beaches can be found all along the coast.

Fishing, boating, hiking, surfing, swimming, exploring the redwoods, golfing, the usual sports: soccer, baseball, basketball, football, gymnastics. New skate parks. Miles of park land. Promenade along the shore in City of Santa Cruz. Rollerblading, walking the dog. Even beaches for dogs.

Restaurants, fast to fine, sidewalk cafes, saloons, coffee houses. Wine tastings. The county has about 1,200 acres in vineyards, of which about 25 percent is dedicated to pinots.

Dance studios. Art galleries. Antique stores.

Plays. Movies. Bookstores. Poetry readings. Classes and activities at the college and the university.

Touristy stuff that the locals turn up their noses at but fun, the boardwalk, roller coaster, the games.

Not a helluva lot of shopping but enough to keep life easy: boutiques, a Costco, Macys, supermarkets, the giant office and home improvement stores. For big-ticket items, head for Stanford Shopping Center or ValleyFair Mall in San Jose.

People who fight to protect trees, limit or stop development, keep roads narrow (the perverse side of congestion, more beauty). In 1966, residents voted out billboards.

No wonder the locals fight to keep the county close to what it is. But there are some problems.

The Drawbacks

The east border of the county is defined by the San Andreas, mother of all earthquake faults in capacity to do damage. Other faults fracture the county in myriad ways. In 1989, the Loma Prieta quake demolished a good portion of downtown Santa Cruz.

Local phone directories carry information and how to prepare for and survive a quake. Worth reading

Education Level of Population Age 25 & Older
Santa Cruz County

City or Town	ND	HS	SC	AA	BA	Grad
Aptos	6%	13%	30%	9%	24%	17%
Ben Lomond	6	17	37	8	23	9
Boulder Creek	3	15	39	10	25	5
Capitola	6	18	30	9	22	12
Felton	5	16	24	5	29	23
Freedom	15	25	19	3	6	2
Live Oak	8	19	29	8	20	10
Santa Cruz	5	15	23	7	27	18
Scotts Valley	4	16	29	9	28	13
Soquel	5	20	30	8	21	12
Watsonville	15	20	16	4	6	3
Santa Cruz County	7	17	25	7	22	13

Source: 2000 Census. Figures are percent of population age 25 and older, rounded to the nearest whole number. **Key**: ND (Less than 9th grade or some high school but no diploma); HS (adults with high school diploma or GED only, no college); SC (adults with some college education); AA (adults with an associate degree); BA (adults with a bachelor's degree only); Grad (adults with a master's or higher degree).

The City of Santa Cruz is low on crime but high in homeless people. A fair number are down on their luck and priced into the street by the cost of housing.

But some are people whose minds and ambitions, whether by drugs, booze or nature, went south years ago. Can't miss them in downtown Santa Cruz. Many people want to help the less fortunate and every year the City of Santa Cruz finds shelters for the homeless. If you are put off by the homeless and sometimes deranged, this side of the county will not appeal to you.

To limit growth, residents have decided not to widen Highway 17, the main road from Silicon Valley, windy, hilly, heavily traveled by commuters and tourists.

As a result: road from hell, in peak hours congested, infuriating and time devouring. Improvements have been made: more CHPs, more turnouts, better pavement. But there's only so much you can do with two lanes.

In summer and on many weekends, the beaches and some coastal towns are loaded with tourists. Internal traffic crawls.

Highway 1, the coastal road into Santa Cruz, is also a horror.

Market demand high, housing supply low — the perfect formula for soaring prices. Shacks within a few blocks of the beach sell for $600,000. The university took over a five-story hotel in the downtown and in recent years has built more housing on campus.

Santa Cruz County has attracted businesses but not that many. It's tax base is weak. The City of Santa Cruz and the county raise some of their revenue through a tax on utilities that infuriates many residents.

Many liberals, many Greens, many people to the left of liberals. If you're a Republican, you may think yourself among the zanies. If you're Libertarian, you may fit in much better than you dreamed possible. Santa Cruz welcomes government controls when they benefit the environment but dislikes them when they intrude into private life.

If Santa Cruz had its way, it would legalize marijuana. And it would push for a thorough overhaul of U.S. drug policies with the goal of treatment not punishment. If you have a kind thought for President George Bush, you are in for an argument.

Santa Cruz may strike some as insular, perhaps because many of the residents have turned their back on growth and the values and complexities of the metropolis. The electorate numbers about 135,000 and politics divide into factions, often the liberal versus the super liberals.

Counties, Cities and Towns

If you wish to avoid confusing yourself and almost everyone else, you should know the simple differences between a city and a town.

California has 58 counties, each with a "county" government headed by an elected board of supervisors. Boards of supervisors and their agencies are regional governors in charge of such tasks as welfare and medical care.

Supervisors are also municipal governors, responsible for police protection, planning, zoning, and paving streets — but only for rural areas and unincorporated towns. Important distinction.

California also recognizes legal or incorporated cities, run by city councils. These councils, within their jurisdictions, also decide zonings and planning and what roads to pave and parks to build and how many cops to hire and so on.

Where the Confusion Enters

Many people use "town" and "city" as if they were one and the same. If you are buying a home or scouting a business location, it's important to make the distinction.

Cities generally exert tighter supervision over development and planning than county governments. In Santa Cruz County, if the streets have sidewalks, chances are good that you are within a city.

If the homes are rundown and ramshackle, chances are they are in the unincorporated area. County governments usually put little energy into code enforcement or prodding residents to fix up their places. Cities are more vigorous in this matter.

This does not mean that county towns and neighborhoods are universally rundown. Other forces are at work: the discipline of the market, the habits of residents, the influence of homeowner associations, the era of construction.

Aptos, unincorporated, was built for people with money; no sidewalks but lovely homes and lovely town. All the mountain towns are unincorporated. No sidewalks but many pretty homes and streets. New homes or clusters of new homes are built to modern standards.

Much of the City of Santa Cruz was built for people who were poor or blue-collar middle class. The streets have sidewalks but many of the homes are modest bungalows and near the downtown there are a few cottages that if you huffed and puffed and let go with a good whoosh, you would have instant urban renewal. But next door, the homes are new or renovated and up to code and you get the feeling that the city is nudging homeowners to improve.

Cities are much more likely than counties to use redevelopment, a tax diversion-rehabilitation program. All four of the county's cities, using redevelopment, have spruced up their downtowns and brought in businesses. When it comes to attracting firms and getting things done, the four cities are much more energetic than the towns or the county government.

With generalizations, there are exceptions. County officials have used redevelopment to fix up the Live Oak neighborhood with parks and a library. And the county has drawn up development plans for many of the small towns.

Cities have park departments, well staffed, and recreation departments that offer classes and activities.

Counties generally stay out of the park business, except occasionally to buy large parcels that require little maintenance. If you look at a detailed map of the county you will find more small and medium-sized parks in the cities than in the county towns. Sometimes, unincorporated towns form taxing districts to raise money for parks.

Cities field their own police departments and have their officers patrol only within city limits.

Counties field sheriff's deputies who patrol towns and rural areas. City supporters argue that cities have better police protection because, typically, more officers are on patrol within smaller areas.

Both cities and counties "capture" local taxes but cities spend their revenue only within city limits. The county government may obtain tax money from one town and spend it in another.

In cities, when you want something governmental done, you go to city hall or to a city recreation department. In towns, you go to a county agency or see the representative of the district supervisor or the supervisor. Or you go to the special agency.

Cities do a better job on their "identities" and connecting to their pasts.

Benefits of town life

All this may sound like cities are a much better bargain than "county" towns. But if you want to be left alone — many people do — and not pestered by your local bureaucrats, the county government is more likely to ignore you.

Down through the decades, the county towns have spawned community groups that watch out for the towns' interests and make the towns' wishes known to the county government. No dopes, the county supervisors have learned to cultivate the towns.

Santa Cruz County has been fortunate in winning government money and private grants for large parks and preserves because it has beauty and treasures — redwoods, mountains, beaches — that just about everyone wants to save. Many of the public beaches are owned and staffed by the state.

County residents can picnic in city parks and join city activities; many do. And if a park is lacking, often the local school can be pressed into service for its playing fields and multiuse room.

As for crime, the county is generally peaceful. Police officers or sheriff's deputies, who cares? Both are adequate for the job.

Where are we?

Cities have precise boundaries. Towns do not. Some towns are defined by census tracts or school districts or zip codes or roads, some by tradition or history that few remember or care about.

Santa Cruz County started 1900 with 21,512 residents and by 1950 had inched up to 66,534. Most of the county was developed after 1950 and in many instances the new tracts overwhelmed the tiny hamlets or four corners that passed for towns.

Some "towns" and neighborhoods — Soquel, Live Oak and Aptos — flow into one another. For the newcomer and many old timers, it's hard to know where one starts at the other ends. Real estate listings will sometimes break out small neighborhoods — Corralitos, Rio del Mar, La Selva Beach — as if they were something separate and distinct. More precisely, they are small tracts with desirable features, usually on the beach or upscale or nicely maintained.

Thousands of residents live in places that are neither towns nor cities. Many homes are located on two-lane roads that wander through the trees and hills. In these areas, the closest public school, in a weak fashion, sometimes becomes the center of community life.

School Districts

All have precise boundaries, which may not coincide with the borders of the local town or city, In many parts of the U.S., school districts are connected to the municipal government. In California, they stand alone and have their own directly-elected trustees.

Top 30 Baby Names

Santa Cruz County				California			
Boys		**Girls**		**Boys**		**Girls**	
Jose	33	Ashley	19	Daniel	4157	Emily	3388
Angel	29	Emily	18	Anthony	3797	Ashley	2922
Daniel	26	Andrea	16	Andrew	3464	Samantha	2474
Juan	22	Jasmine	16	Jose	3379	Isabella	2435
Jacob	18	Samantha	16	Jacob	3327	Natalie	1942
Jesus	18	Sofia	16	Joshua	3292	Alyssa	1808
Miguel	17	Alondra	15	David	3246	Emma	1740
Andrew	16	Isabella	15	Angel	3232	Sophia	1715
Anthony	16	Elizabeth	13	Matthew	2853	Jessica	1700
Christopher	16	Grace	13	Michael	2844	Jasmine	1666
Jack	16	Ariana	12	Christopher	2754	Elizabeth	1595
Jonathan	16	Jocelyn	12	Jonathan	2541	Madison	1572
Luis	16	Maria	12	Ryan	2511	Jennifer	1483
Diego	15	Sophia	12	Alexander	2440	Kimberly	1460
Edgar	15	Alejandra	11	Joseph	2430	Alexis	1434
Isaac	15	Ella	11	Ethan	2356	Andrea	1374
Alejandro	14	Emma	11	Nathan	2302	Abigail	1314
Alexis	14	Evelyn	11	Brandon	2208	Hannah	1310
Carlos	14	Daniela	10	Kevin	2133	Sarah	1304
Joseph	14	Diana	10	Juan	2106	Vanessa	1299
Benjamin	13	Jacqueline	10	Christian	2022	Mia	1270
Brian	13	Leslie	10	Jesus	2012	Stephanie	1246
Joshua	13	Melissa	10	Nicholas	1999	Brianna	1221
Nathan	13	Alexandra	9	Diego	1977	Michelle	1152
William	13	Alexis	9	Luis	1957	Olivia	1149
Adrian	12	Ava	9	Adrian	1824	Kayla	1147
David	12	Hannah	9	Dylan	1757	Leslie	1137
Gabriel	12	Kayla	9	Gabriel	1735	Grace	1127
John	12	Olivia	9	Isaac	1722	Maria	1099
Ryan	12	Alexa	8	Carlos	1638	Victoria	1083

Source: California Department of Health Services, 2004 birth records. Number of children with the given name. Some names would move higher on the list if the state grouped essentially same names with slightly different spellings, for example, Sarah and Sara. But state computer goes by exact spellings.

History

Spanish sailors discovered Monterey Bay in 1542 and visited the area in 1595 and 1602. But Spanish-Mexican colonists did not explore the region until 1769, when an overland party led by Juan Cabrillo and Father Junipero Serra made their way up from Southern California.

The Spanish first set up quarters in Monterey, then moved north and in 1791, a mission was opened in Santa Cruz. A town followed.

Spanish policy was to subdue and domesticate the Indians and cajole or coerce them into mission life. Well intentioned, the approach failed because the

Indians rebelled and because they died in great numbers from exposure to European diseases.

Distracted by the Napoleonic wars, Spain did not send additional colonists. In 1821, Mexico won its independence from Spain and tried to tighten its control over California but it also failed to dispatch colonists in great numbers. Meanwhile, settlers from the United States were pouring over the mountains and England, having secured western Canada, was eyeing the lands to the south.

The Mexican-American War of 1847 cost Mexico its northern province but the loss probably owed less to the war than the failure to colonize. At the time of the war, only about 7,000 Spanish-Mexicans lived in California, some historians estimate.

The Spanish-Mexican legacy included the Spanish names for many towns and places and a strong inclination toward the mission style in public buildings and homes.

The Gold Rush spurred California's population and many miners wound up in the Bay Region pursuing farming. The redwoods of the county were felled to build the cities of the region.

The small fishing villages grew larger and turned to whaling. Toward the end of the 19th century, Capitola and Santa Cruz began to win fame as resorts. The Pacific waters off of Northern California are chilled by arctic currents. Monterey Bay, directly on the Pacific but sheltered by the curve of the coast, took some of the shivers out of the water. Not many; still pretty cold, but enough to win the swimmers. In the 1950s, the neoprene wet suit, probably not by accident, was invented by a Santa Cruz man. A few miles to the south, near Pacific Grove, the Japanese Current starts blending with the Humboldt (cold) current and warming things up.

The loggers cut roads through the mountains. Stagecoach lines and farmers built other roads and the state constructed what was called the Glenwood Highway to the beach towns. It was long, winding and dangerous. In the 1930s, work began on the present Highway 17.

Meanwhile, the population grew slowly. The county started 1900 with 21,512 residents and greeted 1920 with only 26,269. In the next decade, it added 11,000 residents and the 1930s, about 8,000.

The 1940s were a watershed, not only for Santa Cruz but for Santa Clara County. The war economy kicked the region into high gear and attracted thousands of workers from across the nation. After the war, the veterans flocked back to the West Coast. The G.I. bill underwrote home loans for the vets. The feds and state built freeways and opened the countryside for suburban development.

In the 1940s, the county increased its population by 21,000 and in the 1950s by 18,000. In each of the following three decades Santa Cruz added 40,000 to 50,000 residents and by 1990 the population stood at 229,734. In the 1990s, the county, despite great pressure, held its expansion to about 26,000 people.

When the university was opened in the mid-1960s, it was envisioned as the powerful engine that would drive the economy of the region. Enrollment was projected to grow to about 28,000.

But the 1960s saw the start statewide and nationally of an environmental movement that in Santa Cruz County grew stronger year by year. The university brought in the highly educated and this helped attract the tech firms. But the professors and the students embraced conservation and slow growth, very slow.

Thousands of acres slated for residential development went into parkland. The infrastructure necessary to grow, notably a widened Highway 17, never was built. So pronounced was the movement toward conservation that it probably touched something felt deeply by many residents. About 1900, a few people, upset about the destruction of the redwoods, formed the Sempervirens Club to raise money to buy forests and to lobby, connive and beg for their salvation. A few of the big landowners deeded into conservation some of the remaining forests. The club is still active in the service of the trees.

The future: many arguments, continual pressures to develop, continual moves to preserve and to find a balance among the tree, the ocean and the tractor.

Whether home prices hold up is anyone's guess. But with coastal land in short supply, it is quite likely that Santa Cruz will remain up market.

Santa Cruz County Voter Registration

City	Demo	Repub	NP
Capitola	2,947	1,242	1,122
Santa Cruz	20,406	4,318	6,774
Scotts Valley	2,718	2,567	1,166
Watsonville	8,207	2,377	1,945
Unincorporated	38,551	19,002	13,621
County	72,829	29,506	24,628

Source: County registrar of voters,2004. Key: Demo (Democrat), Repub (Republican), NP declined to state. Note: voter registration peaks at presidential elections, then falls off, often sharply, and changes from election to election. These figures are from the presidential election.

Chapter **5a**

State School Rankings

HERE ARE COMPARISON RANKINGS from the 2005 STAR tests taken by almost every public-school student in California. This test is administered annually by the California Department of Education.

We have broken out the results in a way that makes comparisons between schools easy.

The rankings, based on the scores, range from 1 (the lowest) to 99 (the highest). A school that scores in the 20th percentile is landing in the bottom 20 percent of the state. A school that scores in the 95th percentile is placing among the top 5 percent of schools in the state.

These rankings should be considered rough measures of how the schools and their students are performing.

Many low- and middle-scoring schools have students who score high. Many high-scoring schools have students who land below the 25th percentile.

A few schools post average scores but turn out many high-scoring students. These schools often will have many students at the bottom and many at the top and few in the middle.

For more information, visit the school or go on the web and check out reports about individual schools. For more test results, go to www.star.cde.ca.gov. See also the school accountability reports.

To flesh out these scores, we are including in Chapter 2B a ranking system issued by the California Department of Education and in Chapter 3 the SAT scores, math and verbal, for the regular high schools. These scores and a chart that presents SAT scores by state will give you some idea of how local schools compare to schools nationwide.

Scores range from 1-99. A school scoring 75 has done better than 75 percent of other public schools in California.
Key: Eng (English), Ma (Math), Sci (Science).

Bonny Doon Union Elem. School Dist.
Bonny Doon Elem. (Bonny Doon)

Grade	Eng	Ma	Sci
2	74	77	
3	78	73	
4	87	78	
5	95	98	90
6	68	52	

Happy Valley Elem. School Dist.
Happy Valley Elem. (Santa Cruz)

Grade	Eng	Ma	Sci
2	88	85	
3	89	81	
4	86	82	
5	96	80	93
6	96	92	

Live Oak Elem. School Dist.
Cypress Char. High (Santa Cruz)

Grade	Eng	Ma	Sci
9	83		
10	70		

Del Mar Elem. (Live Oak)

Grade	Eng	Ma	Sci
2	41	54	
3	55	74	
4	45	41	
5	56	61	64

Green Acres Elem. (Live Oak)

Grade	Eng	Ma	Sci
2	46	57	
3	44	41	
4	46	17	
5	67	67	72

Live Oak Elem. (Live Oak)

Grade	Eng	Ma	Sci
2	28	43	
3	37	44	
4	57	36	
5	55	35	53

Shoreline Middle (Live Oak)

Grade	Eng	Ma	Sci
6	53	42	
7	52	45	
8	58	83	

Tierra Pacifica Char. (Live Oak)

Grade	Eng	Ma	Sci
4	91	93	
5	89	78	77
8	99		

Mountain Elem. School Dist.
Mountain Elem. (Santa Cruz Mtns.)

Grade	Eng	Ma	Sci
2	64	59	
3	65	43	
4	91	66	
5	88	69	89
6	93	89	

Pacific Elem. School Dist.
Pacific Elem.

Grade	Eng	Ma	Sci
3	85	41	
5	82	61	85
6	83	90	

Pajaro Valley Unified School Dist.
Academic/Vocational Char. (Watsonville)

Grade	Eng	Ma	Sci
10	24		
11	11		

Alianza Char. (Watsonville)

Grade	Eng	Ma	Sci
2	2	2	
3	3	4	
4	3	3	
5	3	3	11
6	4	9	
7	12	16	

Amesti Elem. (Watsonville)

Grade	Eng	Ma	Sci
2	10	34	
3	15	19	
4	21	36	
5	20	12	16

Aptos High (Aptos)

Grade	Eng	Ma	Sci
9	85		56
10	79		39
11	86		38

Aptos Jr. High (Aptos)

Grade	Eng	Ma	Sci
7	81	80	
8	82		

Bradley Elem. (Santa Cruz Mtns.)

Grade	Eng	Ma	Sci
2	43	45	
3	59	79	
4	78	73	
5	77	71	68
6	89	85	

Calabasas Elem. (Watsonville)

Grade	Eng	Ma	Sci
2	4	4	
3	11	10	
4	14	12	
5	18	7	12
6	10	5	

Freedom Elem. (Watsonville)

Grade	Eng	Ma	Sci
2	5	18	
3	19	56	
4	19	29	
5	11	17	11

Hall District Elem. (Santa Cruz Mtns.)

Grade	Eng	Ma	Sci
2	14	27	
3	8	15	
4	27	37	
5	23	33	21

Hall Middle (Santa Cruz Mtns.)

Grade	Eng	Ma	Sci
6	7	6	
7	14	16	
8	16		

Hyde Elem. (Watsonville)

Grade	Eng	Ma	Sci
2	7	32	
3	5	4	
4	13	17	
5	21	11	24

Lakeview Middle (Watsonville)

Grade	Eng	Ma	Sci
6	9	17	
7	11	12	
8	22		

Scores range from 1-99. A school scoring 75 has done better than 75 percent of other public schools in California.
Key: Eng (English), Ma (Math), Sci (Science).

Grade	Eng	Ma	Sci
Landmark Elem. (Watsonville)			
2	3	2	
3	3	3	
4	15	20	
5	12	16	19
Linscott Char. (Watsonville)			
2	94	90	
3	86	83	
4	82	90	
5	90	86	96
6	96	90	
7	83	84	
8	77		
Macquiddy Elem. (Watsonville)			
2	5	9	
3	10	5	
4	16	19	
5	30	16	39
Mar Vista Elem. (Aptos)			
2	71	53	
3	77	70	
4	64	58	
5	76	61	72
6	70	49	
Mintie White Elem. (Watsonville)			
2	3	2	
3	7	14	
4	8	26	
5	29	48	31
Ohlone Elem. (Watsonville)			
2	6	43	
3	2	3	
4	2	7	
5	3	5	5
Pacific Coast Char. (Watsonville)			
6	88	87	
7	69	43	
8	58		
10	83		
11	69		
Pajaro Middle (Watsonville)			
6	8	25	
7	14	14	
8	19		
Pajaro Valley High (Watsonville)			
9	28		
Radcliff Elem. (Watsonville)			
2	2	6	
3	2	2	
4	2	4	
5	3	3	2
Renaissance High (Cont.) (Watsonville)			
10	19		
11	34		
Rio del Mar Elem. (Rio del Mar)			
2	75	84	
3	90	89	
4	93	96	
5	95	84	88
6	89	93	

Grade	Eng	Ma	Sci
Rolling Hills Middle (Watsonville)			
6	7	4	
7	13	10	
8	23		
Soldo Elem. (Watsonville)			
2	6	7	
3	9	5	
4	10	9	
5	27	41	24
Starlight Elem. (Watsonville)			
2	3	21	
3	6	6	
4	12	28	
5	16	24	11
Valencia Elem. (Aptos)			
2	62	66	
3	95	91	
4	82	77	
5	89	85	87
6	82	74	
Watsonville Elem.			
2	87	84	
3	62	18	
4	50	45	
5	64	64	71
6	68	63	
7	69	49	
Watsonville High			
9	32		
10	40		
11	45		

San Lorenzo Valley Unified Sch. Dist.

Grade	Eng	Ma	Sci
Boulder Creek Elem. (Boulder Creek)			
2	72	74	
3	88	74	
4	78	69	
5	77	56	70
6	88	90	
San Lorenzo Valley Elem. (Felton)			
2	60	59	
3	74	60	
4	83	78	
5	82	93	82
6	83	80	
San Lorenzo Valley High (Felton)			
9	85		
10	90		
11	90		
San Lorenzo Valley Jr. High (Felton)			
7	72	65	
8	79		

Scores range from 1-99. A school scoring 75 has done better than 75 percent of other public schools in California.
Key: Eng (English), Ma (Math), Sci (Science).

SLVUSD Char. (Ben Lomond)

Grade	Eng	Ma	Sci
2	19	9	
3	61	12	
4	54	12	
5	52	4	54
6	81	51	
7	87	75	
8	81		
9	60		
10	70		
11	55		

Santa Cruz City Elem. School Dist. (Santa Cruz)

Bay View Elem.

Grade	Eng	Ma	Sci
2	50	47	
3	62	40	
4	55	53	
5	58	35	64

De Laveaga Elem.

Grade	Eng	Ma	Sci
2	49	67	
3	59	52	
4	76	63	
5	71	73	67

Gault Elem.

Grade	Eng	Ma	Sci
2	20	19	
3	61	48	
4	30	27	
5	65	36	74

Westlake Elem.

Grade	Eng	Ma	Sci
2	86	79	
3	87	83	
4	95	88	
5	94	85	95

Santa Cruz City High School Dist. (Santa Cruz)

Ark Ind. Studies

Grade	Eng	Ma	Sci
9	34		
10	33		
11	51		

Branciforte Middle

Grade	Eng	Ma	Sci
6	58	41	
7	57	37	
8	78		

Delta Char.

Grade	Eng	Ma	Sci
9	5		
10	25		
11	14		

Harbor High

Grade	Eng	Ma	Sci
9	87		88
10	90		93
11	93		95

Loma Prieta High (Cont.)

Grade	Eng	Ma	Sci
10	19		
11	8		16

Mission Hill Middle

Grade	Eng	Ma	Sci
6	82	64	
7	65	62	
8	82		

Pacific Collegiate Charter

Grade	Eng	Ma	Sci
7	99	96	
8	99		
9	99		
10	99		
11	99		

Santa Cruz High

Grade	Eng	Ma	Sci
9	91		
10	87		
11	88		

Soquel High (Soquel)

Grade	Eng	Ma	Sci
9	83		
10	86		
11	74		

Scotts Valley Unified School Dist.

Brook Knoll Elem. (Scotts Valley)

Grade	Eng	Ma	Sci
2	79	89	
3	95	97	
4	93	92	
5	90	75	91

Scotts Valley High

Grade	Eng	Ma	Sci
9	85		
10	78		
11	87		

Scotts Valley Middle

Grade	Eng	Ma	Sci
6	88	86	
7	87	83	
8	90		

Vine Hill Elem. (Scotts Valley)

Grade	Eng	Ma	Sci
2	68	80	
3	88	80	
4	93	90	
5	84	78	87

Soquel Union Elem. School Dist.

Main St. Elem. (Soquel)

Grade	Eng	Ma	Sci
2	89	81	
3	69	56	
4	81	64	
5	85	80	83

New Brighton Middle (Capitola)

Grade	Eng	Ma	Sci
6	69	67	
7	85	78	
8	85		

Santa Cruz Gardens Elem. (Santa Cruz)

Grade	Eng	Ma	Sci
2	73	71	
3	74	75	
4	69	31	
5	60	51	66

Soquel Elem. (Soquel)

Grade	Eng	Ma	Sci
2	68	84	
3	70	47	
4	63	35	
5	59	48	55

Chapter **5b**

State 1 to 10 Rankings

FOR EASE OF COMPREHENSION, the California Department of Education has worked out a system to rank schools by their test scores.

This system takes several forms, the simplest of which is a ranking of 1 to 10.

One is the lowest score, ten is the highest.

This chapter lists the rankings for just about every school in the county.

Keep in mind that this is a crude representation of how the schools are scoring. If you combine this data with the rankings in Chapter 2a and the SAT scores and other data in Chapter 7, you will have a more rounded picture of the scores at each school.

Nonetheless, the scores can still mislead. Almost every school, even those at the bottom, will graduate students who score at the top.

Almost every school with scores at the top will graduate kids who score at the bottom and the middle.

For a general discussion of scores and what they mean, read the chapter on How Public Schools Work.

School	District	City/Town	Rank
Bonny Doon Elem.	Bonny Doon Elem.	Bonny Doon	9
Happy Valley Elem.	Happy Valley Elem.	Santa Cruz	10
Del Mar Elem.	Live Oak Elem.	Santa Cruz	4
Green Acres Elem.	Live Oak Elem.	Santa Cruz	5
Live Oak Elem.	Live Oak Elem.	Santa Cruz	5
Shoreline Middle	Live Oak Elem.	Santa Cruz	6
Mountain Elem.	Mountain Elem.	Soquel	8
Alianza Elem.	Pajaro Valley Unified	Watsonville	1
Amesti Elem.	Pajaro Valley Unified	Watsonville	2
Bradley Elem.	Pajaro Valley Unified	Watsonville	8
Calabasas Elem.	Pajaro Valley Unified	Watsonville	1
Freedom Elem.	Pajaro Valley Unified	Freedom	2
Hall District Elem.	Pajaro Valley Unified	Watsonville	1
Hyde Elem.	Pajaro Valley Unified	Watsonville	1
Linscott Charter	Pajaro Valley Unified	Watsonville	9
Macquiddy Elem.	Pajaro Valley Unified	Watsonville	2
Mar Vista Elem.	Pajaro Valley Unified	Aptos	6
Mintie White Elem.	Pajaro Valley Unified	Watsonville	2
Ohlone Elem.	Pajaro Valley Unified	Watsonville	1
Rio del Mar Elem.	Pajaro Valley Unified	Aptos	10
Salsipuedes Elem.	Pajaro Valley Unified	Watsonville	2
Soldo Elem.	Pajaro Valley Unified	Watsonville	1
Starlight Elem.	Pajaro Valley Unified	Watsonville	1
Valencia Elem.	Pajaro Valley Unified	Aptos	8
Aptos Jr. High	Pajaro Valley Unified	Aptos	8
Hall Middle	Pajaro Valley Unified	Watsonville	1
Lakeview Middle	Pajaro Valley Unified	Watsonville	2
Pajaro Middle	Pajaro Valley Unified	Watsonville	1
Rolling Hills Middle	Pajaro Valley Unified	Watsonville	1
Aptos High	Pajaro Valley Unified	Aptos	7
Watsonville High	Pajaro Valley Unified	Watsonville	2
Boulder Creek Elem.	San Lorenzo Valley Unif.	Boulder Creek	9
San Lorenzo Valley Elem.	San Lorenzo Valley Unif.	Felton	8
San Lorenzo Valley Jr. High	San Lorenzo Valley Unif.	Felton	8
San Lorenzo Valley High	San Lorenzo Valley Unif.	Felton	8
Pacific Collegiate	Santa Cruz Co. Off. of Ed.	Santa Cruz	10
Bay View Elem.	Santa Cruz City Elem.	Santa Cruz	7
Branciforte Elem.	Santa Cruz City Elem.	Santa Cruz	3

School	District	City/Town	Rank
De Laveaga Elem.	Santa Cruz City Elem.	Santa Cruz	9
Gault Elem.	Santa Cruz City Elem.	Santa Cruz	5
Natural Bridges Elem.	Santa Cruz City Elem.	Santa Cruz	7
Westlake Elem.	Santa Cruz City Elem.	Santa Cruz	9
Branciforte Middle	Santa Cruz City High	Santa Cruz	7
Mission Hill Middle	Santa Cruz City High	Santa Cruz	8
Harbor High	Santa Cruz City High	Santa Cruz	7
Santa Cruz High	Santa Cruz City High	Santa Cruz	7
Soquel High	Santa Cruz City High	Soquel	6
Brook Knoll Elem.	Scotts Valley Unified	Santa Cruz	10
Vine Hill Elem.	Scotts Valley Unified	Scotts Valley	9
Scotts Valley Middle	Scotts Valley Unified	Scotts Valley	9
Scotts Valley High	Scotts Valley Unified	Scotts Valley	9
Capitola Elem.	Soquel Union Elem.	Capitola	7
Main St. Elem.	Soquel Union Elem.	Soquel	9
Santa Cruz Gardens Elem.	Soquel Union Elem.	Santa Cruz	7
Soquel Elem.	Soquel Union Elem.	Soquel	8
New Brighton Middle	Soquel Union Elem.	Capitola	9

Chapter 6

City & Town Profiles Santa Cruz County

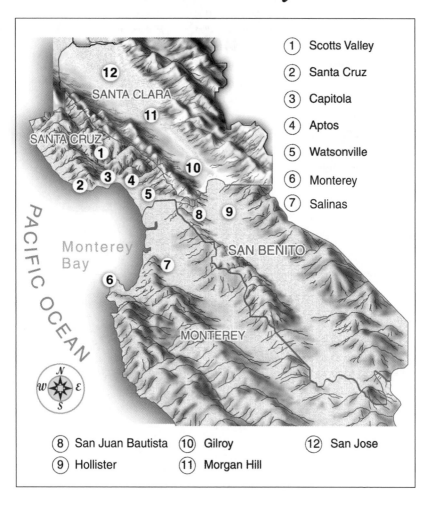

1. Scotts Valley
2. Santa Cruz
3. Capitola
4. Aptos
5. Watsonville
6. Monterey
7. Salinas
8. San Juan Bautista
9. Hollister
10. Gilroy
11. Morgan Hill
12. San Jose

APTOS

UPSCALE TOWN that straddles Highway 1, east of Capitola. State beach, fishing pier, many custom and lovely homes built around the Seascape Golf Course. Country feeling, tall trees, no sidewalks. Borders Soquel Community College on its west side.

Unincorporated; vague boundaries. On many maps, Aptos seems to be located north of Highway 1, removed from the beach. Maps also break out Rio Del Mar and La Selva Beach, nearby neighborhoods, as separate entities.

But as suburban growth has blurred the distinctions between the neighborhoods, this guide places the entire area under Aptos. The 2000 census counted 9,396 residents in Aptos but if you add in the other sections, the number will probably hit 24,000 to 28,000.

Aptos came from Spanish, who applied it to local Indian tribe or settlement. Early maps or records spelled the name Outos, Atos and Ortos.

The 2000 census put the median age of residents at 41. Kids and teens under 18 make up 19 percent of the residents. People over age 55 account for 24 percent of the village. Translation: many empty nesters, town getting older.

Children generally attend Valencia, Rio Del Mar and Mar Vista Elementary schools, then move up to Aptos Middle and Aptos High School, all in the Pajaro Valley School District. Scores range from the 70th to the 90th percentile, the top 30 percent in the state, and some classes score in the 90th percentile. The high school was crowded but in 2005 relief came in with the opening of another high school in Watsonville.

Housing ranges from plain suburban to custom lovely. Tall trees grace the winding streets around the golf course and give the neighborhood an air of rustic affluence. Some mansions hide behind hedges and ornate gates. Many of coastal homes and apartments are situated on bluffs and have nice views of Monterey Bay. State beaches, easily reached, run along most of the coast. The blend of trees, golf and Pacific adds to the charms of the region.

Very little new construction. In 2002, the county Board of Supervisors, after four years and hearings and arguments, approved the construction of 26 homes, half of what the developer first requested. By Aptos standards, this was a major project.

A large park (New Brighton) with another state beach is located on the west side, near Capitola. North of the freeway, a smaller golf course amuses the duffers. A long narrow trail from Aptos Village Park leads up to Forest of Nisene Marks State Park, which has many second-growth redwoods.

Mrs. Marks was an immigrant whose family farmed and purchased land. When she died, her children donated the park, about 10,000 acres, to the state in her memory. Nice tribute. The 1989 Loma Prieta quake was centered in the park.

A few restaurants and shops near the water. Small shopping plaza with Gottschalks at Highway 1. Town has its own newspaper.

North of Highway 1, streets wind off into the hills and ravines. At least some of the residents in this area will have an "Aptos" mailing address.

Regarding Rio Del Mar and La Selva Beach, realty magazines and listings will often use these neighborhood names. Both are located on the east side of Aptos. Rio Del Mar has many custom homes with lovely and imaginative landscaping. La Selva Beach is a small neighborhood of homes and cottages on Lundborg and Manresa beaches. Palm trees line the main street, Playa Boulevard, which has a planted median strip. Cliff provides a sweeping vista of beaches and Pacific.

Cabrillo Community College a real plus. Many classes and activities open to locals. Theater used by community groups. The campus recently built more classrooms, a science lab, a computer lab, a bookstore, faculty and counseling offices, a theater and arts building, a sports facility and a horticultural center.

Park and Ride lot to ease the commute. For the everyday commute, Highway 1 to Highway 17.

At Seacliff Beach, the remains of the *Palo Alto,* a cement ship built for use in World War I but unfinished at war's end. It was towed to Seacliff, flooded down to the sand, and turned into a casino with a dance floor. After this venture failed, the *Palo Alto* became a fishing pier.

• Getting some riled but it has its supporters: a tourist trolley from Capitola to Aptos. It would run along an old rail line.

• In 2005, Rio Del Mar Elementary School won a national Blue Ribbon for academic excellence. Hip, hip, hooray and well done!

BEN LOMOND, BOULDER CREEK, BROOKDALE, FELTON, MOUNT HERMON

SMALL TOWNS along Highway 9, the old logging-stagecoach road through the redwoods. Several got their start as mill towns. The two-lane highway runs parallel to the San Lorenzo River, which has carved a long valley through the mountains.

The 2000 census broke out Ben Lomond, 2,364 residents, Boulder Creek, 4,081, and Felton, 1,051. But when you add in the outlying streets and hamlets, the region's population ranges from 30,000 to 40,000.

Many trees, many redwoods. Many homes live in almost perpetual shade. Some virgin giant redwoods remain but most are second and third growth. But even the second-growth redwoods are often tall and majestic. Also pines and assorted other trees. Besides traffic, possibly the only downside is the weather. Redwoods thrive in fogs and moisture. Winters are often wet and damp.

Many year-round residents but also many people who take their summers at a cabin in the woods or put up at a motel. Or rent a cabin or home.

It's customary to describe these towns by their histories and their ornaments. Felton has a teen center and a covered wooden bridge, Brookdale a large mural of James Dean. An old steam train starts at Felton and winds through the redwoods, one of the most scenic amusements of the county. Old stores have been remodeled into modern efficiency while retaining their historic charm.

But it's also misleading to describe the towns in this way. Many of the homes are located on streets that snake off of Highway 9 and have little connection to the past. You'll find old homes and cabins, many small, many old. But the majority of homes are modern or fairly modern, built to custom or tract designs. A few apartment complexes and mobile home parks also can be found along Highway 9.

Artisans work their crafts in some of the older buildings but many of the businesses lining Highway 9 make their money by providing the daily necessities — markets, hardware stores, beauty and nail salons, doctor and dental offices, chiropractors, service stations, restaurants, delis and cafes, pizza parlors, post offices, laundries, movie rentals, insurance firms, and so on. Fast-food places are rare, which gives the local cuisine a down-home flavor. A fair number of churches, including one with an onion dome. Also, bed and breakfast places, yoga and spiritual retreats, a swim center, and small establishments where one or several people will teach you or your children how to dance or play a musical instrument. Many artists retreat to the woods and need to make a buck or two. Several vineyards. Antique stores. Summer camps. Cowell Redwoods and Big Basin State parks covers thousands of acres. Campgrounds, trails. Swimming in rivers. Several small parks and schools provide some of the playing fields. One golf course in the region.

Felton and Mount Hermon are located just outside Scotts Valley, which has medium-sized shopping plazas.

If you are working in Silicon Valley and want to make your home in this region, it's not like you are moving to the sticks but the atmosphere is definitely country-forest. Even if you buy in what might pass for a suburban tract, you will often be surrounded by trees. No sidewalks in the residential areas. Utility lines overhead. Feral pigs a problem in some places; when possible, trapped and killed.

Several towns flow into one another, Mount Hermon to Felton, Felton to Ben Lomond, Ben Lomond to Brookdale. The locals know the boundaries but visitors and newcomers may pay them little attention and as more homes are built, the dividing lines will become even more blurred. Purchase a good map and drive the streets. It won't take long and it will give you a feel for the nuances of the towns.

This region has been building homes for well over 100 years so it offers variety. If your budget or inclinations say mountain shack or log cabin, they are there. If you can afford a custom home built on a hilltop, that's there too. If you want privacy and the dark of redwoods, it can be yours. If your idea of pleasure is a short stroll to a coffee shop and a leisurely read of the daily paper, you can secure both with a home near Highway 9. Many people, according to local newspapers, are running businesses out of their homes or mixing regular work with telecommuting.

Most children attend the schools in the San Lorenzo Unified District. In state rankings, the schools score in the 70th to 90th percentile, which indicates upscale demographics and high parental interest in the schools. Losing enrollment, the district recently closed two schools. In 2004, residents passed a bond to renovate the district's schools.

Highway 17 can be picked up in Scotts Valley, which has bus service to Silicon Valley. If you live on the north side near Redwood Grove, it probably is faster to take Highway 9 north into Saratoga and Silicon Valley. On some days you'll pay the penalty of the road's limitations. Highway 9 has its turnouts but it's a two-lane road, full of curves and hills. If the car in front of you takes it pokey slow and doesn't turn out, you're stuck.

Felton, Mount Hermon and Ben Lomond are within 10 minutes of downtown Santa Cruz and university. More restaurants, stores, things to do, surfing, etc. For all the hassles over Highway 17, Santa Cruz is not that big a county. Many communities are within a short drive of one another.

CAPITOLA

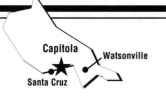

ONE OF THE OLDEST RESORT COMMUNITIES in California. On Monterey Bay. Slow growing. In the last decade, the population dropped by 138 persons. The state in 2005 estimated the number of residents at 9,924.

Lovely beach and old town, which has been overhauled by city. Shops, restaurants, bookstore, art galleries, pizza parlors, hotel, cottage rentals, ice cream parlor. Fishing pier. Most of what is old and quaint is confined to five or six short blocks, where Soquel Creek flows into the ocean.

East of the downtown, the terrain rises into low hills. Many homes have views of the ocean. Few large homes. Many cottages, lovingly fussed over. Flowers. Trees.

West of the downtown, the housing tends to two- and three-bedroom modest homes, well maintained, built over flat land but within a few blocks of the ocean. Typically, the front yards are small. Many have large windows and decks facing toward the ocean and the sunset.

Leaving town on Monterey Avenue going toward Aptos, newer, larger homes show themselves. Well maintained. Capitola also has a trailer park.

In 2005, the town tallied 5,387 housing units, of which 1,977 were single homes, 514 single-attached, 2,246 condos or apartments and 650 mobile homes.

Capitola has the largest mall in the county. It is located back from the beach and within a short drive of Highway 1. Anchor stores are Mervyns, Gottschalks and Macys. Sales tax revenue from the mall helps fund city programs. Trader Joe's.

Three neighborhood parks, city-esplanade beach in downtown, state park on west side, larger state park on east side; it extends to the beach.

Children attend schools in the Soquel district, then move up to Soquel High in the Santa Cruz High district. After failing once, the Soquel District in 2002 won a bond to renovate its schools. Also in 2002, the high-school district won an extension on a parcel tax to maintain its arts and academic programs. A few students may attend Pajaro High School.

When California became a state, many towns competed for the honor of becoming the state capital. A Santa Cruz County group put in its bid and even designated the place for the Capitola — Spanish for capital. Nothing came of the effort.

The town came to life in 1874 when a pioneering land owner erected cottages, bath houses and a stable, and later a hotel, all with the intention of building a resort on the European model. Capitola also served as shipping-farming center for the region. Capitola grew slowly and by the time it incorporated as a legal city in 1949, it mustered about 1,800 residents.

In the 1960s, through annexations and newcomers, the town more than doubled its population, from 2,021 to 5,080. In the 1970s, came another big increase, to 9,095 residents. Then clang went the door: an increase of 1,000 in the 1980s and just about nothing in the 1990s. In the 1990s, according to state estimates, the city added about 350 residential units.

Zero homicides in 2004, one in 2003, zero between 2002 and 1995, with the exception of 1997, one homicide.

Annual begonia festival. Soquel Creek, which flows to the bay, is filled with floats draped with flowers. Art and wine festival in the fall. Cabrillo Community College is located on the town's eastern border. Many classes, activities open to the public.

For commuters, a short drive to Highway 1.

In sum, lovely town, especially in fall when Capitola blooms with foliage trees. Some streets look straight out of New England.

But because of limited housing, not too much comes on the market for newcomers.

Parking a problem in the downtown and near beaches. City, for fee, issues permits to downtown residents.

Under argument, a tourist trolley from Capitola to Aptos.

For information, chamber of commerce (831) 475-6522.

• No smoking, please. In 2004, Capitola outlawed smoking on its beaches.

SANTA CRUZ

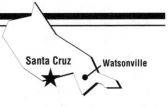

LARGEST AND MOST POPULOUS CITY, 56,451 RESIDENTS, in the county. Place with the most jobs. Lovely in spots, plain in others. Most of the city falls into the category of middle-class presentable.

Crime low but begging and the homeless are issues in local politics. School scores high. Many homes along shore and in hills have delightful views. Majority of housing was built on flat lands, somewhat removed from Monterey Bay. Nonetheless, a strong feeling of sea and sand permeates Santa Cruz, which has dubbed itself Surf City.

College town. The University of California, built over hills and terraces, is located on the northwest border of Santa Cruz. The university is the largest employer in the county.

A town with energy. When the Loma Prieta quake of 1989 leveled the downtown, civic leaders and business people did an excellent job of restoring and rebuilding and, by bringing in new businesses and reviving a movie theater, reshaping the downtown into a vibrant and pleasant center. Bookstores, restaurants, delis and coffee shops add to the allures of the place.

Santa Cruz is the county seat. The courts and the county government bureaucracy are based in the city — many jobs. Santa Cruz has also landed a little high tech to diversify its employment base. Supposedly many people have set up home offices.

Nonetheless, Santa Cruz follows the prevailing sentiment of the county's residents — restricted development. In the 1990s, the city added about 2,000 residential units, about half of them single homes. This came in a decade where Silicon Valley was begging for more land for housing. The university resorted to buying a hotel and an apartment complex to house students.

Many residents see anti-growth as their duty to protect the bay, the ocean, the trees and the natural beauties. Some people, no doubt, envy Silicon Valley and wish Santa Cruz had more high-tech but a greater number see Santa Cruz as a refuge from the bustle and congestion and noise of Silicon Valley. Over the last few years, as California wrestled with budget deficits and a sluggish economy, Santa Cruz, sometimes called the People's Republic of Surf City, has felt the pain and vows to be friendlier to big-box stores (a former enemy), shops and restaurants. But regarding residential construction, the county remains anti-growth. In 2005, Santa Cruz counted 23,133 residential units, of which 12,289 were single homes, 1,954 single-attached, 8,450 apartments, condos or hotel rooms and 440 mobile homes.

Until recently, the children attended schools in an elementary district, then moved up to a high school district. Both are now one, the Santa Cruz Unified School District. Bonds have been passed to renovate buildings and upgrade their technology and parcel taxes passed to maintain the quality of programs.

After much arguing, the district voted in 2004 to "close" Natural Bridges and Branciforte elementaries. The reasons: declining enrollments and the success of a public charter school called Pacific Collegiate, which is open to students from throughout the region and decides some admissions by lottery.

Several years ago parents who were dissatisfied with the local public schools won permission to open a public charter, grades 7-12, that stressed academics, required parents to volunteer at least 40 hours a year and made it clear that parents had to help raise money for programs. Pacific Collegiate was formed under the loose control of the County Office of Education; it is not part of Santa Cruz Unified School District. In effect, Pacific Collegiate governs itself through its parents committee and staff.

Lacking a campus, Pacific Collegiate rented space at Natural Bridges School, a neighborhood elementary of the Santa Cruz district. Soon Pacific Collegiate was posting the highest scores in the county, making it all the more attractive to parents. They moved their kids out of the neighborhood schools, weakening their finances. Fewer kids, fewer dollars from the state. This ultimately made it impossible for the Santa Cruz Unified District to keep open Branciforte and Natural Bridges as neighborhood schools.

Natural Bridges was taken over by Pacific Collegiate. This sounds like a clear-cut transition but it aroused animosity. The new school served some children from the immediate neighborhood but not as many as before. In some quarters Pacific Collegiate was seen as elitist. On the other side, the Pac Col parents were fighting for tougher academics. The dispute perhaps was not unexpected in a collegiate town where many parents are sensitive to the pace of learning.

In and around Santa Cruz, private schools educate about 1,000 kids.

Explored by the Spanish in 1769, Santa Cruz was one of the mission towns of the crown. For most of its modern life, its prosperity was built around farming, fishing and resorts. By 1900, the population stood at 5,600, by 1940, at 17,000. After World War II, towns up and down California boomed into suburban life and saw their populations rise dramatically. Business and civic leaders hoped that Santa Cruz would follow this course. When the University of California broke ground in the 1960s, the regents anticipated that great day when the campus would hold 27,500 students. But the opening coincided with the movement to slow growth and protect the environment. The university now enrolls only 15,000 students (but plans to expand).

Nonetheless, Santa Cruz did increase its population. By 1960, the town claimed 25,500 residents and by 1980, it counted 41,500. By 1990, the tally stood at 49,000. In the 1990s, Santa Cruz added about 6,000 residents, the census reported. The Association of Monterey Bay Area Governments predicts the city will inch up to 64,000 residents by 2020.

Housing styles can be divided roughly into old and ornate (some lovely Victorians), old and plain and occasionally rundown, bungalows (the design of the 1910s to the 1940s), middle-class tract (circa 1950 to 1970), and upper-middle custom or executive, the new homes and the homes of the 1990s.

Many of the homes near or on the beach were built at time when Santa Cruz was a sleepy burg that catered to the working middle class and summer vacationers. These homes run generally to two and three bedrooms. On the west side, some upscale custom homes, pretty, have shouldered their way on to Cliff Drive on the ocean but just behind them the streets are filled with two- and three-bedroom tract models.

Many of the large new homes are located north of Highway 1 in a hollow with views of the hills (but not the bay).

Intimate town. You get the feeling that people really know their neighbors. Except for the few ramshackle homes in the downtown — and these may be gone in a few years — the streets and homes show a lot of care.

Santa Cruz is a town that requires a good map. The streets zig and zag and deadend at San Lorenzo Creek or Highway 1 or some other obstacle, such as the harbor.

The city sits at the top of Monterey Bay and is sheltered not only by the curve of the Bay but by a little protuberance to the west of the downtown, where the Boardwalk (amusement park) and the city's main beaches are located. On the minus side, the golden sunsets that San Francisco enjoys are hidden from many Santa Cruz residents. The sun, as it were, sets over the right shoulder of the town.

Scads to do. Beaches, the Boardwalk, a popular resort in Northern California, brings in big-name performers. Large marina, fishing, swimming, surfing, usual sports (baseball, basketball, soccer, etc.), City hall sponsors after-school programs for kids and teenagers, and such activities as dance (ballet, tap, line, swing), gymnastics, arts and crafts, sports camps. For older teens and adults, there's yoga, aerobics, fencing, massage and more. Also activities for seniors. The university and the community college present plays, lectures, concerts and art exhibits. Three libraries with reading programs for kids. Bookstores, cafes, delis, movies, restaurants, dance halls, shops in downtown. Costco and Trader Joe's. Concerts at community center. Shakespeare festival. McPherson Art and History at Santa Cruz County Art Museum. Short drive to redwood country. Mall in Capitola, the next town to the east. Home Depot into Soquel.

Great town for strolling and gazing. Pelicans and other birds circle the harbor and dive for fish.

On Mission Hill, overlooking downtown, the Santa Cruz Mission State Historic Park preserves some of the earliest Spanish history in the region. An 1824 adobe, constructed primarily by Yokuts Indians, is all that remains of the original 17 structures. The adobe is the only surviving Indian mission housing in California. During some weekends, mission docents in period costumes conduct tours and teach crafts —adobe brick making, tule reed basket weaving, tortilla making, etc.

Beach-resort towns, in their commercial sections, get more than their share of the rowdy and the light-fingered. In its residential neighborhoods, however, Santa Cruz falls into the category of quite safe. After many complaints, the city council made it tougher for beggars and for vagrants who congregate on Pacific Avenue, the main street. One homicide in 2004, four each in 2003 and 2002. Zero in 2001, three in 2000, one in 1999. Counts for previous years are two, one, two, four, three.

Lousy commute. Highway 17 ends its tortured path in Santa Cruz. Bus service over the mountain to Silicon Valley. If you have a local job, the commute may be a little snarled but you'll arrive at the job and at home long before the Silicon Valley sufferers.

In politics, liberal-libertarian. The city council voted to legalize marijuana for medicinal purposes and just about anything President George Bush does, finds disfavor.

- University mascot: the Banana Slug, a slimy, bright yellow mollusk that resides in the redwoods. The slug was chosen in 1965, when the university opened and to many it will come across as a Sixties thing. In the 1980s, dissidents tried to replace the slug with the Sea Lion. But put to a campus vote, the slug won and is now generally accepted.

- Beach choices: for dogs, no leash, Its Beach in Santa Cruz; for nudists, Red, White and Blue beach, just north of Santa Cruz.

- Thousands and thousands of butterflies spend the winter clustered in eucalyptus trees outside Santa Cruz. Visitors flock to Natural Bridges State Park to see swarms of Monarchs.

- Pooper scoopers required in City of Santa Cruz and other urban areas.

- Party poopers. In 2005, city council passed a law that raised fines for loud and unruly parties. UC students protested but lost.

- Greased. Feds put up $75,000 to find out whether it's financially feasible to run buses on cooking oil from restaurants.

Chamber of commerce (831) 457-3713.

SCOTTS VALLEY

Scotts Valley ★

Watsonville

Santa Cruz

SMALL, UPSCALE CITY that straddles Highway 17. Population about 11,571. Crime low, school scores high.

The first major (by Santa Cruz County standards) burg over the hill from Silicon Valley and for that reason considered one of the best commutes in the county — a dubious honor. Highway 17 often snarls long before it reaches Scotts Valley but locals say that even on bad days, you can make Silicon Valley in about 45 minutes.

If you say, "I live in Scotts Valley," people in Silicon Valley generally will conclude that you love trees and have a lot of money. Scotts Valley sits in a bowl surrounded by hills with redwoods and other tall trees and appears to be one of those places that nature designated for the affluent — only it didn't quite turn out this way.

The area was named after Hiram Scott of Maine. As a young man, he took to the sea, jumped ship at Monterey Bay in 1846, hit it big in the Gold Rush, returned to Santa Cruz in 1852, purchased for $25,000 a land grant that includes the present Scotts V., and went into hay, horses and potatoes.

For the next 100 years or so, Scotts Valley remained a farming center but, attracted by the beauty of the region and the closeness of Highway 17, people bought parcels and built houses and developed small tracts, some for mobile-home parks. At that time, Silicon Valley had yet to bloom and people built small and modest. Stores and service businesses followed. In the 1960s, residents decided to bring planning under local control and make sense out of what development they had. So in 1966, they incorporated as a legal city. The 1970 census counted 3,621 residents, the 1980 census, 6,891, an increase of 90 percent. In the 1980s, the city added 1,700 residents and in the last decade, about 2,300. Not exactly rip-roaring growth but these numbers are misleading.

Scotts Valley's streets wander off into the unincorporated countryside, miles of roads that spin off other roads that curl and connect to obscure streets or deadend against some hill. Thousands of homes have been built along these streets and lacking any other point of reference, the residents say they live in Scotts Valley. Many of these homes are custom jobs, handsomely done. This has elevated the reputation of the town. And so has the newer housing within city limits. The new stuff is not knock-out opulent but the homes are much larger than in years past and many are situated on view lots.

Most of the housing in the City of Scotts Valley is located on the south side and about the mid north on both sides of Highway 17. The south side rises into steep hills and cliffs. Woodsy. Good place for kids to practice rock climbing. The mid-north also rises into wooded hills but not as steep. The homes here are older than the ones on the south side. The mobile homes are situated about midtown. In 2005, the state tallied 4,616 housing units, of which 2,482 were single-detached homes, 415 single-attached, 914 apartments or condos and 805 mobile homes. The town is leery about more housing but some happens.

Through redevelopment, the city gradually is fixing up its main drag, Scotts Valley Boulevard, a four-lane road with a planted median strip. Shops and businesses are located along the boulevard but most stores, including a Gottschalks, are to be found along Mount Hermon Boulevard on the south. The offerings include supermarkets, a movie plex, doctor and dental offices, video rentals, a McDonalds, other restaurants, bakery and all that is necessary, within reason, to make basic shopping convenient for residents. At the south entrance to the city is a hotel, which serves tourists and visitors connected to the city's few high-tech businesses.

Santa Cruz and all it offers is about five minutes down road and many residents probably load up at the Costco in Santa Cruz. Mount Hermon Road connects to Highway 9 and Felton and large state parks with many redwoods and tall trees.

Education by Scotts Valley Unified School District, which recently built a high school. Scores in all schools are landing generally in the 80th and 90th percentiles, the top 20 percent in the state. The school district's boundaries extend far beyond city limits, especially on the east and north side. If you buy a home close to Scotts Valley, chances are your children will attend a Scotts Valley school. Lawsuit filed over the construction-design of the high school.

Lowest crime rate of county's four cities. Zero homicides between 1999 and 2004.

Four parks, the newest with three soccer fields. The city works with the school district to provide activities and playing fields. City rec departments sponsors such activities as soccer, how to swim, baby play, tennis, fitness workouts. Scotts Valley Dance Center (private) teaches kids and adults how to dance. New skate park. Other activities in City of Santa Cruz.

Just south of town is a parking lot-bus stop. Park your car and commute by bus over the mountains to downtown San Jose. The nerves you save may be your own. Chamber of commerce (831) 438-1010.

SOQUEL, LIVE OAK

Watsonville

Soquel, Live Oak

UNINCORPORATED COMMUNITIES with a mix of housing, some of it quite modest but often still expensive.

Live Oak, population 16,628, is situated south of Highway 1 and down to the ocean, between the cities of Santa Cruz and Capitola. Many oaks used to grow in the area — the inspiration for the name. Within Live Oak, some maps break out small neighborhoods near the ocean, Twin Lakes and Opal Cliffs.

Soquel (so-kell), population 5,081, is located east of Santa Cruz and north of Highway 1, Live Oak and Capitola. It stretches from about De Laveaga Park to Cabrillo Community College. The Spanish called one of the Indian villages or tribes, Soquel.

Both populations need to be taken with a grain of salt as boundaries are vague.

Live Oak and Soquel lack centers or buildings that unify the community. Both are under the jurisdiction of the county government, which is to say both lack councils that can exert tight controls over development and build civic or town centers. County governments rarely develop strong municipal agencies; the county sees it role as regional governor. For the most part, county governments let market forces determine how unincorporated communities grow and add houses. This said, the county, through redevelopment, has borrowed money to build parks and a library in Live Oak and make general improvements.

When Live Oak developed, the market supported small homes and cottages. This is what you will find all over this community and many of the homes show their age. No sidewalks. Utility lines overhead. Country relaxed. Some people park their cars on what passes for the front lawn.

But many exceptions. In the recent years, the market has favored upscale housing. In Live Oak, it's possible to find small tracts of new middle-plus housing (two story, tile roofs, sidewalks, utilities underground) sitting side by side with rundown cottages. The market is also nudging homeowners to remodel and expand.

Near the ocean, housing quality notches up because of the location. The beach area has many modest "resort" homes constructed in an era when Americans didn't have much money.

Home Price Sampler from Classified Ads

Aptos
- 2BR/1BA, $619,000
- 3BR/2.5BA, ocean views, $1.1 mil.

Ben Lomond
- 3BR/2.5BA, tri-level, $690,000
- 3BR/2BA, good location, $549,000

Boulder Creek
- 3BR/2BA, $599,000
- 1BR/1BA, cottage, $429,000

Capitola
- 2BR/1BA, ranch style, $649,000
- 3BR/2.5BA, $1.4 mil.

Corralitos
- 4BR/2BA, $899,000

Felton
- 5BR/3BA, $860,000
- 3BR/2BA, $1.3 mil.
- 2BR/1BA, $479,000

Rio Del Mar (Aptos)
- 3BR/2BA, townhouse, $659,000
- 3BR/2BA, $1.1 mil.
- 3BR/2BA, $739,000

Santa Cruz
- 4BR/3BA, $2.7 mil.
- 2BR/2BA, $700,000
- 2BR/2.5BA, $539,000

Scotts Valley
- 3BR/2BA, $719,000
- 2BR/1.5BA, $675,000
- 3BR/2.5BA, $1.3 mil.

Soquel
- 4BR/2BA, $749,000
- 2BR/1BA, $650,000

Watsonville
- 5BR/3BA, $800,000
- 3BR/2BA, $899,000

Live Oak is built over gentle hills and ravines, which adds to the country flavor. If you are shopping for a home or a lot, Live Oak is an easy drive. The neighborhood runs about 20 blocks east to west and 20-25 blocks north to south.

Soquel got its start in 1852 as a general store-post office and within 10 years another store and a hotel had opened. Well into the 20th century decades, it functioned as sort of a four-corners hamlet, meeting the needs of travelers and selling supplies to farmers.

When suburbia rolled in after 1950, Soquel's identity was blurred almost to extinction. The county laid in street after street and home after home without trying to make any sense out of Soquel.

Many small stores are located along Soquel Drive but for bigger items and more variety residents head for Capitola and Santa Cruz. Highway 1 split off a portion of the community. Many streets wander off into the hills.

To some extent, both towns can be delineated by the boundaries of their elementary districts and roughly by their zip codes.

Soquel has its rundown and modest homes, but having developed later than Live Oak, more of its homes run to tract models. New homes are mixed in with old. Some mobile home parks.

About 10 parks in both towns. Large parks nearby. Public beaches. Short drive to all that Santa Cruz and Capitola offer. Many classes and activities at Cabrillo Community College. Dominican Hospital in Soquel.

Education by Live Oak Elementary District and Soquel Elementary District. Students attend either Soquel High or Harbor High in the Santa Cruz district. Scores in the Live Oak District, state comparison, land generally in the 50th and 60th percentiles, and in the Soquel District, generally in the 60th to 80th percentile. Some schools score lower. In demographic terms, these numbers translate into middle class and middle plus. All districts have passed bonds to renovate their schools. See Santa Cruz for information about the high schools.

Santa Cruz County Single Home Resale Prices

City	Sales	Lowest	Median	Highest	Average
Aptos	99	$175,000	$840,000	$3,175,000	930,784
Ben Lomond	40	130,000	622,500	1,089,000	631,938
Boulder Creek	58	100,000	539,000	950,000	553,545
Brookdale	2	800,000	850,000	900,000	850,000
Capitola	20	30,000	799,000	1,150,000	768,200
Felton	46	137,500	565,000	839,000	549,700
Freedom	12	267,000	655,000	1,800,000	776,182
Santa Cruz	239	87,500	778,500	3,700,000	891,502
Scotts Valley	45	469,000	839,000	2,320,000	964,756
Soquel	38	515,000	880,000	2,700,000	1,039,392
Watsonville	156	71,500	700,500	1,595,000	715,787

Source: DataQuick Information Systems, LaJolla: Single Family residence sales from May 2005 through July 31, 2005. Median means halfway. In 100 homes, the 50th is the median.

WATSONVILLE

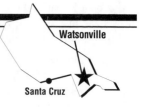

FARM TOWN-SUBURB. Second-largest city in the county and the only city predicted to add a fair number of people but arguments over development are many. Open a long-awaited high school in 2005, relieving crowding at the other schools.

Located at base of hills on flat and gently rolling land. An inland city. No ocean frontage, no tall groves of trees. Much of the land surrounding the town is devoted to farming. Row crops on south side, apple orchards on north. Population 49,601. Over the next 25 years, the city expects to add 20,000 residents.

In its own way, a place with charm. Unlike Capitola and the City of Santa Cruz, Watsonville never had a resort economy. And until recently, it lacked the suburban tracts found in towns throughout California.

Named after a founding pioneer, Watsonville for almost all its life was a farm community, not isolated from outside influences but less dependent on them than other cities. It had its neighborhoods for the rich, the middle class and the poor, many of them migrants working the farms, and it had its downtown where just about everyone shopped and mingled and went to the movies or to church or to service clubs. When visitors came to town, they stayed at the downtown hotels. Watsonville incorporated itself as a city in 1868. It has been electing its own leaders and governing itself for over 135 years and until modern times almost everyone who held public office was tied financially to the success of the town or region, if only because everyone worked locally.

Watsonville grew slowly. It started 1900 with 3,500 residents and 40 years later, on the eve of World War II, claimed 9,000 people. Over the next three decades, while much of the West Coast was roaring into suburbia, Watsonville added only 5,000 residents. Not until the 1970s did suburbia arrive. In that decade, the population jumped from 14,569 to 23,662 and in the 1980s to 31,099. In the 1990s, the city added about 7,000 people, which brought the 2000 population to 44,265. In 2005, the state tallied 13,463 residential units of which 7,100 were single homes, 1,594 were single-attached, 3,869 were apartments or condos and 900 mobile homes.

On its east, Watsonville borders the Pajaro (Pa-Ha-Row) River and Monterey County. The city cannot annex in this direction. Environmentalists have fought, pretty successfully so far, to keep the land west of Highway 1 (toward the ocean) in farming. This has pushed development slightly to the north but mostly to the east of the old downtown.

The result: a city that divides between old and new. The city, through redevelopment, has pumped a lot of money into the downtown to remodel buildings and attract businesses, including a Gottshalks. But the new neighborhoods have their own shopping centers on Main Street and Green Valley Road (supermarkets, Staples, Target, Starbucks, video, bagels, delis, movies, etc). Many people throughout the town shop these stores.

Compared to other towns, Watsonville remains fairly cohesive. No freeway divides the town; Highway 1 skirts the southside. Old housing flows into new, cheap housing into middle and middle into upper and in some areas, the difference between high and low income is only a block or two. For the new stuff, stucco and red-tile roofs, drive Green Valley Road. For the low income, drive the neighborhoods around and to the south of the downtown. For the old middle and old rich or the fairly old, take Lake Avenue north out of the downtown and drive the streets in and around Martinelli Street, Crestview Drive and Brewerton Avenue. Some streets have lovely Victorians, some ornamental street lights. Many buildings in the downtown have been remodeled and fitted with modern wiring and plumbing. Packing and food-processing firms are located south of the downtown.

Two homicides in 2004, three in 2003, zero in 2002, four in 2001.

About a dozen parks, including one with a gigantic tent used to shield soccer fields from rains and allow evening play. New turf recently laid. Usual sports: football, basketball, etc. Pacific and state beach about three miles to west. Restaurants in downtown. Library and on outskirts. Cabrillo College runs a branch campus in downtown. To north of towns, the county fairgrounds and a large park with a lake and boating.

Education by Pajaro Valley Unified School District, which also takes in Aptos and the bordering communities, and a small piece of Monterey County. School rankings bounce all over but many are low. This should improve as the demographics of the town move up. The new high school is located west of Highway 1. Several charter schools in district, including one devoted to the arts. Two Christian schools, one enrolling over 1,000 students. Small Catholic high school. Private school.

- Two unincorporated neighborhoods north of Watsonville. Freedom, 6,000 residents, Corralitos, 2,431. Spread out over hills and valleys.

- Large airport to west. If moving into west side, check for noise.

- Highway 152 runs over the east mountains and drops into Gilroy in southern Santa Clara Valley. For some, this will be the fastest way to get to Silicon Valley.

- City is sprucing up town plaza and adding parking. General plan calls for more parks and buildings that blend shops with housing and cut down on use of the car. For more info, city hall. Chamber of commerce, (831) 724-3900.

Chapter *7*

How Public Schools Work

SCORES MEASURE ACADEMIC success but they have their shortcomings. Some students know the material but are not adept at taking tests and some tests are so poorly designed that they fail to assess what has been taught. The rankings in the previous chapters do not break out students as individuals. A basic exam tests the least the children should know, not the most. Scores cannot assess goodness, kindness or wisdom or predict how helpful students will be to society.

There are other legitimate criticisms of probably every test given to California school children. Nonetheless, the tests have their value and except for a few cases probably give an accurate picture of how the schools are doing academically. Students who do well in elementary school generally do well in high school and score high on the SAT and go on to succeed in college. With rare exceptions, the scores correlate with teacher assessments, and so on. The exceptions cannot be ignored. A student who does poorly in one educational arrangement may thrive in another.

When your children attend a school with high test scores, they are not assured of success. These schools have their failures. Neither can you be certain that your children will get the best teachers or the right programs. Other schools with lower scores might do better on these points. What you can be certain of is that your children are entering a setting that has proven successful for many students.

The main problem with making sense out of scores concerns what is called socioeconomics, a theory educators love, hate and widely believe.

Socioeconomics

In its crudest form, socioeconomics means rich kids score high, middle-class kids score about the middle and poor kids score low. Not all the time, not predictably by individual. Many children from poor and middle-class homes succeed in school and attend the best colleges. But as a general rule socioeconomics enjoys much statistical support.

Compare the rankings in Chapter 2 with income by cities, Chapter 1, page 15. Los Altos Hills and Los Gatos, rich or well-to-do, high scores; Alum Rock

$15.95

McCormack's GUIDES

How California Schools Work

A PRACTICAL
GUIDE FOR
PARENTS

FROM THE EDITORS OF McCormack's Guides

www.mccormacks.com
1-800-222-3602

Scholastic Aptitude Test (SAT) Scores
Santa Clara County

High School	*Enrollment	% Tested	Verbal	Math
Cupertino	298	67	548	623
Del Mar	260	35	498	508
Fremont	374	60	492	546
Gilroy	493	38	502	494
Gunderson	242	36	464	493
Gunn	429	90	607	642
Hill	458	37	439	485
Homestead	358	72	566	618
Independence	986	35	462	509
Leigh	360	53	534	559
Leland	419	78	551	603
Lick	265	13	441	472
Lincoln	380	45	538	522
Live Oak	567	38	511	529
Los Altos	341	75	553	586
Los Gatos	379	76	586	610
Lynbrook	382	94	595	656
Milpitas	605	56	489	540
Monta Vista	519	88	590	666
Mountain View	349	73	563	594
Mt. Pleasant	537	48	462	488
Oak Grove	585	34	489	511
Overfelt	400	25	412	456
Palo Alto	390	83	608	630
Piedmont Hills	481	61	498	538
Pioneer	285	50	528	542
Prospect	265	37	538	550
San Jose Acad.	214	38	482	499
Santa Clara	348	46	480	499
Santa Teresa	521	44	515	525
Saratoga	331	89	621	659
Silver Creek	619	44	461	509
Westmont	342	44	521	547
Wilcox	439	52	476	524
Willow Glen	289	36	477	483
Yerba Buena	371	33	431	491

Source: California Dept. of Education, 2004 tests. SAT scores are greatly influenced by who and how many take the test. The state education department has been pushing schools to have more students take the SAT. A school that has more marginal students taking the test will, by one line of reasoning, be doing a good job, but the scores are likely to be lower. *Senior class.

Elementary School District (East San Jose), low income or poor, low scores; Morgan Hill and Milpitas, middle-class towns, middling to middling-plus scores. The SAT scores reflect the basic test scores.

The same pattern shows up in neighboring Alameda County. The schools in the poorer neighborhoods of Oakland score low; well-to-do Piedmont scores

Scholastic Aptitude Test (SAT) Scores
Santa Cruz County

High School	*Enrollment	% Tested	Verbal	Math
Aptos	430	47	509	521
Harbor	235	39	539	552
San Lorenzo Valley	264	53	545	547
Santa Cruz	282	52	546	552
Soquel	309	45	535	557
Watsonville	643	28	431	461

San Benito County

High School	*Enrollment	% Tested	Verbal	Math
Anzar	57	51	525	510
San Benito	528	34	490	503

Source: California Dept. of Education, 2004 tests. SAT scores are greatly influenced by who and how many take the test. The state education department has been pushing schools to have more students take the SAT. A school that has more marginal students taking the test will, by one line of reasoning, be doing a good job, but the scores are likely to be lower. *Senior class.

high. And the pattern shows up around the Bay Area, the country and in other countries. The federal study, "Japanese Education Today," notes a "solid correlation between poverty and poor school performance ...."

Family and Culture

In its refined form, socioeconomics moves away from the buck and toward culture and family influence.

Note the charts on pages 24 and 112. The towns with the highest number of college educated are generally also the towns with the highest scores. If your mom or dad attended college, chances are you will attend college or do well at school because in a thousand ways while you were growing up they and their milieu pushed you in this direction. Emphasis on "chances are." Nothing is certain when dealing with human beings.

What if mom and dad never got beyond the third grade? Or can't even speak English?

In many statistical studies, scores correlate closely with family income and education. So thoroughly does the California Department of Education believe in these correlations that it has worked socioeconomics into a mathematical model. Teachers collect data on almost all students: Are they on welfare, do they have language problems (immigrants), how educated are their parents? The information is fed to computers and used to predict how students will score on tests.

Top SAT Math Scores-2004

Public high schools in California scoring over 600 in math

High School	County	City	Math
Whitney	Los Angeles	Cerritos	710
Monta Vista	Santa Clara	Cupertino	670
Gunn (Henry M.)	Santa Clara	Palo Alto	667
Saratoga	Santa Clara	Saratoga	665
Troy	Orange	Fullerton	665
Mission San Jose	Alameda	Fremont	664
Lynbrook	Santa Clara	San Jose	662
University	Orange	Irvine	657
Palo Alto	Santa Clara	Cupertino	650
Lowell	San Francisco	San Francisco	644
San Marino	Los Angeles	San Marino	644
Piedmont	Alameda	Piedmont	637
Arcadia	Los Angeles	Arcadia	632
Palos Verdes Peninsula	Los Angeles	Rolling Hills Estates	628
Pacific Collegiate Charter	Santa Cruz	Santa Cruz	627
La Cañada	Los Angeles	La Cañada	625
Oxford	Orange	Cypress	625
Arthur Anderson Comm. Lrng.	Alameda	Alameda	623
Northwood	Orange	Irvine	622
South Pasadena	Los Angeles	South Pasadena	622
Campolindo	Contra Costa	Moraga	621
Homestead	Santa Clara	Cupertino	619
Cupertino	Santa Clara	Cupertino	619
Miramonte	Contra Costa	Orinda	617
Albany	Alameda	Albany	616
Acalanes	Contra Costa	Lafayette	616
Davis	Yolo	Davis	615
Beverly Hills	Los Angeles	Beverly Hills	614
Sunny Hills	Orange	Fullerton	612
Northgate	Contra Costa	Walnut Creek	611
Torrey Pines	San Diego	San Diego	609
Woodbridge	Orange	Irvine	607
Cerritos	Los Angeles	Cerritos	607
Cal. Acad. of Math & Sci.	Los Angeles	Carson	606
Monte Vista	Contra Costa	Danville	603
Los Altos	Santa Clara	Los Altos	601
Walnut	Los Angeles	Walnut	600

Source: Calif. Dept. of Education, 2004 tests.

These correlations cannot be ignored — often they predict scores accurately — but they have contradictions. Historically, many poor and immigrant children have succeeded at school. Asian kids are the latest example of poor kids succeeding but we can also point to the children of peasant Europeans and Africans brought to this country as slaves. This suggests that the money correlation — rich kids score high, middle at the middle, poor at the low end

National Scholastic Aptitude Test (SAT) Scores

State	*Tested (%)	Verbal	Math
Alabama	10	560	553
Alaska	53	518	514
Arizona	32	523	524
Arkansas	6	569	555
California	**49**	**501**	**519**
Colorado	27	554	553
Connecticut	85	515	515
Delaware	73	500	499
Dist. of Columbia	77	489	476
Florida	67	499	499
Georgia	73	494	493
Hawaii	60	487	514
Idaho	20	540	539
Illinois	10	585	597
Indiana	64	501	506
Iowa	5	593	602
Kansas	9	584	585
Kentucky	12	559	557
Louisiana	8	564	561
Maine	76	505	501
Maryland	68	511	515
Massachusetts	85	518	523
Michigan	11	563	573
Minnesota	10	587	593
Mississippi	5	562	547
Missouri	8	587	585
Montana	29	537	539
Nebraska	8	569	576
Nevada	40	507	514
New Hampshire	80	522	521
New Jersey	83	501	514
New Mexico	14	554	543
New York	87	497	510
North Carolina	70	499	507
North Dakota	5	582	601
Ohio	28	538	542
Oklahoma	7	569	566
Oregon	56	527	528
Pennsylvania	74	501	502
Rhode Island	72	503	502
South Carolina	62	491	495
South Dakota	5	594	597
Tennessee	16	567	557
Texas	52	493	499
Utah	7	565	556
Vermont	66	516	512
Virginia	71	515	509
Washington	52	528	531
West Virginia	19	524	514
Wisconsin	7	587	596
Wyoming	12	551	546
Nationwide	**48**	**508**	**518**

Source: California Dept. of Education, 2004 tests. *Percentage of class taking the test.

— is more complicated than first appears. Money is certainly a factor but so is tradition and culture, family and neighborhood history and stability, the influence of peers, the values of the times, and technology. Before television and radio, people got much of their news and sports information from newspapers. Like it or not, you had to read just about every day. In modern times, you don't have to read to get the news or scores, and this has weakened perhaps the most important fundamental of school success, ability to read.

One of the biggest problems California schools have is children who enter school unprepared to do the rudimentary academics required in kindergarten or the first grade. The children start behind and often stay behind.

Does it make a difference if the child is English proficient? Immigrant children unfamiliar with English will have more difficulties with literature and language-proficient courses than native-born children. They will need extra or special help in schools.

Another Socioeconomic Flaw

If you carry the logic of socioeconomics too far, you may conclude that schools and teachers and teaching methods don't matter: Students succeed or fail according to their family or societal backgrounds.

Just not the case! No matter how dedicated or well-intentioned the parent, if the teacher is grossly inept the child probably will learn little. If material or textbooks are out-of-date or inaccurate, what the student learns will be useless or damaging.

Conversely, if the teacher is dedicated and knowledgeable, if the material is well-presented and appropriate, what the child comes away with will be helpful and, to society, more likely to be beneficial.

The late Albert Shanker, president of the American Federation of Teachers, argued that U.S. students would improve remarkably if schools refused to tolerate disruptive behavior, if national or state academic standards were adopted, if external agencies (not the schools themselves) tested students and if colleges and employers, in admissions and hiring, rewarded academic achievement and penalized failure. These four reforms do little or nothing to address socioeconomics but many educators believe they have merit.

Admittedly, however, this is a contentious area. Theories abound as to what is wrong with our schools and what should be done to fix them.

Where the Confusion Enters

It's very difficult, if not impossible, to separate the influence of home-society and schools. Many parents try hard with disappointing results. Some experts argue that friends and peer groups exercise greater influence than the home.

When scores go up, often principals or superintendents credit this or that instructional program, or extra efforts by teachers. But the scores may have risen because mom and dad cracked down on excessive TV. Or a city with old and faded low-income housing (low scores) approves a high-end development. The new residents are more middle class, more demographically inclined to push their kids academically.

One last joker-in-the deck, mobility. Johnny is doing great at his school, which has low to middling scores, but programs that seem to be working. And his family is doing better. Mom has a job, Dad a promotion. What does the family do? It moves. Happens all the time in the U.S.A. and this also makes precise interpretation of scores difficult.

Back to Scores

If a school's scores are middling, it may still be capable of doing an excellent job, if it has dedicated teachers and sound programs. The middling scores may reflect socioeconomics, not instructional quality.

Don't judge us by our overall scores, many schools say. Judge us by our ability to deliver for your son or daughter.

This gets tricky because children do influence one another and high-income parents often interact differently with schools than low-income parents. To some extent, the school must structure its programs to the abilities of the students. But schools with middling and middling-plus grades can point to many successes.

Basic Instruction-Ability Grouping

California and American schools attempt to meet the needs of students by providing a good basic education and by addressing individual and subgroup needs by special classes and ability grouping.

In the first six years in an average school, children receive some special help according to ability but for the most part they share the same class experiences and get the same instruction.

About the seventh grade, until recently, students were divided into classes for low achievers, middling students and high achievers, or low-middle and advanced — tracking. Texts, homework and expectations were different for each group. The high achievers were on the college track, the low, the vocational.

Pressured by the state, schools have curtailed this practice but many schools retain accelerated English and math classes for advanced seventh and eighth graders. Parents can always request a transfer from one group to another (whether they can get it is another matter).

In the last 40 years or so schools introduced into the early grades special programs aimed at low achievers or children with learning difficulties. Although they vary greatly, these programs typically pull the children out of class for instruction in small groups then return them to the regular class.

California College Admissions of Public School Graduates

Santa Clara County

High School	UC	CSU	CC
Branham (San Jose)	19	63	63
Cupertino	59	38	95
Del Mar (San Jose)	20	30	77
Downtown College Prep. (San Jose)	2	27	NA
Fremont (Sunnyvale)	52	64	183
Gilroy	27	42	205
Gunderson (San Jose)	19	28	63
Gunn (Palo Alto)	126	22	66
Hill (San Jose)	38	47	126
Homestead (Cupertino)	85	44	102
Independence (San Jose)	67	103	334
Leigh (San Jose)	32	NA	91
Leland (San Jose)	104	75	100
Lick (San Jose)	2	24	60
Lincoln (San Jose)	26	42	125
Live Oak (Morgan Hill)	30	60	200
Los Altos	72	40	90
Los Gatos	49	66	61
Lynbrook (San Jose)	156	29	59
Milpitas	81	80	222
Monta Vista (Cupertino)	172	49	87
Mt. Pleasant (San Jose)	32	72	165
Mtn. View	55	52	91
Oak Grove (San Jose)	38	50	195
Overfelt (San Jose)	12	39	94
Palo Alto	77	23	75
Piedmont Hills (San Jose)	53	75	101
Pioneer (San Jose)	30	43	74
Prospect (Saratoga)	22	21	71
San Jose	18	13	22
Santa Clara	16	52	70
Santa Teresa (San Jose)	25	55	111
Saratoga	107	19	35
Silver Creek (San Jose)	59	79	89
Sunnyvale	NA	1	5
Westmont (Campbell)	28	28	83
Wilcox (Santa Clara)	33	85	87
Willow Glen (San Jose)	20	20	35
Yerba Buena (San Jose)	16	35	60

Source: California Department of Education. The chart lists the local public high schools and shows how many students advanced in the year 2004 into California public colleges and universities. The state does not track graduates enrolling in private or out-of-state colleges. Continuation schools not included in list. **Key**: UC (University of California system); CSU (Cal State system); CC (Community College).

California College Admissions of Public School Graduates

Santa Cruz County

High School	UC	CSU	CC
Aptos	34	47	154
Harbor (Santa Cruz)	21	21	95
Pacific Collegiate	12	1	NA
San Lorenzo Valley (Felton)	16	44	94
Santa Cruz	35	33	97
Scotts Valley High	34	33	20
Soquel	29	38	122
Watsonville	25	46	274

San Benito County

High School	UC	CSU	CC
Anzar	3	8	7
San Benito	21	53	205

Source: California Department of Education. The chart lists the local public high schools and shows how many students they advanced in the year 2004 into California public colleges and universities. The state does not track graduates enrolling in private or out-of-state colleges. Continuation schools not included in list. **Key**: UC (University of California system); CSU (Cal State system); CC (Community Colleges).

Many schools also pull out gifted (high I.Q.) students and a few cluster them in their own classes.

College Influence

So many local students attend the University of California and California State University schools that public and private high schools must of necessity teach the classes demanded by these institutions.

So the typical high school will have a prep program that meets University of California requirements. The school also will offer general education classes in math and English but these will not be as tough as the prep courses and will not be recognized by the state universities. And usually the school will teach some trades so those inclined can secure jobs upon graduation.

Can a school with mediocre or even low basic scores field a successful college prep program? With comprehensive programs, the answer is yes.

How Middling Schools Succeed — College Admissions

Freshmen attending a California State University, a public community college or a University of California (Berkeley, Los Angeles, San Diego, Davis, etc.) are asked to identify their high schools. In this way and others, the state finds out how many students individual high schools are advancing to college.

The charts on pages 152-153 and 157-158 break out the high schools in Santa Clara, Santa Cruz and San Benito counties (data collected fall 2004) and shows how many students from each school went on to the public colleges. For an idea of the size of the graduating class, see the SAT chart on page 140-141

The UCs generally restrict themselves to the top 13 percent in the state. The Cal States take the top third.

Every school on the chart is graduating kids into college but obviously some are more successful at it than others. Does this mean that the "lesser" schools have awful teachers or misguided programs? We have no idea. It simply may be demographics at work.

Parents with college ambitions for their children should find out as much as possible about prospective schools and their programs and make sure that their kids get into the college-track classes.

Where does the chart mislead? For starters, the Cal States and UCs run on academics, the community colleges run on academics and vocational classes. Just because a student attends a community college does not mean he or she is pursuing a bachelor's degree.

Secondly, students who qualify for a Cal State or even a UC often take their freshman and sophomore years at a community college. It's cheaper and closer to home. The chart suggests that middle- and low-income communities send more kids proportionally to community colleges than high-income towns.

To secure a more diverse student mix, the UCs have lowered their admission scores, a practice that has critics and supporters. The numbers mentioned above and listed in the accompanying chart do not consist of the top students as defined by tests and grade point. In 2004, the UCs raised their admission scores but the last word has not been said on this matter.

The chart does not track private colleges. It doesn't tell us how many local students went to Mills College or the University of Santa Clara or Stanford or Harvard. Or public colleges out of the state.

Many college students drop out. These numbers are not included.

The chart does confirm the influence of socioeconomics: the rich towns, the educated towns or neighborhoods, send more kids to the UCs than the poorer ones.

But socioeconomics does not sweep the field. Not every student from a high-scoring school goes on to college. Many students from low- and middle-income towns come through.

Dissatisfaction

If high schools can deliver on college education and train students for vocations, why are so many people dissatisfied with public schools? These schools can cite other accomplishments: Textbooks and curriculums have been improved, the dropout rate has been decreased and proficiency tests have been adopted to force high school students to meet minimum academic standards.

Yet almost every few years or so, some group releases a study showing many California children are scoring below expectations or doing poorly as compared to Japanese or European children.

The California system is expensive, over $55 billion annually just for the K-12 system.

Comparisons between countries are tricky. If Japanese or European high school students fail or do poorly on their tests, they are often denied admission to college. Those who do well, however, are marked not only for college but the higher-paying jobs. Our system gives second and third chances and allows easy admission to colleges, but bears down on students during college and after they graduate. Then they have to prove themselves at work to get ahead, and this forces many to return to college or get training. Their system pressures teenagers; ours pressures young adults. Some studies suggest that by age 30 the differences even out.

As intriguing as this theory is, many parents and teachers would feel much better if the learning curve showed a sharper rise for the high-school scholars and, of course, our top universities — Cal, Stanford, Harvard — demand top scores for admission.

Registering For School

To get into kindergarten, your child must turn five before Dec. 3 of the year he or she enters the grade. For first grade, your child must be six before Dec. 3. If he is six on Dec. 4, if she is a mature Jan. 6 birthday girl, speak to the school. There may be some wiggle room. In 2000, the state changed the law to allow school to admit children who turn five or six before Sept. 2. But to take advantage of this law, a school must offer pre-kindergarten instruction. Many don't. The law also gives schools some say over whether the child is mature enough for school. Talk to the school.

For registration, you are required to show proof of immunization for polio, diphtheria, hepatitis B, tetanus, pertussis (whooping cough), measles, rubella and mumps. If the kid is seven or older, you can skip mumps and whooping cough. Continuing students entering the seventh grade must show proof of being immunized against hepatitis B.

Register Early

Just because you enroll your child first does not necessarily mean that you will get your first choice of schools or teachers.

But in some school districts first-come does mean first-served. Enrollment and transfer policies change from year to year in some districts, depending on the number of children enrolled and the space available. When new schools are opened, attendance boundaries are often changed. The same when they are closed.

Even if the school district says, "There's plenty of time to register," do it as soon as possible. If a dispute arises over attendance — the school might get an unexpected influx of students — early registration might give you a leg up in any negotiations. Persistence sometimes helps in trying for transfers.

Choosing the "Right" School

Almost all public schools have attendance zones, usually the immediate neighborhood. The school comes with the neighborhood; usually you have no choice. Your address determines your school.

Always call the school district to find out what school your children will be attending. Sometimes school districts change attendance boundaries and do not inform local Realtors. Sometimes crowding forces kids out of their neighborhood schools. It's always good to go to the first source.

Just say something like, "I'm Mrs. Jones and we're thinking about moving into 1234 Main Street. What school will my six-year-old attend?"

Ask what elementary school your child will attend and what middle school and high school. In the three counties, many children attend elementary and middle school or junior high in one school district then move up to a high school in a different district.

Keep in mind that although a district scores high, not all the schools in the district may score high. In some districts, scores vary widely. School districts legally are separate from municipalities and quite often school district and city boundaries will differ. Just because you move into the City of San Jose does not mean your children will attend the schools of the San Jose Unified School District.

Transfers

If you don't like your neighborhood school, you can request a transfer to another school in the district or to a school outside the district. But the school won't provide transportation.

Transfers to schools inside the district are easier to get than transfers outside the district. New laws supposedly make it easier to transfer children to other districts. In reality, the more popular (high scoring) districts and schools, lacking space, rarely accept "outside" students. This is a changing picture. New federal laws supposedly make it easier to transfer out of schools that do not meet academic standards. And some high-scoring schools, because of demographics, are seeing enrollments drop.

A few parents use the address of a friend or relative to smuggle their child into a high-scoring school or district. Some districts make an effort to ferret out these students and give them the boot.

If your child has a special problem that may demand your attention, speak to the school administrators about a transfer to a school close to your job. If

UCs Chosen by Public School Graduates
Santa Clara County

School	Berk	Davis	Irv	UCLA	RIV	SD	SB	SC	Total
Branham	3	6	1	0	1	3	4	1	19
Cupertino	9	18	7	5	4	10	3	3	59
Del Mar	3	5	0	0	0	1	5	6	20
Fremont	4	15	2	3	1	5	9	13	52
Gilroy	3	8	1	1	1	0	4	9	27
Gunderson	3	4	0	0	1	8	2	1	19
Gunn	17	34	6	16	3	16	16	18	126
Hill	4	14	3	3	2	7	1	4	38
Homestead	17	19	7	7	2	18	9	6	85
Independence	6	22	5	1	3	13	4	13	67
Leigh	6	5	4	2	1	1	6	7	32
Leland	17	26	8	17	4	14	12	6	104
Lick	0	0	0	0	0	2	0	0	2
Lincoln	5	6	3	2	1	1	3	5	26
Live Oak	3	6	2	0	2	2	6	9	30
Los Altos	10	13	2	19	8	11	2	7	72
Los Gatos	7	11	3	7	0	9	4	8	49
Lynbrook	41	24	21	14	12	20	8	16	156
Milpitas	15	26	10	0	12	6	5	7	81
Monta Vista	32	26	14	27	17	30	12	14	172
Mt. Pleasant	3	10	3	4	3	7	1	1	32
Mtn. View	5	8	1	10	3	17	9	2	55
Oak Grove	5	9	3	2	4	7	3	5	38
Overfelt	3	7	0	0	0	0	2	0	12
Palo Alto	5	12	1	15	4	17	9	14	77
Piedmont Hills	7	17	8	4	8	3	3	3	53
Pioneer	7	4	7	3	0	1	2	6	30
Prospect	4	2	2	1	0	3	1	9	22
San Jose	5	5	2	0	0	3	2	1	18
Santa Clara	4	3	0	0	3	1	1	4	16
Santa Teresa	4	4	2	3	3	4	2	3	25
Saratoga	26	21	9	17	3	19	7	5	107
Silver Creek	6	13	6	4	6	7	2	15	59
Westmont	0	5	2	1	4	6	7	3	28
Wilcox	5	17	2	1	1	2	1	4	33
Willow Glen	7	4	1	0	0	0	3	5	20
Yerba Buena	0	10	0	3	0	2	0	1	16

Source: California Dept. of Education. The chart shows the University of California choices by local public high school graduates of 2004. The state does not track graduates enrolling in private colleges or out-of-state colleges.
Key: Berk (Berkeley), Irv (Irvine), SD (San Diego), SB (Santa Barbara), River (Riverside), SC (Santa Cruz).

UCs Chosen by Public School Graduates

Santa Cruz County

School	Berk	Davis	Irv	UCLA	RIV	SD	SB	SC	Total
Aptos	4	2	0	4	0	2	9	13	34
Harbor	2	0	0	2	1	1	5	10	21
San Lorenzo	3	3	3	0	0	0	2	5	16
Santa Cruz	4	5	1	3	0	3	3	16	35
Scotts Valley	2	0	0	1	0	4	2	25	34
Soquel	2	1	0	1	0	0	12	13	29
Watsonville	6	7	0	2	0	1	3	6	25

San Benito County

School	Berk	Davis	Irv	UCLA	RIV	SD	SB	SC	Total
Anzar	1	0	0	0	0	0	0	2	3
San Benito	0	3	1	1	1	3	5	7	21

Source: California Dept. of Education. The chart shows the University of California choices of by local public high school graduates of 2004. The state does not track graduates enrolling in private colleges or out-of-state colleges.
Key: Berk (Berkeley), Irv (Irvine), SD (San Diego), SB (Santa Barbara), RIV (Riverside), SC (Santa Cruz).

your child's ethnicity adds some diversity to a school or district, it might bend its rules. Never hurts to ask.

Does a Different School Make a Difference?

This may sound like a dumb question but it pays to understand the thinking behind choosing one school or district over another. Two stories:

Researching earlier editions, we contacted a school district that refused to give us test results. This stuff is public information.

In so many words, the school administrator said, look, our scores are lousy because our demographics are awful: low income, parents poorly educated, etc. But our programs and staff are great. I'm not giving out the scores because parents will get the wrong idea about our district and keep their kids out of our schools (He later changed his mind and gave us the scores.)

Second story, while working as a reporter, one of our editors covered a large urban school district and heard about a principal who was considered top notch. An interview was set up and the fellow seemed as good as his reputation: friendly, hardworking, supportive of his staff, a great role model for his students, many of whom he knew by their first names. But scores at the school were running in the 10th to 20th percentile, very low.

Although neither person said this, the clear implication was that if the demographics were different, scores would be much higher. And they're probably right. If these schools got an influx of middle- and upper middle-class children, their scores would dramatically increase.

Why don't schools tell this to the public, to parents? Probably because socioeconomics is difficult to explain. Teachers want to work with parents, not alienate them with accusations of neglect. Some educators argue that even with poor socioeconomics, teachers should be able to do an effective job — controversy. Socioeconomics focuses attention on the problems of home and society to the possible detriment of schools (which also need help and funds). School, after all, is a limited activity: about six hours a day, 180 teaching days a year.

When you strip away the fluff, schools seem to be saying that they are in the business of schools, not in reforming the larger society, and that they should be held accountable only for what they can influence: the children during the school day, on school grounds.

For these reasons — this is our opinion — many teachers and school administrators think that scores mislead and that parents often pay too much attention to scores and not enough to programs and the background and training of personnel. This is not to say that teachers ignore scores and measurements of accomplishment. They would love to see their students succeed. And schools find tests useful to determine whether their programs need changes.

No matter how low the scores, if you, as a parent, go into any school and ask — can my child get a good education here — you will be told, probably invariably, often enthusiastically, yes. First, there's the obvious reason: if the principal said no, his or her staff and bosses would be upset and angry. Second, by the reasoning common to public schools, "yes" means that the principal believes that the school and its teachers have the knowledge, training and dedication to turn out accomplished students. And the programs. Schools stress programs.

Is all this valid? Yes. Programs and training are important. Many schools with middling scores do turn out students that attend the best universities.

But this approach has its skeptics. Many parents and educators believe that schools must be judged by their scores, that scores are the true test of quality.

Some parents fear that if their child or children are placed in classes with low-achieving or even middle-achieving children they will not try as hard as they would if their friends or classmates were more academic, or that in some situations their children will be enticed into mischief. In some inner-city districts, the children, for misguided reasons, pressure each other not to do well in school.

Some parents do not believe that a school with many low-scoring students can do justice to its few middle- and high-scoring students. To meet the needs of the majority, instruction might have to be slowed for everyone.

Discipline is another problem. Teachers in low-scoring schools might have to spend more time on problem kids than teachers in high-scoring schools.

There's much more but basically it comes down to the belief that schools do not stand alone, that they and their students are influenced by the values of parents, of classmates and of the immediate neighborhood.

To continue this logic, schools and school districts are different from one another and for this reason it pays to move into a neighborhood with high-scoring schools or one with at least middling-plus scores. Or to somehow secure a transfer to one of the schools in these neighborhoods.

To an unknown extent, the marketplace has reinforced this belief. It rewards neighborhoods and towns with high-scoring schools by increasing the value (the price) of their homes.

The parents who seem to do best at this business find out as much as possible about the schools, make decisions or compromises based on good information and work with the schools and teachers to advance their children's interests. Each school should be publishing an "accountability report" or report card. Ask for it or look for it on the web, under the name of the school or school district.

Year-Round Schools

Year-round schools are employed by some districts as a way to handle rapidly increasing enrollments. Schedules, called "tracks," vary from district to district but all students attend a full academic year.

Traditional holidays are observed. One group may start in summer, one in late summer and so on. A typical pattern is 12 weeks on, four weeks off. One track is always off, allowing another track to use its class space. Some school districts run a "year-round" program called modified traditional: two months summer vacation, three two-week breaks in the school year.

Families with several children on different tracks are sometimes forced to do quite a bit of juggling for vacation and child care. Call your school for information.

Ability Grouping

Ask about the school's advancement or grouping policy or gifted classes.

Without getting into the pros and cons of these practices, schools often tiptoe around them because they upset some parents and frankly because some children have to be slighted. Say the ideal in a middle school is three levels of math: low, middle and high. But funds will allow only two levels. So low is combined with middle or middle with high. If you know the school is making compromises, you might choose to pay for tutoring to bridge the gap.

Miscellaneous

- For much of the 1990s, California, in a tough economy, pulled the purse strings tight against school spending. Teacher salaries fell behind what was paid in other states. Programs were cut. Quality, many believe, suffered. In the late 1990s, the economy came roaring back and pushed billions of extra dollars into the state treasury.

The state put a lot of this money back into the public schools. Salaries were raised (now tops in the U.S.), class sizes in the first three grades were lowered (to 20-1), programs were restored. The state also gave extra money to the lowest-scoring schools and threatened to close them or take them over if they didn't raise scores.

- About 2001, the economy tanked and within a few years California had burned through its surplus and was saddled with a large deficit. We have entered another era of stingy spending that is spilling into cuts for education.

- On the positive side, several years ago voters dropped the approval vote for local bonds for school construction from two-thirds of ballots cast to 55 percent. School districts that had lost several bond elections went back to the voters and won approval. On the state level, voters in 2002 and 2004 approved construction bonds worth $24 billion. Many school districts have become skilled at squeezing developers for building costs.

- The contradiction: after decades of neglect, California has renovated thousands of its schools and building more. The state in 2004 settled a law suit that will inject more fixing-up money into the poorest and most run-down schools. At the same time, school districts are finding it harder to come up with operational funds — salaries, programs, books, etc. Extra operational money generally requires a two-thirds vote; hard to win. Many school districts have turned to parental and community fund raising to come up with operational money. This often amounts to a parental tax, usually collected by a "foundation" run by the parents.

- Private vs. public. A complex battle, it boils down to one side saying public schools are the best and fairest way to educate all children versus the other side saying public education is inefficient and will never reform until it has meaningful competition. The state has allowed about 560 schools to restructure their programs according to local needs — an effort at eliminating unnecessary rules. These institutions are called charter schools.

- Over the past several years, the state Dept. of Education has adopted standards for science, history, math and reading and other subjects. These standards define what the students are supposed to master at every grade level. Now the state has introduced texts and tests based on the standards. If students don't pass the tests, they may not be promoted. How much of this will be implemented remains to be seen. The feds, through No Child Left Behind, are demanding tougher penalties on low-scoring schools and programs that do not improve. Testing is touchy in California.

- Courts and school districts have sorted out Proposition 227, which curtailed non-English instruction in public schools. Parents can request a waiver, which under certain conditions allows instruction in the native language. Some schools are embracing dual immersion as a way to teach Spanish and English. The kids start with almost all Spanish and gradually introduce English until the ratio is 50-50.

- What if you or your neighborhood can't afford voluntary fees? Shop for bargains. Community colleges, in the summer, often run academic programs for children. Local tutors might work with small groups. Specific tutoring, say just in math, might be used to get the student over the rough spots. For information on tutors, look in the Yellow Pages under "Tutoring."

- Busing. School districts can charge and several do. Some low-income and special education kids ride free.

- Uniforms. Schools have the discretion to require uniforms, an effort to discourage gang colors and get the kids to pay more attention to school than to how they look. "Uniforms" are generally interpreted to mean modest dress; for example, dark pants and shirts for boys, plaid skirts and light blouse for girls.

- Closed campus vs. open campus. The former stops the students from leaving at lunch or at any time during the school day. The latter allows the kids to leave. Kids love open, parents love closed.

- Grad night. Not too many years ago, graduating seniors would whoop it up on grad night and some would drink and then drive and get injured or killed. At many high schools now, parents stage a grad night party at the school, load it with games, raffles and prizes, and lock the kids in until dawn. A lot of work but it keeps the darlings healthy.

- T-P. California tradition. Your son or daughter joins a school team and it wins a few games or the cheerleaders win some prize — any excuse will do — and some parent will drive the kids around and they will fling toilet paper over your house, car, trees and shrubs. Damn nuisance but the kids love it.

- Open Houses, Parents Nights. One study, done at Stanford, concluded that if parents will attend these events, the students, or at least some of them, will be impressed enough to pay more attention to school.

- Magnet Schools. Some school districts use magnet or enriched schools to promote integration. With the enriched programs, educators open to draw the students out of neighborhood schools that have too many of one ethnic group and too few of another.

- Rather than lug around books, lunches, gym gear, etc., students these days are using rolling suitcases similar to carry-on luggage. "They help your

(Continued on page 166)

School Accountability Report Card

Want more information about a particular school or school district?

Every public school and district in the state is required by law to issue an annual School Accountability Report Card.

The everyday name is the SARC report or the SARC card (pronounced SARK). SARCs are supposed to include:

- The ethnic makeup of the school and school district.

- Test results. The results may be presented in several ways but almost without exception the formats follow the presentation methods of the California Dept. of Education.

- A description of the curriculum and the programs.

- Class sizes, teacher-pupil ratios.

- Description of the teaching staff. How many have teaching credentials.

- Description of facilities.

To obtain a SARC, call the school and if the person answering the phone can't help you, ask for the superintendent's secretary or the curriculum department. Almost all schools now post their SARCS on the internet.

If you don't know the name of the neighborhood school, start with the school district.

Here are the phone numbers of the districts and the towns they serve.

School Districts, next page. Unified school districts include elementary, middle and high schools, the whole ball of wax. Palo Alto, San Jose, Santa Clara, Morgan Hill and Gilroy run unified districts. In the other arrangements, elementary school districts, as individual political agencies, educate the children up to the eighth grade. Then the students move up to high schools run by high school districts, also politically independent. For example, students from Cupertino, Montebello, and Sunnyvale elementary districts move up to high schools in the Fremont Union High School District. Attendance policies vary by district. For information about attendance, call the school districts.

Santa Clara County

Alum Rock Union Elementary (San Jose) (408) 928-6800

Berryessa Union Elementary (San Jose) (408) 923-1800

Cambrian Elementary (San Jose) (408) 377-2103

Campbell Union Elementary (408) 364-4200

Santa Clara County

ELEMENTARY, HIGH SCHOOL & UNIFIED SCHOOL DISTRICTS

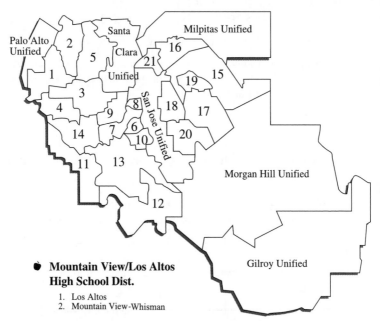

Mountain View/Los Altos High School Dist.

   1. Los Altos
   2. Mountain View-Whisman

Fremont Union High School Dist.

   3. Cupertino
   4. Montebello
   5. Sunnyvale

Campbell High School Dist.

   6. Cambrian
   7. Campbell
   8. Luthur Burbank
   9. Moreland
   10. Union

Los Gatos-Saratoga School Dist.

   11. Lakeside
   12. Loma Prieta
   13. Los Gatos
   14. Saratoga

Gilroy Unified School Dist.

East Side Union High School Dist.

   15. Alum Rock
   16. Berryessa
   17. Evergreen
   18. Franklin McKinley
   19. Mount Pleasant
   20. Oak Grove
   21. Orchard

Palo Alto Unified School Dist.

San Jose Unified School Dist.

Santa Clara Unified School Dist.

Morgan Hill Unified School Dist.

Milpitas Unified School Dist.

Campbell Union High (408) 371-0960
Cupertino Union (408) 252-3000
East Side Union High (San Jose)
(408) 347-5000
Evergreen Elementary (San Jose)
(408) 270-6800
Franklin-McKinley Elementary (San
Jose) (408) 283-6000
Fremont Union High (Sunnyvale)
(408) 522-2200
Gilroy Unified (408) 847-2700
Lakeside Joint (Los Gatos) (408)
354-2372
Loma Prieta Joint Union Elementary
(Los Gatos) (408) 353-1101
Los Altos Elementary (650) 947-1150
Los Gatos-Saratoga Joint High
(408) 354-2520
Los Gatos Union Elementary (408)
335-2000
Luther Burbank (San Jose) (408)
295-2450
Milpitas Unified (408) 945-2300
Montebello Elementary (Cupertino)
(408) 867-3628
Moreland Elementary (San Jose)
(408) 874-2900
Morgan Hill Unified (408) 779-5272
Mt. Pleasant Elementary (San Jose)
(408) 223-3700
Mountain View-Whisman Elementary
(650) 526-3500
Mountain View-Los Altos Union High
(650) 940-4650
Oak Grove Elementary (San Jose)
(408) 227-8300
Orchard Elementary (San Jose)
(408) 944-0397
Palo Alto Unified (650) 329-3700
San Jose Unified (408) 535-6000
Santa Clara Unified (408) 983-2000

Saratoga Union Elementary (408)
867-3424
Sunnyvale Elementary (408) 522-
8200
Union Elementary (San Jose) (408)
377-8010

Santa Cruz County

Bonny Doon Union (831) 427-2300
Happy Valley Elementary (831) 429-
1456
Live Oak Elementary (831) 475-6333
Mountain Elementary (831) 475-6812
Pacific Elementary (831) 425-7002
Pajaro Valley Unified (831) 728-6200
San Lorenzo Valley Unified (831)
336-9526
Santa Cruz City Schools (831) 429-
3410
Scotts Valley Unified (831) 438-1820
Soquel Union Elementary (831) 464-
5630

San Benito County

Aromas-San Juan Unified (831) 623-
4500
Bitterwater-Tully Union Elementary
(831) 385-5339
Cienega Union Elementary (831)
637-3821
Hollister Elementary (831) 634-2000
Jefferson Elementary (831) 389-4593
North County Joint Union Elemen-
tary (831) 637-5574
Panoche Elementary (831) 628-3438
San Benito High (831) 637-5831
Southside Elementary (831) 637-
4439
Tres Pinos Union Elementary (831)
637-0503
Willow Grove Union Elementary
(831) 628-3256

(Continued from page 163)

back," said one student. The outfits seem to be particularly popular in schools that have done away with lockers.

- Special education. Sore point in California education. When the feds and the state passed laws requiring schools to meet the special needs of students, they promised funding that never materialized. This forced school districts to take money from their regular programs and fund the special programs. Arguments and lawsuits followed accusing school districts of shorting special ed kids. In 2000, the state agreed to increase funding for these programs but arguments continue.

- More kids are being pushed into algebra, not only in high school but in the seventh and eighth grades. New law requires all students to take algebra before graduating from high school.

- Exit exam. Starting in 2006, students must pass an exit exam to receive a high school diploma. To get the kids prepared, all of them must take the exam by their sophomore year. If they fail, the high school will offer extra help.

- The California Dept. of Education recently named the following Santa Clara County schools as "Distinguished," meaning the state thinks they are well run: Monroe Middle, Lincoln High – San Jose, Rolling Hills Middle – Los Gatos, Westmont High – Campbell, Rancho Milpitas Middle, Russell Middle – Milpitas, Wilcox High – Santa Clara.

- In 2005, the national Blue Ribbon for academic excellence, a rare award, went to Marshall Lane Elem. in Saratoga and Rio del Mar Elem. in Aptos.

Chapter 8

Private Schools

ALTHOUGH PRIVATE SCHOOLS often enjoy a better reputation than public, they are not without problems. The typical private or parochial school is funded way below its public school counterpart. In size, facilities and playing fields, and in programs, public schools usually far outstrip private schools. Private school teachers earn less than public school teachers.

"Typical" has to be emphasized. Some private schools are well-equipped, offer exceptional programs, pay their teachers competitively and limit class sizes to fewer than 15 students. Private schools vary widely in funding.

But even when "typical," private schools enjoy certain advantages over public schools.

The Advantages

Public schools must accept all students, have almost no power to dismiss incompetent teachers and are at the mercy of their neighborhoods for the quality of students — the socioeconomic correlation. The unruly often cannot be expelled or effectively disciplined.

Much has been said about the ability of private schools to rid themselves of problem children and screen them out in the first place. But tuition, even when modest, probably does more than anything else to assure private schools quality students.

Parents who pay extra for their child's education and often agree to work closely with the school are, usually, demanding parents. The result: fewer discipline problems, fewer distractions in the class, more of a willingness to learn.

When you place your child in a good private school, you are, to a large extent, buying him or her scholastic classmates. They may not be the smartest children — many private schools accept children of varying ability — but generally they will have someone at home breathing down their necks to succeed in academics.

The same attitude, a reflection of family values, is found in the high-achieving public schools. When a child in one of these schools or a private

Public Colleges-Univ. Chosen by Private School Graduates

Santa Clara County

School	UC	CSU	CC
Archbishop Mitty (San Jose)	51	49	26
Bellarmine (San Jose)	81	39	20
Castilleja (Palo Alto)	7	0	2
Harker (San Jose)	30	NA	NA
King's Acad (Sunnyvale)	12	NA	3
Liberty Baptist (San Jose)	3	NA	2
Mountain View	4	0	9
Notre Dame (San Jose)	19	30	24
Presentation (San Jose)	27	43	20
St. Francis (San Jose)	80	66	29
St. Lawrence (Santa Clara)	6	0	16
Valley Christian (San Jose)	22	0	33

Santa Cruz County

School	UC	CSU	CC
Georgiana Bruce Kirby (Santa Cruz)	12	0	NA
Monte Vista Christian (Watsonville)	13	35	54
Monterey Bay Acad.(La Selva Beach)	1	0	9
Mt. Madonna (Watsonville)	2	0	NA

Source: California Dept. of Education. The chart tracks California public colleges or universities, and high school graduates from private schools. It shows how many students from these high schools enrolled as college freshmen in fall 2004. The state does not track graduates enrolling in private colleges or out-of-state colleges. **Key**: UC (University of California), CSU (California State University), CC (Community Colleges).

school turns to his left and right, he will see and later talk to children who read books and newspapers.

A child in a low-achieving school, public or private, will talk to classmates who watch a lot of television and rarely read.

(These are, necessarily, broad generalizations. Much depends on whom a child picks for friends. High-achieving students certainly watch television but, studies show, much less than low-achieving students. Many critics contend that even high-scoring schools are graduating students poorly prepared for college.)

The Quality of Teaching

Do private schools have better teachers than public schools? Impossible to tell. Both sectors sing the praises of their teachers.

Private schools, compared to public, have much more freedom to dismiss teachers but this can be abused. The private schools themselves advise parents to avoid schools with excessive teacher turnover.

Although most can't pay as much as public schools, private institutions claim to attract people fed up with the limitations of public schools, particu-

(Continued on Page 171)

A Profile of Catholic Schools

THE LARGEST PRIVATE school system in the three counties, Catholic schools enroll 16,388 students in Santa Clara County, 973 in Santa Cruz and 418 in San Benito. The following information is based on interviews with Catholic educators and reviewed by the San Jose diocese. Data from 2001-2002 school year.

- Santa Clara County, 29 elementary schools, one kindergarten, six high schools; Santa Cruz County, four elementary schools, high school opened in 2002 in Watsonville.

"The Catholic community values Catholic education, and they want it," according to a Catholic education administrator.

- All races, creeds welcome. Where schools are full, preference is given first to Catholic children from families active in parish. After that, to active Catholics unable to get into own parish schools.

High schools recruit regionally for students. Admissions and placement tests but all accept average students. Standards vary by school. Recommendations by parish pastors, principals, eighth-grade teachers carry clout.

Enrollment in 2002 was 9,937 elementary and 6,165 secondary.

- Why parents send kids to Catholic schools. A survey: 1. Religious tradition, moral and spiritual values. 2. Academics. 3. Discipline.

- Curriculum. Elementary schools cover same basic subjects as public schools but weave in religious-moral viewpoint. "Philosophy based in Jesus Christ. Religious values are integral to learning experience." State textbooks often used. Each school picks texts from list approved by diocese. High school instruction, although varied, is greatly influenced by requirements of University of California. Strong emphasis on technology in elementary and secondary schools.

Educators advise parents to approach high schools as they would any educational institution: ask about grades, what percentage of students go on to college.

- Non-Catholics. Get same instruction as Catholics, including history of Church and scripture. Attend Mass but not required to take sacraments. "We don't try to convert them," said one nun.

- Corporal punishment. Thing of past. More aware now of child abuse. Stress positive discipline, name on board, detention, probation. Try to work problems through, few expulsions.

(Continued on Next Page)

Catholic Schools

(Continued from Previous Page)

- Class sizes. Before 40, now 30 to 32. Somewhat smaller for high schools because of special classes, e.g. French.

  Would like smaller but point out that with well-behaved students, teachers can accomplish a lot. Matter of economics. If parents wanted smaller classes, they would have to pay more. "We want to keep affordable prices so all people can choose us, not just rich."

- Call schools. See directory of private schools at the end of this chapter.

- Schedule. Similar to public schools. 180 teaching days, minimum of five hours, 10 minutes a day. Many go longer.

- Ability grouping. In elementary grades (K-8) not done by class. Grouping within classes, advanced children working at one level, slow children at another. Tutoring after class. "You're not going to walk in and find 35 children on the same page."

  All high schools run prep programs, tend to attract prep students, but will accept remedial students, if they have remedial instruction. Admission standards vary by high school.

- Homework. Each school sets policy but diocese suggests guidelines: Grades one and two, 20 minutes; three and four, 30-45 minutes; five and six, 45 to 60 minutes; seven and eight, 60-90 minutes. None on weekends and vacations. High schools require more homework, may assign on weekends and holidays. Teacher's choice.

- Report cards. Four a year plus results of diocesan tests. Parents are expected to attend conferences, back-to-school nights.

- Teacher quality. Bachelor's degree required. Most credentialed. Hired for competence, commitment to Catholic educational philosophy. A few non-Catholic teachers but system tends to attract Catholic educators.

- Uniforms. Yes. Generally plaid skirts, blouses and sweaters for girls, collared shirts, sweaters and cords for boys.

- Extended care. All Santa Clara schools offer before- and after-school care, 7 a.m. to 6 p.m. Ask.

- Drugs. "Not major problem but when it happens we do everything to work with student."

- Extracurricular activities. Although campuses small, schools try to offer variety of activities, sports, arts, music. At elementary school, much

CATHOLIC SCHOOLS

depends on work of parents. "Parents are expected to do a lot." High schools offer good variety: music, band, arts, intramural sports, many club activities, computers, science. Catholic high schools usually field very competitive football and basketball teams.

- For more information, admissions, call school directly. Most registrations in spring but earlier for high schools. Waiting list for many primary grades. Education office at San Jose diocese, (408) 983-0185.

(Continued from Page 168)

larly restrictions on disciplining and ejecting unruly children. Some proponents argue that private schools attract teachers "who really want to teach."

Religion and Private Schools

Some private schools are as secular as any public institution. But many are religious-oriented and talk in depth about religion or ethics, or teach a specific creed. Or possibly they teach values within a framework of western civilization or some other philosophy.

Until recently public schools almost never talked about religion or religious figures. They now teach the history of major religions and the basic tenets of each, and they try to inculcate in the children a respect for all religions. It's hard, if not impossible, however, for public schools to talk about values within a framework of religion or a system of ethics. Often, it's difficult for them to talk about values. Some people argue that this is a major failing.

Many religious schools accept students of different religions or no religion. Some schools offer these students broad courses in religion — less dogma. Ask about the program.

Money

Private-school parents pay taxes for public schools and they pay tuition. Public-school parents pay taxes but not tuition. Big difference.

Ethnic Diversity

Many private schools are integrated and the great majority of private-school principals — the editor knows no exceptions — welcome minorities. Some principals fret over tuition, believing that it keeps many poor students out of private schools. Money, the lack of it, weighs heavily on private schools. Scholarships are awarded, adjustments made, family rates offered. Ask.

UCs Chosen by Private School Graduates

Santa Clara County

School	Berk	Davis	Irv	UCLA	Riv	SD	SB	SC	Total
Archbishop Mitty	6	6	8	6	1	5	7	12	51
Bellarmine	10	16	9	11	2	14	11	8	81
Castilleja	2	0	0	2	0	1	2	0	7
Harker	12	2	1	3	1	7	1	3	30
King's Acad	1	2	0	3	0	4	1	1	12
Liberty Baptist	0	1	1	0	0	0	0	1	3
Mid-Pen. Ctr.	0	0	1	0	0	0	0	1	2
Mtn. View Acad.	0	0	2	0	0	1	1	0	4
Notre Dame	3	4	4	0	1	0	1	6	19
Presentation	2	3	0	1	1	6	7	7	27
St. Francis	12	18	5	8	5	2	25	5	80
St. Lawrence	1	0	0	0	1	1	1	2	6
Valley Christian	2	6	5	3	1	2	3	0	22

Santa Cruz County

School	Berk	Davis	Irv	UCLA	Riv	SD	SB	SC	Total
Georg. Bruce Kirby	1	1	0	0	0	1	0	99	12
Monte Vista	0	1	1	0	3	1	3	4	13
Monterey Bay	0	0	1	0	0	0	0	0	1
Mt. Madonna	1	0	0	1	0	0	0	0	2

Source: Calif. Dept. of Education. The chart tracks Universities of California and high school graduates from private schools. It shows how many students from these schools enrolled as UC freshmen in fall 2004.The state does not track graduates enrolling in private colleges or out-of-state colleges. **Key**: Berk (Berkeley), Irv (Irvine), SD (San Diego), SB (Santa Barbara), Riv (Riverside), SC (Santa Cruz).

What's in the two counties

The two counties have about 150 private schools but many of them are one-family schools, mother and father teaching their own children at home. A support network that supplies books and materials has grown up for these people.

Some regular private schools have low teacher-pupil ratios, fewer than 15 students per teacher, occasionally around 10 to 1. Public school classes usually go 25 to 30 per teacher, sometimes higher (new funding has reduced sizes in grades 1-3). Class sizes in Catholic schools, in the upper grades, run close to the public-school ratio, and in some schools higher. Catholic schools, nonetheless, are the most popular, a reflection in part of the high number of Catholics in the three counties. Some Catholic schools have waiting lists.

Private schools come in great variety, Christian, Jewish, Montessori, Carden (schools with different teaching approaches), prep schools, schools that emphasize language or music, boarding and day schools, schools that allow informal dress, schools that require uniforms.

Choosing a Private School

1. Inspect the grounds, the school's buildings, ask plenty of questions. "I would make myself a real pest," advised one private school official. The good schools welcome this kind of attention.

2. Choose a school with a philosophy congenial to your own, and your child's. Carden schools emphasize structure. Montessori schools, while somewhat structured, encourage individual initiative and independence.

   Ask whether the school is accredited. Private schools are free to run almost any program they like, to set any standards they like, which may sound enticing but in some aspects might hurt the schools. A few bad ones spoil the reputation of the good.

   To remedy this, many private schools sign up for inspections by independent agencies, such as the Western Association of Schools and Colleges and the California Association of Independent Schools. These agencies try to make sure that schools meet their own goals. Some good schools do not seek accreditation.

3. Get all details about tuition carefully explained. How is it to be paid? Are there extra fees? Book costs? Is there a refund if the student is withdrawn or dropped from the school?

4. Progress reports. Parent conferences. How often are they scheduled?

5. What are the entrance requirements? When must they be met? Although many schools use entrance tests, often they are employed to place the child in an academic program, not exclude him from the school.

6. For prep schools, what percentage of the students go on to college and to what colleges?

7. How are discipline problems handled?

8. What are the teacher qualifications? What is the teacher turnover rate?

9. How sound financially is the school? How long has it been in existence? There is nothing wrong inherently with new schools. But you want a school that has the wherewithal to do the job.

10. Do parents have to work at school functions? Are they required to "volunteer"?

11. Don't choose in haste but don't wait until the last minute. Some schools fill quickly, some fill certain classes quickly. If you can, call the school the year before your child is to enter, early in the year.

12. Don't assume that because your child attends a private school you can expect everything will go all right, that neither the school nor the student needs your attention. The quality of private schools varies widely.

Directory of Private Schools

The directory contains the most current information available at press time. In California, tuition ranges widely in private schools. Many Catholic elementaries charge from about $2,500 to $3,500 plus. Catholic high schools run $7,000 to $9,000 Some non-denominational schools with low pupil-teacher ratios charge over $12,000 and a few up to $18,000.

Don't let the numbers scare you from calling. Some schools offer scholarships. Discounts are often given for siblings. If strapped, ask about financial help. Day care costs extra.

Santa Clara County

Campbell
Campbell Christian, 1075 W. Campbell Ave., (408) 370-4900, Enroll: 300, K-5th.

Casa di Mir Montessori Elem., 90 E. Latimer, (408) 370-3073, Enroll: 78, K-6th.

Old Orchard Elem., 400 W. Campbell Ave., (408) 378-5935, Enroll: 210, K-8th.

Pioneer Family Acad., 1799 S. Winchester Blvd. #100, (408) 313-5113, Enroll: 359, K-12th.

San Jose Christian, 1300 Sheffield Ave., (408) 371-7741, Enroll: 300, K-8th.

St. Lucy Parish Sch., 76 E. Kennedy Ave., (408) 871-8023, Enroll: 317, K-8th.

W. Valley Christian Sch., 95 Dot Ave., (408) 378-4327, Enroll: 63, K-8th.

Cupertino
Bethel Lutheran Elem., 10181 Finch Ave., (408) 252-8512, Enroll: 98, K-6th.

Lutheran Sch. of Our Savior, 5825 Bollinger Rd., (408) 252-0250, Enroll: 120, PreK-8th.

St. Joseph of Cupertino Elem., 10120 N. DeAnza Blvd., (408) 252-6441, Enroll: 306, K-8th.

Gilroy
Pacific West Christian Acad., 1575 A Mantelli Dr. #A, (408) 847-7922, Enroll: 352, K-9th.

St. Mary Sch., 7900 Church St., (408) 842-2827, Enroll: 314, K-8th.

Los Altos
Canterbury Christian Elem., 101 N. El Monte Ave., (650) 949-0909, Enroll: 106, K-6th.

Los Altos Christian, 625 Magdalena Ave., (650) 948-3738, Enroll: 248, K-6th.

Miramonte Elem., 1175 Altamead Dr., (650) 967-2783, Enroll: 166, K-8th.

Pinewood Pvt. Sch., 327 Fremont Ave., (650) 941-2828, Enroll: 169, 3rd-6th.

Pinewood Pvt. Sch.-Lower Campus, 477 Fremont Ave., (650) 949-5775, Enroll: 130, K-2nd.

St. Simon Elem., 1840 Grant Rd., (650) 968-9952, Enroll: 606, K-8th.

Waldorf Sch. of the Peninsula, 11311 Mora Dr., (650) 948-8433, Enroll: 62, K-8th.

Los Altos Hills
Pinewood Pvt. Sch.-Upper Campus, 26800 Fremont Rd., (650) 941-1532, Enroll: 296, 7th-12th.

St. Nicholas Elem., 12816 S. El Monte Ave., (650) 941-4056, Enroll: 270, K-8.

Los Gatos
Challenger, 220 Belgatos Rd., (408) 402-9766, Enroll: 45, K.

Hillbrook Sch., 300 Marchmont Dr., (408) 356-6116, Enroll: 312, K-8th.

Los Gatos Acad., 220 Belgatos Rd., (408) 358-1046, Enroll: 78, K-12th.

Los Gatos Christian Sch., 16845 Hicks Rd., (408) 997-4676, Enroll: 397, K-8th.

St. Mary's Elem., 30 Lyndon Ave., (408) 354-3944, Enroll: 311, K-8th.

Stratford, 220 Kensingon Way, (408) 371-3020, Enroll: 281, K-6th.

Valley Christian Elem., 1450 Leigh Ave., (408) 559-4400, Enroll: 385, K-5th.

Milpitas

Milpitas Foothill Seventh-Day Adventist, 1991 Landess Ave., (408) 263-2568, Enroll: 94, K-8th.

Milpitas Montessori Sch., 1500 Yosemite Dr., (408) 263-0991, Enroll: 45, K-3rd,

Rainbow Bridge Ctr., 1500 Yosemite Dr., (408) 945-9090, Enroll: 309, K-8th.

St. John the Baptist Catholic, 360 S. Abel St., (408) 262-8110, Enroll: 287, K-8th.

Morgan Hill

Almaden Valley Christian, 16465 Carlson Dr., (408) 776-6691, Enroll: 105, K-12th.

Carden Acad., 410 Llagas Rd., (408) 776-8801, Enroll: 72, K-8th.

Crossroads Christian Sch., 145 Wright Ave., (408) 779-8850, Enroll: 242, K-8th.

Oakwood Country Sch., 105 John Wilson Way, (408) 782-7177, Enroll: 301, K-8th.

St. Catherine Elem., 17500 S. Peak Ave., (408) 779-9950, Enroll: 295, K-8th.

Mountain View

German Int'l Sch. of Silicon Valley, 310 Easy St., (650) 254-0748, Enroll: 66, K-10th.

Girls' Middle Sch., 180 N. Rengstorff, (650) 968-8338, Enroll: 122, 6th-8th.

Mountain View Acad., 360 S. Shoreline Blvd., (650) 967-2324, Enroll: 164, 9th-12th.

St. Francis High, 1885 Miramonte Ave., (650) 968-1213, Enroll: 1,510, 9th-12th.

St. Joseph's Catholic Sch., 1120 Miramonte Ave., (650) 967-1839, Enroll: 263, K-8th.

Yew Chung Int'l Sch., 310 Easy St., (650) 903-0986, Enroll: 25, K-4th.

Palo Alto

Achieve, Inc., 3860 Middlefield Rd., (650) 494-1200, Enroll: 41, 1st-12th.

Castilleja High, 1310 Bryant St., (650) 328-3160, Enroll: 415, 6th-12th.

Challenger Sch., 3880 Middlefield Rd., (650) 213-8245, Enroll: 231, K-6th.

Esther B. Clark Sch. at Children's Health Council, 650 Clark Way, (650) 322-3065, Enroll: 69, 1st-11th.

Children's Int'l, 4000 Middlefield Rd., Ste. L1, (650) 813-9131, Enroll: 119, K-8th.

Emerson Sch., 4251 El Camino Real, (650) 424-1267, Enroll: 48, K-8th.

Gideon Howsner Jewish Day Sch., 4000 Terman Dr., (650) 494-8200, Enroll: 359, K-8th.

Intl. Sch. of the Peninsula, 151 Laura Ln., (650) 251-8500, Enroll: 378, K-8th.

Keys Sch., 2890 Middlefield Rd., (650) 328-1711, Enroll: 176, K- 8th.

Kehillah Jewish High Sch., (650) 213-9600. Jut moved from San Jose.

Living Wisdom Sch., 456 College Ave., (650) 462-8150, Enroll: 50, K-8th.

Palo Alto Prep., 4000 Middlefield Rd., (650) 493-7071, Enroll: 35, 8th-12th.

St. Elizabeth Seton, 1095 Channing Ave., (650) 326-9004, Enroll: 266, K-8th.

Torah Acad., 3070 Louis Rd., (650) 424-9801, Enroll: 41, K-8th.

San Jose

Achievekids, 1212 McGinness, (408) 928-5777, Enroll: 35, Ungraded Special Ed.

Achiever Christian, 540 Sands Dr., (408) 264-6789, Enroll: 456, K-8th.

Almaden Country Sch., 6835 Trinidad Dr., (408) 997-0424, Enroll: 331, K-8th.

Almaden Valley Christian, 6291 Vegas Dr., (408) 776-6691, Enroll: 105, K-12th.

Apostles Luth. Elem., 5828 Santa Teresa Blvd., (408) 578-4800, Enroll: 172, K-8th.

Archbishop Mitty High, 5000 Mitty Way, (408) 252-6610, Enroll: 1,624, 9th-12th.

Beacon, 5670 Camden Ave., (408) 265-8611, Enroll: 59, 5th-12th.

Bellarmine College Prep., 960 W. Hedding St., (408) 294-9224, Enroll: 1,452, 9th-12th.

Calvary Chapel Christian Acad., 1175 Hillsdale Ave., (408) 269-2222, Enroll: 64, K-8th.

Canyon Heights Acad., 3800 Blackford Ave., (408) 984-2600, Enroll: 25, Pre-school, K-8th.

Carden Day Sch. of San Jose, 890 Meridian Way, (408) 286-7323, Enroll: 63, K-8th.

Challenger, 730 Camina Escuela, (408) 213-0083, Enroll: 213, K-5th.

Challenger, 2845 Meridian Ave., (408) 723-0111, Enroll: 491, K-8th.

Challenger, 19950 McKean Rd., (408) 927-5771, Enroll: 330, K-7th.

Challenger, 711 E. Gish Dr., (408) 998-2860, Enroll: 468, K-8th

Christ the King Acad., 2530 Berryessa Rd., # 142, (408) 298-2969, Enroll: 136, 1st-12th.

E. Valley Christian Sch., 2715 S. White Rd., (408) 270-2525, Enroll: 113, K-8th.

Five Wounds Elem., 1390 Five Wounds Ln., (408) 293-0425, Enroll: 232, K-8th.

Grace Christian, 2350 Leigh Ave., (408) 377-2387, Enroll: 25, K-8th.

Harker, 500 Saratoga Ave., (408) 249-2510, Enroll: 1,585, K-12th.

Holy Family Ed. Ctr., 4850 Pearl Ave., (408) 978-1355, Enroll: 536, K-8th.

Holy Spirit, 1198 Redmond Ave., (408) 268-0794, Enroll: 341, K-8th.

Liberty Baptist, 2790 S. King Rd., (408) 274-5613, Enroll: 375, K-12th.

Little Scholars, 3703 Silver Creek Rd., (408) 238-2500, Enroll: 54, K-6th.

Milpitas Christian, 3435 Birchwood Ln., (408) 945-6530, Enroll: 716, K-9th.

Most Holy Trinity Elem., 1940 Cunningham Ave., (408) 729-3431, Enroll: 277, K-8th.

Mulberry, 1980 Hamilton Ave., (408) 377-1595, Enroll: 95, K-5th.

New Covenant Christian, 1975-B Cambrianna Dr., (408) 369-2976, Enroll: 42, K-10th.

Notre Dame High, 596 S. Second St., (408) 294-1113, Enroll: 590, 9th-12th.

One World Montessori, 5331 Dent Ave., (408) 723-5140, Enroll: 52, K-8th.

Piedmont Hills Montessori, 1425 Old Piedmont Rd., (408) 923-5151, Enroll: 50, K-1st.

Pine Hill Sch., 3002 Leigh Ave., (408) 979-8210, Enroll: 65, 1st-12th.

Plantation Christian Sch., 209 Herlong Ave., (408) 972-8211, Enroll: 112, 1st-12th.

Presentation High, 2281 Plummer Ave., (408) 264-1664, Enroll: 749, 9th-12th.

Primary Plus, 3500 Amber Dr., (408) 248-2464, Enroll: 275, K-8th.

Queen of Apostles Elem., 4950 Mitty Way, (408) 252-3659, Enroll: 310, K-8th.

Rainbow Bridge Ctr., 750 N. Capitol Ave., (408) 254-1280, Enroll: 300, K-6th.

Rainbow of Knowledge, 1718 Andover Ln., (408) 377-5730, Enroll: 63, K-5th.

Sacred Heart Nativity, 310 Edwards Ave., (408) 993-1293, Enroll: 54, 6th-8th.

St. Christopher Elem., 2278 Booksin Ave., (408) 723-7223, Enroll: 620, K-8th.

St. Frances Cabrini, 15325 Woodard Rd., (408) 377-6545, Enroll: 573, K-8th.

St. John Vianney, 4601 Hyland Ave., (408) 258-7677, Enroll: 615, K-8th.

St. Leo the Great, 1051 W. San Fernando St., (408) 293-4846, Enroll: 270, K-8th.

St. Martin of Tours Elem., 300 O'Connor Dr., (408) 287-3630, Enroll: 353, K-8th.

St. Patrick Elem., 51 N. Ninth St., (408) 283-5858, Enroll: 241, K-8th.

St. Stephen's Episcopal Sch., 500 Shawnee Ln., (408) 365-2927, Enroll: 126, K-7th.

St. Timothy's Luth., 5100 Camden Ave., (408) 265-0244, Enroll: 123, K-5th.

St. Victor Elem., 3150 Sierra Rd., (408) 251-1740, Enroll: 314, K-8th.

Starlight High Sch., 455 Silicon Valley Blvd., (408) 284-9015, Enroll: 31, 8th-12th.

Tower Acad., 2887 McLaughlin Ave., (408) 578-2830, Enroll: 86, K-5th.

Trinity Christian Sch., 1333 LeFont Dr., (408) 573-7270, Enroll: 56, 1st-12th.

Upper Echelon Academic & Life Skills, 2827 Buena Knoll Ct., (408) 274-5757, Enroll: 56, 6th-12th.

Valley Christian Elem., 1450 Leigh Ave., (408) 559-4400, Enroll: 382, K-5th.

Valley Christian Jr. High, 100 Skyway Dr. #130, (408) 513-2460, Enroll: 524, 6th-8th.

Valley Christian High, 100 Skyway Dr. #100, (408) 513-2400, Enroll: 1,079, 9th-12th.

White Rd. Baptist Acad., 480 S. White Rd., (408) 272-7713, Enroll: 42, 1st-12th.

Willow Veil Christian, 1730 Curtner Ave., (408) 448-0656, Enroll: 75, K-12th.

Santa Clara

Adventures in Lrng., 890 Pomeroy Ave., (408) 247-4769, Enroll: 46, K-6th.

Carden El Encanto Day, 615 Hobart Terr., (408) 244-5041, Enroll: 324, K-8th.

Challenger, 890 Pomeroy Ave., (408) 243-6190, Enroll: 140, K-4th.

Delphi Acad. of S.F. Bay, 890 Pomeroy Ave. #201, (408) 260-2300, Enroll: 110, K-8th.

Granada Islamic, 3003 Scott Blvd., (408) 980-1161, Enroll: 338, K-12th.

Jubilee Acad., 2499 Homestead Rd., (408) 244-9777, Enroll: 43, K-5th.

Morgan Ctr., 400 N. Winchester Blvd., (408) 241-8161, Enroll: 43, K-12th.

North Valley Baptist Sch., 941 Clyde Ave., (408) 988-8883, Enroll: 245, K-12th.

Our Lady of Peace, 2800 Mission College Blvd., (408) 988-4160, Enroll: 28, K.

Santa Clara Christian, 3421 Monroe St., (408) 246-5423, Enroll: 108, K-5th.

Sierra Elem. & High, 220 Blake Ave. #B, (408) 247-4740, Enroll: 55, K-12th.

St. Clare Elem., 760 Washington St., (408) 246-6797, Enroll: 302, K-8th.

St. Justin's, 2655 Homestead Rd., (408) 248-1094, Enroll: 303, K-8th.

St. Lawrence Acad., 2000 Lawrence Ct., (408) 296-3013, Enroll: 335, 9th-12th.

St. Lawrence Elem. & Middle, 1977 St. Lawrence Dr., (408) 296-2260, Enroll: 321, K-8th.

Tican Institute, 220 Blake Ave., No. D, (408) 554-8787, Enroll: 50, K-6th.

Saratoga

Sacred Heart Elem., 13718 Saratoga Ave., (408) 867-9241, Enroll: 308, K-8th.

St. Andrew's Sch., 13601 Saratoga Ave., (408) 867-3785, Enroll: 380, K-8th.

Sunnyvale

Challenger, 1185 Hollenbeck Ave., (408) 245-7170, Enroll: 517, K-8th.

French American School of Silicon Valley, 1522 Lewiston Dr., (408) 746-0460, Enroll: 106, K-5th.

King's Acad., 562 N. Britton Ave., (408) 481-9900, Enroll: 869, K-12th.

Pacific Autism Center for Ed., 572 Dunholme Way, (408) 245-3400, Enroll: 56, K-12th.

Rainbow Montessori Child Dev. Ctr., 790 E. Duane Ave., (408) 738-3261, Enroll: 361, K-6th.

Resurrection Elem., 1395 Hollenbeck Ave., (408) 245-4571, Enroll: 245, K-8th.

S. Peninsula Hebrew Day, 1030 Astoria Dr., (408) 738-3060, Enroll: 158, K-8th.

St. Cyprian, 195 Leota Ave., (408) 738-3444, Enroll: 236, K-8th.

St. Martin's Elem., 597 Central Ave., (408) 736-5534, Enroll: 223, K-8th.

Stratford, 1196 Lime Dr., (408) 732-4424, Enroll: 287, K-7th.

Stratford, 820 W. McKinley Ave., (408) 737-1500, Enroll: 106, K-3rd.

Sunnyvale Christian, 445 S. Mary Ave., (408) 736-3286, Enroll: 88, K-6th.

Santa Cruz County

Aptos

Aptos Acad., 1940 Bonita Dr., (831) 688-1080, Enroll: 76, K-8th.

Magic Apple, 2120 Trout Gulch Rd., (831) 688-1753, Enroll: 44, 2nd-6th.

Santa Cruz Montessori, 6230 Soquel Dr., (831) 476-1646, Enroll: 181, K-9th.

Twin Lakes Christian, 2701 Cabrillo College Dr., (831) 465-3301, Enroll: 235, K-5th.

Corralitos (North of Watsonville)

Salesian Sisters' Elem. & Jr. High, 605 Enos Ln., (831) 728-5518, Enroll: 208, K-8th.

Felton

St. Lawrence Acad., 6180 Hwy. 9, (831) 335-0328, Enroll: 61, K-12th.

La Selva Beach

Monterey Bay Acad., 783 San Andreas Rd., (831) 728-1481, Enroll: 236, 9th-12th.

Santa Cruz

Carden El Encanto, 2500 Soquel Ave., (831) 475-7250, Enroll: 48, K-6th.

Gateway Elem., 126 Eucalyptus Ave., (831) 423-0341, Enroll: 253, K-8th.

Georgiana Bruce Kirby Prep. High, 117 Union St., (831) 423-0658, Enroll: 127, 7th-12th.

Good Shepherd Catholic, 2727 Mattison Ln., (831) 476-4000, Enroll: 215, K-8th.

Holy Cross, 150 Emmet St., (831) 423-4447, Enroll: 219, K-8th.

Outdoor Science Exploration, 150 Lions Field Dr., (831) 423-5925, Enroll: 34, 2nd-8th.

Santa Cruz Children's Sch., 366 Gault St., (831) 429-8444, Enroll: 42, K-6th.

Santa Cruz Waldorf Elem., 2190 Empire Grade, (831) 425-0519, Enroll: 200, K-8th.

Spring Hill Avanced Elem. of Santa Cruz, 250 California St., (831) 427-2641, Enroll: 98, K-6th.

VHM Christian Sch., 427 Capitola Rd. Ext., (831) 475-4762, Enroll: 116, K-8th.

Scotts Valley

Baymonte Christian, 5000 Granite Creek Rd., No. B, (831) 438-0100, Enroll: 400, K-8th.

Soquel

Beach High, 5520 Old San Jose Rd., (831) 462-5867, Enroll: 32, 8th-12th.

Tara Redwood, 5810 Prescott, (831) 462-9632, Enroll: 29, K-3rd.

Watsonville

Green Valley Christian Elem., 376 S. Green Valley Rd., (831) 724-6505, Enroll: 334, K-12th.

Monte Vista Christian, Two School Way, (831) 722-8178, Enroll: 1,080, 6th-12th.

Moreland Notre Dame Catholic, 133 Brennan St., (831) 728-2051, Enroll: 273, K-8th.

Mt. Madonna, 445 Summit Rd., (408) 847-2717, Enroll: 184, K-12th.

St. Francis Central Coast Cath. High Sch., 2400 East Lake Ave., (831) 724-5933, Enroll: 115, 9th-12th.

San Benito County

Hollister

Calvary Christian Sch., 1900 Highland Dr., (831) 637-2909, Enroll: 140, K-12th.

Hollister Seventh - Day Adventist Christian Sch., 2020 Santa Ana Rd., (831) 637-5570, Enroll: 89, K-8th.

Sacred Heart Parish Sch., 670 College St., (831) 637-4157, Enroll: 425, K-8th.

Trinity Lutheran, 2300 Airline Hwy., (831) 636-2821, Enroll: 27, K-12th.

Chapter *9*

Infant-Baby Care

FOR LICENSING, CALIFORNIA divides child-care facilities into several categories:

- Small family: up to 6 children in the providers's home.
- Large family: 7-12 children in the provider's home.
- Nursery schools or child-care centers.

A child is considered an infant from birth to age 2. No category at this time has been established for toddler.

Individual sitters are not licensed and neither are people whom parents arrange for informally to take care of their children but if a person is clearly in the business of child care from more than one family he or she should be licensed. Each of the three categories has certain restrictions. For example, the small-family provider with six children cannot have more than three under the age of 2.

In everyday reality, many of the larger facilities tend to limit enrollments to children over age 2, and some have even higher age limits.

The state and its local umbrella agencies maintain referral lists of local infant and day-care providers. All you have to do is call and they will send a list of the licensed providers and suggestions on how to make a wise choice.

The names of the agencies and their numbers are:

4 Cs Community Coordinated Child Care Development Council of Santa Clara County, Inc., 111 East Gish Rd., San Jose 95112. (408) 487-0747.

Child Care Coordinating Council of San Mateo County, 2121 South El Camino Real, Suite A-100, San Mateo, 94403 (650) 655-6770.

Santa Cruz: Child Care Switchboard. (831) 476-8585.

Here's some advice from one licensing agency:

- Plan ahead. Give yourself one month for searching and screening.
- Contact the appropriate agencies for referrals.

- Once you have identified potential caregivers, phone them to find out about their services and policies. For those that meet your needs, schedule a time to visit while children are present.

- At the site, watch how the children play and interact with one another.

- Contact other parents using the programs. Ask if they are satisfied with the care and if their children are happy and well-cared-for.

- Select the program that best meets your needs. "Trust your feelings and your instincts."

This is a bare-bones approach. The referral centers can supply you with more information. To get you started, we are listing here the names of the infant centers in the county. For the older children, refer to the directory in the next chapter. The infant centers:

Santa Clara County
Campbell
A Special Place, 1260 Erin Way, (408) 559-1566
Campbell Christian Early Childhood Ctr., 1075 W. Campbell Ave., (408) 370-4900
KinderCare, 1806 W. Campbell Ave., (408) 379-8152
Kinderwood Children's Ctr. #2, 1190 W. Latimer, (408) 374-4442
Noah's Ark, 560 N. Harrison Ave., (408) 378-3212
Primary Plus, 1125 W. Campbell Ave., (408) 379-3184
Pukka Beginnings, 453 W. Campbell Ave., (408) 379-0469

Cupertino
Bright Horizons Children's Ctr., 10253 Portal Ave., (408) 366-1963
De Anza College Inf./Toddler Ctr., 21250 Stevens Creek Blvd., (408) 864-8822
Good Samaritan Ed. Enrichment, 19624 Homestead Rd., (408) 996-8290
Happy Days CDCtr., 10115 Saich Way, (408) 725-3707

Gilroy
Countryside DC & Presch. Ctr. I, 8985 Monterey Rd., (408) 848-3448
Gavilan College CDCtr., 5055 Santa Teresa Blvd., (408) 848-4814
Goldsmith Seed's Children's Ctr., 2280 Hecker Pass Hwy., (408) 847-6175

Happy Place Montessori, 7360 Alexander St., (408) 848-3819
Los Arroyos CDCtr., 885 Moro Dr., (408) 843-9005
Ochoa CDCtr., 902 Arizona Cir., (408) 842-2201

Los Altos
Baby World, 1715 Grant Rd., (650) 988-8627
Stepping Stones CCCtr., 1575 Holt Ave., (650) 960-1303

Los Gatos
Beginning Steps To Independence, 14969 Los Gatos-Almaden Rd., (408) 371-5620
Kiddie Kampus, 16330 Los Gatos Blvd., (408) 356-6776
Peppertree Sch., 15344 National Ave., (408) 402-9973

Milpitas
Calaveras Montessori Sch., 1331 Calaveras Blvd., (408) 945-1331
Children's World Lrng. Ctr., 860 N. Hillview Dr., (408) 263-0444
Cisco Family Ctr., 800 Barber Ln., (408) 853-8073
KinderCare, 400 S. Abel St., (408) 263-7212
Rainbow Bridge Ctr., 1500 Yosemite Dr., (408) 945-9090

Morgan Hill
A Children's Garden CC, 610 E. Dunne Ave., (408) 778-1977
First Steps, 25 Wright Ave., (408) 778-2529

Kids World, 17535 Del Monte Ave., (408) 779-7678

KinderCare, 605 E. Dunne Ave., (408) 778-1237

Mountain View

Ames CCCtr. at Moffett Field, 923 R. T. Jones Rd., (650) 564-9285

Kiddie Acad., 205 E. Middlefield Rd., (650) 960-6900

KinderCare, 2065 W. El Camino Real, (650) 967-4430

Primary Plus, 333 Eunice Ave., (650) 967-3780

Palo Alto

Children First at Palo Alto Square, 3000 El Camino, (650) 493-3777

Children's Creative Lrng. Ctr., 848 Ramona Dr., (650) 473-1100

Children's Presch. Ctr., 4000 Middlefield Rd., (650) 855-5770

Covenant Children's Ctr., 670 E. Meadow Dr., (650) 493-9505

Good Neighbor Montessori, 4000 Middlefield Rd., (650) 493-2777

Headsup CDCtr., 4251 El Camino Real, (650) 424-1221

Knowledge Beginnings, 625 Clark Way, (650) 723-8700

Learning Ctr., 459 Kingsley, (650) 325-6683

Lilliput Inf./Toddler Ctr., 3789 Park Blvd., (650) 857-1736

Mini Inf. Ctr., 3149 Waverly St., (650) 424-9170

Neighborhhod Inf./Toddler Ctr., 311 N. California Ave., (650) 321-3493

Palo Alto Inf./Toddler Ctr., 4111 Alma St., (650) 493-2240

Sojourner Truth CD & Inf. Ctr., 3990 Ventura Ct., (650) 493-5990

Whistle Stop, 3801 Miranda Ave., (650) 852-3497

San Jose

A Special Place, 3124 Williamsburg Dr., (408) 374-4980

Action Day Nursery, 2146 Lincoln Ave., (408) 266-8952

Action Day Nursery, 3030 Moorpark Ave., (408) 249-0668

Associated Students CDCtr., 460 S. 8th St., (408) 924-6988

Atypical Inf. Motivation Prog., 4115 Jacksol Dr., (408) 559-1400

Bright Horizons, 6120 Liska Ln., (408) 225-3276

Center for Employment Training-CDCtr., 701 Vine St., (408) 295-4566

Children's Creative Lrng. Ctr., 521 W. Capitol Express Way, (408) 978-1500

De Colores CC, 7026 Santa Teresa Blvd., (408) 229-2000

Early Lrng. Ctr., 921 Fox Ln., (408) 944-0395

Eden Palms CDCtr., 5398 Monterey Rd., (408) 972-4106

Emmanuel's CDCtr., 467 N. White Rd., (408) 272-1360

ESO CDCtr., 2055 Summerside Dr., (408) 971-0888

Familiar Footsteps, 301 Cottle Rd., (408) 225-0289

Future Assests CD, 7245 Sharon Dr., (408) 252-0203

Good Samaritan Hospital CCCtr., 2425 Samaritan Dr., (408) 559-2454

Headsup CDCtr., 2841 Junction Ave., (650) 432-1644

Kidango-Ohlone Chynoweth CDCtr., 5312 Terner Way, (408) 979-1670

Kidango-Valley Medical Ctr. CCCtr., 730 Empey Way, (408) 297-9044

Kidz Acad., 1224 N. Winchester, (408) 224-1465

KinderCare., 1081 Foxworthy Ave., (408) 265-7380

KinderCare, 3320 San Felipe Rd., (408) 270-0980

Kinderwood Children's Ctr., 5560 Entrada Cedros, (408) 363-1366

Neighborhood Christian Presch., 2575 Coit Dr., (408) 371-4222

One World Montessori Sch., 5331 Dent Ave., (408) 723-5140

Primary Plus, 801 Hibiscus Ln., (408) 985-5998

Rainbow Bridge Ctr., 750 N. Capitol Ave., (408) 254-1280

Rosa Elena CCCtr., 2380 Enborg Ln., (408) 279-7515

San Jose Day Nursery, 33 N. 8th St., (408) 295-2752

San Jose Job Corps CDCtr., 3485 East Hills Dr., (408) 254-5627

San Juan Bautista CDCtr., 1945 Terilyn Ave., (408) 259-4796

St. Elizabeth's Day Home, 1544 McKinley Ave., (408) 295-3456

Births — History & Projections

Santa Clara County

Year	Births	Year	Births	Year	Births
1981	21,902	1991	27,881	2001	27,076
1982	22,538	1992	27,481	2002	27,060
1983	22,698	1993	26,975	2003	26,997
1984	23,681	1994	26,639	2004	26,887
1985	24,110	1995	25,983	2005	26,711
1986	24,400	1996	26,646	2006	26,530
1987	24,518	1997	26,416	2007	26,382
1988	26,274	1998	26,659	2008	26,252
1989	26,805	1999	26,266	2009	26,121
1990	28,080	2000	27,612	2010	25,975

Santa Cruz County

Year	Births	Year	Births	Year	Births
1981	3,195	1991	4,125	2001	3,470
1982	3,329	1992	4,037	2002	3,334
1983	3,338	1993	3,888	2003	3,453
1984	3,657	1994	3,676	2004	3,462
1985	3,582	1995	3,475	2005	3,463
1986	3,710	1996	3,419	2006	3,465
1987	3,803	1997	3,559	2007	3,470
1988	3,978	1998	3,421	2008	3,479
1989	4,093	1999	3,446	2009	3,489
1990	4,397	2000	3,505	2010	3,497

San Benito County

Year	Births	Year	Births	Year	Births
1981	576	1991	730	2001	978
1982	496	1992	755	2002	920
1983	517	1993	806	2003	869
1984	547	1994	740	2004	881
1985	621	1995	796	2005	891
1986	603	1996	798	2006	902
1987	594	1997	888	2007	914
1988	692	1998	891	2008	927
1989	698	1999	974	2009	940
1990	732	2000	876	2010	953

Source: California Dept. of Finance, Demographic Research Unit.

Tamian CCCtr., 1197 Lick Ave., (408) 271-1980

Tomorrow Montessori Sch., 2466 Almaden Rd., (408) 979-1164

Trinity CCCtr., 3151 Union Ave., (408) 377-2342

Voyager's DCCtr., 1590 Las Plumas Ave., (408) 926-8885

Wonder Years, 1411 Piedmont Rd., (408) 926-1234

YWCA-Villa Nueva CCCtr., 375 S. 3rd St., (408) 295-4011

Santa Clara

Happy Days CDCtr., 220 Blake Ave., (408) 296-5770

Kids on Campus, 2705 The Alameda, (408) 554-5563

KinderCare, 840 Bing Dr., (408) 246-2141

Mission College CDCtr., 3000 Mission College Blvd., (408) 855-5175
MCA Granada Islamic Sch., 3003 Scott Blvd., (408) 980-1161

Saratoga

Creative Corner CC, 20300 Herriman Dr., (408) 354-8700
My Preschool, 1472 Saratoga Ave., (408) 376-0385
Primary Plus, 18720 Bucknall Rd., (408) 370-0350

Stanford

Children's Ctr. of Stanford, 695 Pampas Ln., (650) 853-3090
Stanford Arboretum Children's Ctr., 215 Quarry Rd., (650) 725-6322

Sunnyvale

California Young World, 1110 Fairwood Ave., (408) 245-7285
Caring Hearts CDCtr., 645 W. Fremont Ave., (408) 245-6356
Children's Creative Lrng. Ctr., 794 E. Duane Ave., (408) 732-2288
DeLor Montessori Sch., 1510 Lewiston Dr., (408) 773-0200
Early Horizons, 1510 Lewiston Dr., (408) 746-3020
Little Rascals CCCtr., 494 S. Bernardo Ave., (408) 730-9900
Mother's Day Out, 728 W. Fremont Ave., (408) 736-2511
New World CDCtr., 730 E. Homestead Rd., (408) 255-5330
Prodigy CDCtr., 1155 E. Arques Ave., (408) 245-3276
Rainbow Montessori CDCtr., 790 E. Duane Ave., (408) 738-3261

Santa Cruz County

Aptos

Cabrillo College Children/Inf. Ctr., 6500 Soquel Dr., (831) 479-6352
Simcha Presch., 3055 Porter Gulch Rd., (831) 479-3449

Ben Lomond

Children's Ctr. of San Lorenzo Valley, 8500 Hwy. 9, (831) 336-2857

Freedom (Watsonville)

Freedom Migrant Head Start, 37 Holly Dr., (831) 728-8199

Santa Cruz

A Child's Reflection, 327 Church St., (831) 426-3655
Good Beginnings Toddler Ctr., 111 Errett Cir., (831) 688-8840
Harvey West Children's Ctr., 191-B Harvey West Blvd., (831) 469-9358
Kids' Klub, 1114 Water St., (831) 469-0403
Santa Cruz Toddler Care Ctr., 1738 16th Ave., (831) 476-4120
Tam Inf. Ctr., 120 Weeks St., (831) 429-3050
UCSC Children's Ctr., 599 Koshland Way, (831) 459-2967

Scotts Valley

Scotts Valley Children's Ctr., 255-B Mt. Hermon Rd., (831) 461-9330

Soquel

Mid-County Children's Ctr., 305 Alturas Way, (831) 476-8890

Watsonville

Bradley Migrant Head Start, 321 Corralitos Rd., (831) 728-6955
Buena Vista Inf. Children's Ctr., 201 Tierra Alta, (831) 728-6428
Calabasas Inf./Toddler Ctr., 202 Calabasas Rd., (831) 761-6185
H.A Hyde Inf./Toddler Ctr., 125 Alta Vista Ave., (831) 761-6179
Louise Blanchard CCCtr., 175 Lawrence Ave., (831) 724-9234
Ohlone Inf./Toddler Ctr., 24 Bay Farms Rd., (831) 728-6955
Pajaro Valley Children's Ctr., 234 Montecito St., (831) 722-3737
Salispuedes Inf./Toddler Ctr., 115 Casserly Rd., (831) 761-6182

San Benito County

Hollister

Countryside DC, 331 Gateway, (831) 638-0599
Paddington School, 1431 Santa Ana Rd., (831) 637-5065

Chapter **10**

Day Care

SEE THE PRECEDING chapter on baby care for more information about how local baby and child care is provided and who provides it.

For insights on how to pick a day-care center or provider, here is some advice offered by a person who runs a day-care center.

- Ask about age restrictions. Many centers and family-care providers will not take care of children under age two or not toilet trained. See previous chapter for infant centers.

- Give the center or home a visual check. Is it clean? In good condition or in need of repairs? Is there a plan for repairs when needed?

- Find out if the person in charge is the owner or a hired manager. Nothing wrong with the latter but you should know who is setting policy and who has the final say on matters.

- Ask about the qualifications of the people who will be working directly with your child. How long have they worked in day care? Training? Education? Many community colleges now offer training in early child-hood and after-school care.

- What philosophy or approach does the center use. The Piaget approach believes children move through three stages and by exploring the child will naturally move through them. The job of the teacher is to provide activities appropriate to the right stage. For example, from age 2-7, many children master drawing and language; from 7-11, they begin to think logically. For the younger child art and sorting and language games would be appropriate; multiplication would not.

  Montessori believes that if given the right materials and placed in the right setting, children will learn pretty much by themselves through trial and error. Montessorians employ specific toys for teaching.

  Traditional emphasizes structure and repetition.

  These descriptions are oversimplified and do not do justice to these approaches or others. Our only purpose here is to point out that day-care providers vary in methods and thinking, and in choosing a center, you also choose a distinct philosophy of education.

- For family day-care providers. Some set up a small preschool setting in the home. Often your child will be welcomed into the family as an extended member. Is this what you want?

- Discipline. Johnny throws a snit. How is it handled? Does the provider have a method or a plan? Do you agree with it?

- Tuition. How much? When it is due? Penalty for picking up child late? Penalty for paying late?

- Hours of operation. If you have to be on the road at 5:30 a.m. and the day-care center doesn't open until 6, you may have to look elsewhere or make different arrangements. Some centers limit their hours of operation, e.g., 10 hours.

- Holidays. For family providers, when will the family take a vacation or not be available? For the centers, winter breaks? Summer vacations?

- Communication. Ask how you will be kept informed about progress and problems. Regular meetings? Notes? Calls? Newsletters?

- Classes-Tips for parents. Opportunities to socialize with other parents? Activities for whole family?

- Field trips and classes. Outside activities. Your son and daughter play soccer, an activity outside the day-care center. How will they get to practice? What's offered on site? Gymnastics? Dance?

- Siestas. How much sleep will the children get? When do they nap? Does this fit in with your child's schedule?

- Activities. What are they? How much time on them? Goals?

- Diapers, bottles, cribs, formula, extra clothes. Who supplies what?

- Food, lunches. What does the center serve? What snacks are available?

Remember, day-care centers and providers are in business. The people who staff and manage these facilities and homes may have the best intentions toward the children but if they can't make a profit or meet payrolls, they will fail or be unable to provide quality care. Even "nonprofits" must be run in a businesslike way or they won't survive.

Some centers may offer a rich array of services but for fees beyond your budget. You have to decide the tradeoffs.

For licensing, the state divides child care into several categories, including infant, licensed family, child-care centers, and school-age centers for older children. The previous chapter lists the infant providers. This chapter will list the large day-care centers, for both pre-school and school-age children.

For a list of family-care providers, call the Community Coordinated Child Development Council of Santa Clara at (408) 487-0747; for Santa Cruz, call the Child Care Switchboard at (831) 476-8585. For San Benito, call local schools.

Santa Clara County

Campbell

A Special Place-Camden, 1260 Erin Way, (408) 559-1566

Aurora CDCtr., 995 Apricot Ave., (408) 371-2605

Bright Days Presch., 1675 Winchester Blvd., (408) 378-8422

Bright Ideas CDCtr., 1063 Fewtrell Dr., (408) 371-9310

Campbell Christian Early Childhood Ctr., 1075 W. Campbell Ave., (408) 370-4900

Campbell Parents Participation Presch., 528 N. Harrison St., (408) 866-7223

Capri Presch., 850 Chapman Dr., (408) 364-4260

Casa Di Mir Montessori Elem. Sch., 90 E. Latimer Ave., (408) 370-3073

Discoveryland, 600 W. Campbell Ave., (408) 379-6636

Early Years CDCtr., 3225 S. Winchester Blvd., (408) 378-9000

Hazelwood Presch. & Ext. Day, 775 Waldo Rd., Rm. 28, (408) 341-7000

KinderCare, 1806 W. Campbell Ave., (408) 379-8152

Kinderwood Children's Ctr. #2, 1190 W. Latimer Ave., (408) 374-4442

Montessori Acad., 177 E. Rincon Ave., (408) 871-1801

New Generation Presch. & DC, 1291 Elam Ave., (408) 866-5422

Noah's Ark Lrng. Ctr., 560 N. Harrison Ave., (408) 378-3212

Primary Plus, 1125 W. Campbell Ave., (408) 379-3184

Pukka Beginnings, 453 W. Campbell Ave., (408) 379-0469

Rosemary Presch., 401 W. Hamilton Ave., (408) 341-7000

Rosemary State Presch., 401 W. Hamilton Ave., (408) 374-1158

San Jose Montessori Sch., 1300 Sheffield Ave., (408) 377-9888

Sunnymont Nursery Sch., 771 Waldo Rd., (408) 871-7300

Cupertino

Bethel Luth. Ch. Nursery Sch., 10181 Finch Way, (408) 252-8512

Bright Horizons Children's Ctr., 10253 Portal Ave., (408) 366-1963

Collins Sch. Age CDCtr., 10401 Vista Dr., (408) 446-5428

De Anza CDCtr., 21250 Stevens Creek Blvd., (408) 864-8863

Eaton Sch. Age CDCtr., 20220 Suisun Dr., (408) 257-3570

Faria Sch. Age CDCtr., 10155 Barbara Ln., (408) 973-0325

Garden Gate CDCtr., 10500 Ann Arbor Ave., (408) 725-0269

Good Samaritan Enrichment, 19624 Homestead Rd., (408) 996-8290

Happy Days CDCtr., 10115 Saich Way, (408) 725-3707

Kinder Land CDCtr., 10352 N. Stelling Rd., (408) 861-0160

Little People Christian DCCtr., 20900 McClellan Rd., (408) 257-1212

Play and Learn Presch. & DC, 10067 Byrne Ave., (408) 253-7081

Portal Sch. CDCtr., 10300 Blaney Ave., (408) 996-1547

Sedgwick State Presch. & CDCtr., 19200 Phil Ln., (408) 252-3103

TLC Of Cupertino, 10038 Bret Ave., (408) 996-1866

Vallco CDCtr., 10123 N. Wolfe Rd., (408) 446-4136

Villa Montessori II, 20900 Stevens Creek Blvd., (408) 257-3374

Village Little, 10100 N. Stelling Rd., (408) 252-2050

YMCA-Stevens Creek, 10300 Ainsworth Dr., (408) 736-5041

Gilroy

Christopher Ranch Head Start, 305 Bloomfield Ave., (408) 847-3110

Countryside DC & Presch. I, 8985 Monterey Rd., (408) 848-3444

Creative Play Lrng. Ctr., 95 4th St., (408) 846-9551

Del Buono Head Start, 245 Farrell Ave., (408) 410-0300

Gavilan College CDCtr., 5055 Santa Teresa Blvd., (408) 848-4815

Gilroy Unified State Presch., 475 W. 9th St., (408) 842-4486

Glenview Head Start, 480 8th St., (408) 410-0254

Goldsmith Seed's Children's Ctr. Presch., 2280 Hecker Pass Hwy., (408) 847-6175

Happy Place Montessori, 7360 & 7350 Alexander St., (408) 848-3819

Harmony Christian Presch., 651 Broadway, (408) 842-4415

Leavsley Head Start, 7871 Murray Ave., (408) 410-0251

Los Arroyos CDCtr., 885 Moro Dr., (408) 843-9005

Medallion Champions-Del Buono, 9300 Wren Ave., (408) 847-5322

Medallion Champions-El Roble, 930 3rd St., (408) 842-1093

Medallion Champions-Luigi Aprea, 9225 Calle Del Rey, (408) 842-7150

Medallion Champions-Rod Kelley, 8755 Kern Ave., (408) 847-2036

Oasis Head Start, 7871 Murray Ave., (408) 410-0251

Ochoa CDCtr., 902 Arizona Cir., (408) 842-2201

One World Presch. & CCCtr., 8387 Wren Ave., (408) 842-4148

Vineyard Presch., 1735 Hecker Pass Hwy., (408) 347-8462

Wonderland Chinese Sch., 10931 Maxine Ave., (408) 245-3288

Los Altos

Abracadabra CCCtr., 1120 Rose Ave., (650) 965-0695

Children's Creative Lrng. Ctr., 700 Los Altos Ave., (650) 917-9300

Children's Creative Lrng. Ctr., 2310 Homestead Rd., (408) 736-7400

Children's House of Los Altos, 770 Berry Ave., (650) 968-9052

Joan Bourriague's Presch., 1040 Border Rd., (650) 941-1662

Los Altos Christian Presch., 625 Magdalena Ave., (650) 948-2907

Los Altos-Mtn. View Children's Corner, 97 Hillview Ave., (415) 948-8950

Los Altos Parent Presch., 199 Almond Ave., (650) 947-9371

Los Altos United Methodist Ch. CC, 655 Magdalena Ave., (650) 941-5411

Monarch Christian Sch., 2420 Foothill Blvd., (408) 773-8543

Montclaire Sch. Age CDCtr., 1160 St. Joseph Ave., (650) 965-7169

Montecito Presch., 1468 Grant Rd., (650) 968-5957

Stepping Stones CCCtr., 1575 Holt Ave., (650) 960-1303

YMCA Kids Place-Almond, 550 Almond Ave., (650) 941-8102

YMCA Kids Place-Oak, 1122 Covington Rd., (650) 969-6865

Los Gatos

Addison Penzak Jewish Comm. Ctr., 14855 Oka Rd., (408) 358-5339

Beginning Steps to Independence, 14969 Los Gatos-Almaden Rd., (408) 371-5620

Challenger Sch., 220 Belgatos Rd., (408) 402-9766

Eitz Chaim Acad., 16555 Shannon Rd., (408) 402-0264

Green Hills Presch., 16195 George St., (408) 356-8911

Growing Footprints & Growing Footsteps, 16575 Shannon Rd., (408) 356-4442

Harwood Hills Country Sch., 16220 Harwood Rd., (408) 266-2400

Holy Cross Luth. Children's Ctr., 15885 Los Gatos-Almaden Rd., (408) 356-6828

Kiddie Kampus DCCtr., 16330 Los Gatos Blvd., (408) 356-6776

Los Gatos Acad., 220 Belgatos Rd., (408) 358-1046

Mariposa Montessori Sch., 16548 Ferris Ave., (408) 266-5683

Oak Tree Children's Club, 17765 Daves Ave., (408) 395-6144

Peppertree Presch., 5344 National Ave., (408) 402-9973

Shannon Nursery Sch., 16575 Shannon Rd., (408) 358-3936

Stratford Sch., 220 Kensington Way, (408) 371-3020

Milpitas

Calaveras Montessori Sch., 1331 Calaveras Blvd., (408) 945-1331

Children's World Lrng. Ctr., 860 N. Hillview Dr., (408) 263-0444

Cisco Family Ctr., 800 Barber Ln., (408) 853-8073

Crossing Early CC & Lrng. Ctr., 757 E. Capitol Ave., (408) 262-5530

Day Star Montessori Sch., 215 Dempsey Rd., (408) 263-1618

First Years CCCtr., 1400 S. Main St., (408) 934-0581

Footprints Presch., 1651 N. Milpitas Blvd., (408) 719-9329

Golden Harvest Montessori Sch., 1905 N. Milpitas Blvd., (408) 719-1686

Hands on Lrng. Ctr., 637 S. Main St., (408) 946-5622

KinderCare, 400 S. Abel St., (408) 263-7212

Milpitas Christian Presch. & DC, 200 Abbott Rd., (408) 946-5795

Milpitas Christian Sch., 1000 S. Park Victoria Dr., (408) 262-2630

Milpitas Discoveryland, 1991 Landess Ave., (408) 263-7626

Milpitas Montessori, 1500 Yosemite Dr., (408) 263-0991

Milpitas Parents Presch., 355 E. Dixon Rd., (408) 263-3950

Milpitas Rose Head Start, 250 Roswell Dr., (408) 262-3641

Monarch Christian Sch., 1715 Calaveras Blvd., (408) 263-4840

Rainbow Bridge Ctr., 123 Corning Ave., (408) 946-2812

Rainbow Bridge Ctr., 1500 Yosemite Dr., (408) 945-9090

Randall Child Dev., 1300 Edsel Dr., (408) 945-5591

Rose CDCtr., 250-A Roswell Dr., (408) 945-5583

Spangler Child Dev., 140 N. Abbott Ave., (408) 945-5591

St. John the Baptist Sch., 360 S. Abel St., (408) 262-8110

Sunnyhills CDCtr., 356 Dixon Rd., (408) 945-5577

YMCA Pomeroy, 1505 Escuela Pkwy, (408) 263-8032

Morgan Hill

Bright Beginnings Presch. & DC, 15345 Calle Enrique, (408) 776-9000

Burnett CDCtr.-State Presch., 85 Tilton Ave., (408) 779-6016

Children's Garden, 610 E. Dunne Ave., (408) 778-1977

Countryside DC Presch. Ctr. #2, 174 W. Main Ave., (408) 779-1220

El Toro CDCtr.-State Presch., 455 E. Main St., (408) 778-1402

First Steps Presch., 25 Wright Ave., (408) 778-2529

Kids World CCCtr., 17535 Del Monte Ave., (408) 779-7678

KinderCare, 605 E. Dunne Ave., (408) 778-1237

Little Sonshine Schoolhouse, 16970 DeWitt Ave., (408) 779-6788

Montessori Lrng. for Living, 16900 DeWitt Ave., (408) 779-6488

Morgan Hill Parent Child Nursery Sch., 16870 Murphy Ave., (408) 779-4515

Morgan Hill Presch. Acad., 17780 Monterey Rd., (408) 226-2857

Morgan Hill Ranch CDCtr., 18555 Butterfield Rd., (408) 778-2930

Morgan Hill Presch. at Galvan Park, 17666 Crest Ave., (408) 779-6553

Nordstrom State Presch. & CDCtr., 1425 E. Dunne Ave., (408) 778-2821

P.A. Walsh CDCtr. & State Presch., 353 W. Main St., (408) 778-2896

St. John Episcopal Presch., 17740 Peak Ave., (408) 782-9994

YMCA-Barrett, 895 Barrett, (408) 778-3225

YMCA-Jackson, 2700 Fountain Oaks Dr., (408) 779-8854

YMCA-Paradise Valley, 1400 La Crosse Dr., (408) 778-5711

Mountain View

Abracadabra CCCtr., 201 Covington, (650) 949-1796

Ames CCCtr. at Moffett Field, Gate 17, (650) 564-9285

Canyon Heights Presch., 310 Easy St., (650) 691-9373

Castro State Presch., 505 Escuela Ave., (650) 526-3590

Creative Lrng. Ctr., 675 Escuela Ave., (650) 564-9907

German Sch., 310 Easy St., (650) 254-0748

Hobbledehoy Montessori Presch., 2321 Jane Ln., (650) 968-1155

Kiddie Acad., 205 E. Middlefield Rd., (650) 960-6900

KinderCare, 2065 W. El Camino Real, (650) 967-4430

Little Acorn Sch., 1667 Miramonte Ave., (650) 964-8445

Mt. View Parent Nursery Sch., 1299 Bryant Ave., (650) 969-9506

Mt. View Sch. Dist. State Presch., 325 Gladys Ave., (650) 964-8089

Oaktree Nursery Sch. III, 2100 University Ave., (650) 493-1905

Primary Plus, 333 Eunice Ave., (650) 967-3780

St. Paul Luth. CDCtr., 1075 El Monte Ave., (650) 969-2696

St. Timothy's Nursery Sch., 2094 Grant Rd., (650) 967-4724

Walnut Grove Children's Ctr., 84 Murlagan Ave., (650) 960-1826

Wedgwood Presch., 1710 Miramonte Ave., (650) 938-1323

Western Montessori Day Sch., 323 Moorpark Way, (650) 961-4131

Wonder World Presch., 2015 Latham St., (650) 964-7784

Yeu Chung Int'l Sch., 310 Easy St., (650) 903-0986

YMCA Kid's Place-Bubb, 525 Hans St., (650) 965-2922

YMCA Kid's Place-Huff, 253 Martens Ave., (650) 567-9928

YMCA Kid's Place-Landels, 115 W. Dana St., (650) 965-2008

YMCA Kid's Place-Slater, 325 Gladys Ave., (650) 965-8002

YMCA Kid's Place-Theuerkauf, 1625 San Luis Ave., (650) 961-7076

YMCA of the East Bay CDCtr., 750 San Pierre Way, (650) 969-9622

YMCA Way To Grow Presch., 115 W. Dana St., (650) 965-2008

Palo Alto

Addison Kids Corner, 650 Addison Ave., (650) 323-6806

Albert L. Schultz Jewish Comm. Ctr., 4120 Middlefield Rd., (650) 493-9400

Barron Park Children's Ctr., 800 Barron Ave., (650) 493-2361

Barron Park Presch., 3650 La Donna St., (650) 493-7597

Besse Bolton Kid's Club, 500 E. Meadow Dr., (650) 856-0847

Casa Dei Bambini Sch., 463 College, (650) 473-9401

Challenger School, 3880 Middlefield Rd., (650) 213-8245

Children's Creative Lrng. Ctr., 848 Ramona Dr., (650) 473-1100

Children First at Palo Alto Square, 3000 El Camino, Ste. 3-110, (650) 493-3777

Children's Presch. Ctr., 4000 Middlefield Rd., (650) 855-5770

College Terrace Presch. Ctr., 2300 Wellesley St., (650) 858-1580

Comm. Assoc. for Rehabilitation, 3864 Middlefield Rd., (650) 494-0550

Covenant Children's Ctr., 670 E. Meadow Dr., (650) 493-9505

Crescent Park Comm. CC, 888 Boyce Ave., (650) 322-9668

Discovery Children's House, 303 Parkside Dr., (650) 570-5038

Downtown Children's Ctr., 555 Waverly St., (650) 321-9578

Duveneck Kids Club, 705 Alester Ave., (650) 328-8356

El Carmelo Kids Corner, 3024 Bryant St., (650) 856-6150

Ellen Thacher Children's Ctr., 505 E. Charleston Rd., (650) 493-2361

Escondido Kid's Club, 890 Escondido Rd., (650) 855-9828

First Congregational Ch. Nursery Sch., 1985 Louis Rd., (650) 856-6662

First School, 625 Hamilton Ave., (650) 323-6167

Good Neighbor Montessori, 4000 Middlefield Rd., (650) 493-2777

Grace Luth. Presch., 3149 Waverly St., (650) 494-1212

Headsup CDCtr., 4251 El Camino Real, Bldg. A, (650) 424-1221

Heffalump Coop. Nursery Sch., 3990 Ventura Ct., (650) 856-4321

Int'l. Sch. of the Peninsula, 3233 Cowper St., (650) 852-0264

Juana Briones Kid's Club, 4100 Orme St., (650) 856-3874

Knowledge Beginnings, 625 Clark Way, (650) 723-8700

Learning Ctr., 459 Kingsley Ave., (650) 325-6683

Love-n-Care Christian Presch. & DCCtr., 2490 Middlefield Rd., (650) 322-1872

Montessori Sch. of Los Altos, 4161 Alma St., (650) 493-7200

Ohlone Kids Club, 950 Amarillo Ave., (650) 493-0774

Palo Alto Friends Nursery Sch., 957 Colorado St., (650) 856-6152

Palo Alto Montessori Sch., 575 Arastradero Rd., (650) 493-5930

Palo Verde Kid's Corner, 3450 Louise Rd., (650) 856-1672

Peninsula DCCtr., 525 San Antonio Rd., (650) 494-1880

Redwood Enrichment Ctr, 445 E. Charleston Rd., (650) 320-9001

Sojourner Truth Child Dev. Presch., 3990 Ventura Ct., (650) 493-5990

Walter Hayes Kids Club, 1525 Middlefield Rd., (650) 325-5350

Whistle Stop, 3801 Miranda Ave., (650) 852-3497

Young Life Christian Presch. Ctr., 687 Arastradero Rd., (650) 494-7885

San Jose

3 D Presch., 5370 Snell Ave., (408) 507-9623

A Place to Grow, 3001 Ross Ave., (408) 265-2994

A Special Place-Williamsburg, 3124 Williamsburg Dr., (408) 374-4980

A Special Trinity Union, 3151 Union Ave., (408) 377-2342

A T.L.C. Presch., 1975 Cambrianna Dr., (408) 371-2573

ABC Lrng. Montessori, 1115 Kimberly Dr., (408) 448-4578

Achieve Therapeutic Presch., 1212 McGinness Ave., (408) 928-5777

Achiever Christian Sch., 820 Ironwood Dr., (408) 264-2345

Action Day Nursery, 2146-2148 Lincoln Ave., (408) 266-8952

Action Day Nursery, 3030 Moorpark Ave., (408) 247-6972

After Sch. Adventures-Steindorf Play Society, 3001 Ross Ave., #9, (408) 264-8400

Almaden Country Sch. Begindergarten Prog., 6835 Trinidad Dr., (408) 997-0424

Almaden Head Start, 1200 Blossom Hill Rd., (408) 265-6251

Almaden Parents Presch., 5805 Cahalan Ave., (408) 225-7211

Almaden Presch., 1295 Dentwood Dr., (408) 535-6207

Alphabet Soup, 1191 DeAnza Blvd., (408) 253-6660

Alum Rock Head Start, 30 Kirk Ave., (408) 453-6900

Anderson Sch. Age CDCtr., 5800 Calpine Dr., (408) 972-5373

Andrew Hill Children's Ctr., 3200 Senter Rd., (408) 347-4198

Anne Darling Elem. Presch., 333 N. 33rd St., (408) 535-6209

Anne Darling Sch. Age CDCtr., 333 N. 33rd St., (408) 347-8026

Arbor Park CDCtr., 899 N. King Rd., (408) 272-1588

Arbuckle CDCtr., 1910 Cinderella Ln., (408) 259-8340

Arbuckle-Sunset Head Start, 1970 Cinderella Ln., (408) 251-4062

Associated Students CDCtr., 460 S. 8th St., (408) 924-6988

Bachrodt CDCtr., 1471 Keoncrest Rd., (408) 453-0511

Bachrodt Sch. Age CDCtr., 102 Sonora Ave., (408) 453-7533

Ballard Montessori Sch., 2555 Moorpark Ave., (408) 260-1888

Berryessa State Presch., 2760 Trimble Rd., (408) 923-1944

Bethel CCCtr., 1201 S. Winchester Blvd., (408) 246-6945

Blackford Sch. Age CDCtr., 1970 Willow St., (408) 723-9363

Bright Beginnings Presch. & DCCtr., 637 Calero Ave., (408) 227-1771

Bright Horizons Presch., 6120 Liska Ln., (408) 225-3276

Building Block Presch., 6350 Rainbow Dr., (408) 996-2477

Building Kids Care, 280 Martinvale Ln., (408) 629-6532

Canyon Heights Presch., 3800 Blackford Dr., (408) 984-2600

Carter Ave. Nursery Sch., 5303 Carter Ave., (408) 265-3580

CAS-Los Arboles Head Start, 455 Los Arboles Ln., (408) 363-9016

Cassell CDCtr., 1300 Tallahassee Dr., (408) 259-4796

Caterpillars to Butterflies, Inc., 935 Piedmont Rd., (408) 926-1264

Cathedral of Faith Lrng. Ctr., 2315 Canoas Garden Ave., (408) 979-3025

Center for Early Lrng., 2174 Lincoln Ave., (408) 723-1234

Central Nursery Sch., 1177 Naglee Ave., (408) 287-0266

Challenger Presch. #2, 18811 Cox Ave., (408) 378-0444

Challenger Presch. #3, 4977 Dent Ave., (408) 266-7073

Challenger School, 19950 McKean Rd., (408) 377-2300

Challenger School, 711 E. Gish Rd., (408) 998-2860

Challenger School, 730 Camina Escuela, (408) 973-8787

Challenger School, 2845 Meridian Ave., (408) 377-2300

Champions-Miner, 511 Cozy Dr., (408) 887-1505

Chandler Tripp-Head Start, 780 Thornton Way, (408) 293-8404

Cherrywood Ext. DC Prog., 2550 Greengate Dr., (408) 259-9739

Child Kingdom, 4160 Senter Rd., (408) 365-1236

Childcare Ctr. at Calvary Chapel, 1175 Hillsdale Ave., (408) 978-2357

Chlidren's Creative Lrng. Ctrs., 521 W. Capitol Expwy., (408) 978-1500

Church of the Chimes Children's Ctr., 1447 Bryan Ave., (408) 445-2445

Clement Presch., 955 Branham Ln., (408) 256-2226

Congregation Sinai Nursery Sch., 1556 Willowbrae Ave., (408) 264-8486

Cornerstone Presch. & Ext. Care, 6601 Camden Ave., (408) 268-7595

Cory CDCtr., 897 Broadleaf Ln., (408) 247-3938

Country Lane Tiny Tots, 5140 Country Ln., (408) 874-3471

Creative Beginnings Presch., 14834 Leigh Ave., (408) 559-3247

Cupertino House of Montessori, 1211-D & E Kentwood Ave., (408) 255-8905

De Colores CC, 7026 Santa Teresa Blvd., (408) 229-2000

De Vargas Sch. Age CDCtr., 5050 Moorpark Ave., (408) 725-0278

Del Roble CDCtr., 5345 Avenida Almendros, (408) 972-8335

Discovery Parent-Child Presch., 1919 Gunston Way, (408) 377-5390

Early Lrng. Ctr., 921 Fox Ln., (408) 944-0395

East Hills Presch., 14845 Story Rd., (408) 923-8616

Easter Seals Bay Area, 730 Empey Way, (408) 295-0228

Easthills-Lyndale Head Start, 13901 Nordyke Dr., (408) 258-1523

Eastside Presch., 2490 Story Rd., (408) 926-5884

Edenvale-Head Start, 5319 Carryback Ave., (408) 363-1823

Eden Comm. Presch. & Kind., 3275 Williams Rd., (408) 243-0236

Eden Palms CDCtr., 5398 Monterey Rd., (408) 972-4106

El Rancho Verde CDCtr., 318 El Rancho Verde Dr., (408) 254-1717

Emmanuel's CDCtr., 467 N. White Rd., (408) 272-9310

Empire Gardens At Watson Park, 550 N. 22nd St., (408) 535-6221

Ernesto Galarza State Presch., 1610 Bird Ave., (408) 535-6671

ESO CDCtr., 2055 Summerside Dr., (408) 298-8656

Estrella Family Svcs., 611 Willis Ave., (408) 998-1343

Evergreen Valley College CDCtr., 3095 Yerba Buena Rd., (408) 270-6452

Evergreen Valley Presch., 3122 Fowler Rd., (408) 238-4001

Explorer Parent Participation Presch., 2700 Booksin Ave., (408) 723-0779

Familiar Footsteps, 301 Cottle Rd., (408) 225-0289

Familiar Footsteps, 420 Calero Ave., (408) 227-3464

Family of Christ Presch., 3412 Sierra Rd., (408) 259-1670

Foothill Christian Presch. & DC, 5301 McKee Rd., (408) 258-2171

Forest Hill Ext. Day & Presch., 4450 McCoy, (408) 364-4279

Franklin Head Start, 420 Tully Rd., (408) 410-0278

Franklin House Head Start, 451 Baltic Way, (408) 293-3558

Fred Marten Head Start, 14271 Story Rd., (408) 453-6900

Future Assets CDCtr., 7245 Sharon Dr., (408) 252-0203

Gardner Presch., 502 Illinois Ave., (408) 535-6508

Genesis Presch. & CC, 10160 Clayton Rd., (408) 251-7793

Good Samaritan Hospital CCCtr., 2425 Samaritan Dr., (408) 559-2454

Grant Presch., 470 E. Jackson St., (408) 293-7955

Graystone CDCtr., 6982 Shearwater Dr., (408) 997-1980

Green Valley Children's Ctr., 302 Checkers Dr., (408) 923-1130

Green Valley CDCtr., 525 Giuffrida Ave., (408) 371-9900

Grove CDCtr., 510 E. Branham Ln., (408) 226-3640

Growing Together Nursery Sch., 935 Piedmont Rd., (408) 926-1264

Hayes State Presch. & CDCtr., 5035 Poston Dr., (408) 629-1185

Headsup CDCtr., 2841 Junction Ave., (408) 432-1644

Hellyer Head Start, 725 Hellyer Ave., (408) 225-8534

Hillsdale Presch., 3200 Water St., (408) 360-8904

Holy Cross Luth. Children's Ctr., 5410 Taft Dr., (408) 356-4777

Holy Family Ed. Ctr., 4850 Pearl Ave., (408) 978-1355

James Lick Children's Ctr., 2955 Alum Rock Ave., (408) 347-5310

Job Corps Head Start, 3485 E. Hills Dr., (408) 937-3276

Jordan Sch., 5102 Alum Rock Ave., (408) 258-7387

Joyful Noise Presch. & K, 1229 Naglee St., (408) 288-5433

Julian/26th St. Head Start, 333 N. 26th St., (408) 453-6900

K's Quality Children Ctr., 15063 Union Ave., (408) 377-6660

Kennedy Presch., 1602 Lucretia Ave., (408) 536-0330

Kid Connection, 410 Sautner Dr., (408) 226-8600

Kidango-Arbuckle Ctr., 1910 Cinderella Ln., (408) 258-3710

Kidango-Hubbard Ctr., 1745 June Ave., (408) 258-5488

Kidagno-Linda Vista, 65 Gordon Ave., (408) 277-1286

Kidango-Ohlone Chynoweth, 5312 Terner Way, (408) 979-1670

Kidango-Valley Medical Ctr., 730 Empey Way, (408) 297-9044

Kidango-Veronica Forbes CDCtr., 2005 E. San Antonio St., (408) 258-3673

Kidango-VMC Ctr., 730 Empy Way, (408) 297-9044

Kiddie Kollege, 5386 Alum Rock Ave., (408) 259-1188

Kiddie Kountry, 2715 S. White Rd., (408) 274-2040

Kids Ext. Care, 280 Martinvale Ln., (408) 629-6532

Kids' Korner, 1515 Kooser Rd., (408) 267-3706

Kids' Korner Christian CCCtr., 2920 Fowler Rd., (408) 270-2000

Kidspark, 2858 Stevens Creek Blvd., (408) 281-8880

Kidspark, 5440 Thornwood Dr., (408) 281-8880

Kidz Acad., 1224 N. Winchester, (408) 406-0988

KinderCare, 3320 San Felipe Rd., (408) 270-0980

KinderCare, 1081 Foxworthy Ave., (408) 265-7380

Kinderwood Children's Ctr., 5560 Entrada Cedros, (408) 363-1366

Las Plumas Head Start, 1590 Las Plumas Dr., (408) 258-8524

Learning Co. #2, 5670 Camden Ave., (408) 723-1131

Legend Lrng. Ctr., 3412 Sierra Rd., (408) 923-8804

Legend Lrng. Ctr., 1025 S. De Anza Blvd., (408) 253-6944

Linda Vista CDCtr., 65 Gordon Ave., (408) 928-7780

Little Friends Presch., 2720 S. Bascom Ave., (408) 377-8541

Little Kiddles Swing Set Groups, 286 Sorrento Way, (408) 227-5758

Little Oak Presch., 1921 Clarinda Way, (408) 356-7554

Little Scholar Presch. & DC., 3560 Kettmann Rd., (408) 238-1474

Little Scholars Schools, 3703 Silver Creek Rd., (408) 274-4726

Lotus Presch., 639 N. 5th St., (408) 293-1612

Los Arboles Head Start, 455 Los Arboles St., (408) 363-9016

Luther Burbank CDCtr., 4 Wabash Ave., (408) 295-1731

Lyndale Head Start, 13901 Nordyke Dr., (408) 258-1523

MACSA Youth Ctr., 660 Sinclair Dr., (408) 929-1080

Mandala Children's House, 5038 Hyland Ave., (408) 251-8633

Mariposa Montessori Sch., 1550 Meridian Ave., (408) 266-5683

McGinness H.S. Head Start, 1212 McGinness Ave., (408) 937-5203

McKinley Presch. Prog., 651 Macredes, (408) 297-7717

Medallion Champions-Guadalupe, 6044 Vera Cruz Dr., (408) 997-9821

Medallion Champions-Ledesma, 1001 School House Rd., (408) 972-4034

Medallion Champions-Miner, 5629 Lean Ave., (408) 225-2144

Medallion Champions-San Anselmo, 6670 San Anselmo Way, (408) 578-2710

Metro Head Start, 760 Hillsdale Ave., (408) 723-6555

Miller Presch., 1250 S. King Rd., (408) 928-8319

Minigym Explorations, 4115 Jacksol Dr., (408) 559-4616

Monte Alban Head Start, 1322 Santee Dr., (408) 453-6900

Montessori Acad., 1188 Wunderlich Dr., (408) 252-1488

Montessori Acad. III, 495 Massar Ave., (408) 259-5736

Mt. Pleasant Children's Ctr., 1650 S. White Rd., (408) 937-2892

Mulberry Coop. Nursery Sch. & K, 1980 Hamilton Ave., (408) 377-1595

My Little University, 878 Boynton Ave., (408) 296-5582

Neighborhood Christian Presch., 2575 Coit Dr., (408) 371-4222

New Concept Sch., 3800 Blackford Ave., Bldg. 1, (408) 296-6668

New Covenant Christian Presch., 1975 Cambrianna Dr., (408) 369-0233

Noble Ext. DC, 3466 Grossmont Dr., (408) 251-8952

Northwood CDCtr., 2760 Trimble Rd., (408) 923-1943

Olinder Presch., 890 E. William St., (408) 286-4198

One World Montessori Sch., 5331 Dent Ave., (408) 255-3770

Orange Blossom Head Start, 701 Vine St., (408) 292-7160

Over the Rainbow Montessori Sch., 880 Hillsdale Ave., (408) 266-5432

Over the Rainbow Montessori Sch., 3001 Ross Ave., (408) 978-5454

Pacific Montessori Acad. #1, 4115 Jacksol Dr., (408) 246-5432

Park Avenue Presch., 1080 The Alameda, (408) 294-4807

Parkview State Presch. & CDCtr., 330 Bluefield Dr., (408) 363-1901

Parkway CDCtr., 1800 Fruitdale Ave., (408) 297-7717

Phelan Tiny Tots, 801 Hibiscus Ln., (408) 446-4166

Piedmont Hills Montessori Acad., 1425 Old Piedmont Rd., (408) 923-5151

Pioneer Montessori Sch., 3520 San Felipe Rd., (408) 238-8445

Play-n-Learn Presch., 3800 Narvaez Ave., (408) 269-9004

Precious Presch., 12360 Redmond Ave., (408) 268-9000

Presch. DC Dom Dinis, 1395 E. Santa Clara St., (408) 993-0383

Presley Head Start, 1990 Kammerer Ave., (408) 928-7280

Primary Plus, 3500 Amber Dr., (408) 248-2464

Rainbow Bridge Ctr., 750 N. Capitol Ave., (408) 254-1280

Rainbow of Knowledge, 1718 Andover Ln., (408) 377-5730

Randol Sch. Age CDCtr., 762 Sunset Glen Dr., (408) 224-4505

Regard CC Dev. Ctr., 2021 Lincoln Ave., (408) 266-2561

Rex and Lee Lindsey's CDCtr., 1315 McLaughlin Ave., (408) 292-6196

River Glen Presch., 1088 Broadway, (408) 535-6240

Rosa Elena CCCtr., 2380 Enborg, (408) 279-7515

Rouleau Head Start, 1875 Monrovia Dr., (408) 270-4873

San Jose City Coll. Child Dev., 2100 Moorpark Ave., (408) 288-3759

San Jose Day Nursery, 33 N. 8th St., (408) 288-9667

San Jose Job Corps, 1149 E. Julian St., (408) 254-5627

San Jose Head Start, 275 N. 24th St., (408) 410-0232

San Jose Parents Part. Nursery Sch., 2180 Radio Ave., (408) 265-3202

San Jose State University CDCtr., 1 Washington Sq., (408) 924-3727

San Juan Bautista CDCtr., 1945 Terilyn Ave., (408) 259-4796

Santa Teresa State Presch. & CDCtr., 6200 Encinal Dr., (408) 972-4396

Santa Teresa Children's Ctr., 6150 Snell Ave., (408) 347-6280

Santee Head Start, 1399 Santee Dr., (408) 999-0853

Santee State Presch. & CDCtr., 1313 Audubon Dr., (408) 280-6739
Seven Trees Head Start, 3975 Mira Loma Way, (408) 363-8944
Shepherd of the Valley Luth. Ch., 1281 Redmond Ave., (408) 997-4846
Slonaker Ext. DC, 1601 Cunningham Ave., (408) 259-4796
Small World-Athenour, 5200 Dent Ave., (408) 358-9988
Small World-Baker, 4845 Bucknall Rd., (408) 374-6422
Small World-Country Lane, 5140 Country Ln., (408) 379-3200
Small World-Latimer, 4250 Latimer Ave., (408) 379-7459
Small World-Noddin, 1755 Gilda Way, (408) 283-9200
Small World-Payne, 3750 Gleason Ave., (408) 246-1028
Small World-Valley Vista, 2400 Flint Ave., (408) 238-3525
South Valley Children's Ctr.-Carlton, 2421 Carlton Ave., (408) 356-1453
South Valley Children's Ctr.-Oster, 1855 Lencar Way, (408) 269-1676
St. Edward's Presch., 15040 Union Ave., (408) 377-0158
St. Elizabeth's Day Home, 950 St. Elizabeth Dr., (408) 295-3456
St Frances Cabrini Sch., 15325 Woodard Ave., (408) 377-6545
St. Patrick Sch., 51 N. 9th St., (408) 283-5858
St. Stephen's Sch., 500 Shawnee Ln., (408) 365-2927
St. Timothy's Luth. Sch., 5100 Camden Ave., (408) 265-0244
Starbright Sch., 4645 Albany Dr., (408) 985-1460
Steindorf Head Start, 3001 Ross Dr., Rm. 5, (408) 266-0953
Stonegate State Presch. & CDCtr., 2605 Gassman Dr., (408) 225-0678
Story Road Head Start, 1250 Foxdale Loop, (408) 251-8796
Sunrise Kiddie Korral, 5860 Blossom Ave., (408) 227-0831
Sunshine Montessori Sch., 1321 Miller Ave., (408) 996-0856
Tamian CCCtr., 1197 Lick Ave., (408) 271-1980
Temple Emanu-El, 1010 University Ave., (408) 293-8660

Tinytown, 1133 Piedmont Rd., (408) 923-0441
Tomorrow Montessori Sch., 2466 Almaden Rd., (408) 979-1164
Tom Thumb Presch., 668 N. 1st St., (408) 288-8832
Tower Acad., 2887 McLaughlin Ave., (408) 578-2830
Toyon Partners CDCtr., 995 Bard St., (408) 729-8239
Trace Presch., 651 Dana Ave., (408) 535-6257
Villa San Pedro Head Start, 282 Danze Dr., (408) 365-7684
Vine Head Start, 701 Vine St., (408) 920-5750
Voyager's DCCtr., 1590 Las Plumas Ave., (408) 926-8885
Washington Presch., 100 Oak St., (408) 535-6261
W.C. Overfelt Children's Ctr., 1835 Cunningham Ave., (408) 258-3654
Westside Coop. Presch., 3257 Payne Ave., (408) 249-5533
Williams Sch. Age CDCtr., 1150 Rajkovich Way, (408) 997-8703
Willow Glen Acad., 1590 Minnesota Ave., (408) 266-8056
Willow Glen Comm. Ext. Day Prog., 1425 Lincoln Ave., (408) 287-6999
Willow Glen United Meth. Presch. & DC, 1420 Newport Ave., (408) 294-6072
Willow Vale Christian Children's Ctr., 1730 Curtner Ave., (408) 448-0656
Wonder Years, 1411 Piedmont Rd., (408) 926-1234
Wonder Years, 11843 Redmond Ave., (408) 268-5165
Woolcreek Head Start, 645 Woolcreek Dr., (408) 283-6118
Yerba Buena Children's Ctr., 1855 Lucretia Ave., (408) 347-4754
YMCA-Allen, 5845 Allen Ave., (408) 298-3888
YMCA-Anderson, 4000 Rhoda Dr., (408) 244-1962
YMCA-Autumn Wonderland, 505 W. Julian St., (408) 298-1717
YMCA-Booksin, 1590 Dry Creek Rd., (408) 265-3588
YMCA-Easterbrook, 4660 Eastus Dr., (408) 874-3376
YMCA-East Valley Presch., 1975 S. White Rd., (408) 258-4419

YMCA-East Valley Presch., 2995 Rossmore Way, (408) 223-7472
YMCA-Fammatre, 2800 New Jersey Ave., (408) 371-7680
YMCA-Farnham, 15711 Woodard Rd., (408) 371-8377
YMCA-Hacienda Valley View, 1290 Kimberly Dr., (408) 978-1156
YMCA-Lietz, 5300 Carter Ave., (408) 370-1877
YMCA-Los Paseos, 121 Avenida Grande, (408) 972-5132
YMCA-Majestic Way, 1855 Majestic Way, (408) 923-1925
YMCA-Matsumoto, 4121 Mackin Woods Ln., (408) 223-4873
YMCA-Meyerholz, 6990 Melvin Dr., (408) 996-2308
YMCA-Muir, 6550 Hanover Dr., (408) 253-7440
YMCA-Reed, 1524 Jacob Ave., (408) 978-3002
YMCA-Ruskin, 1363 Turlock Ln., (408) 251-6222
YMCA-Sakamoto, 6280 Shadelands Dr., (408) 227-3605
YMCA-Schallenberger, 1280 Koch Ln., (408) 298-3888
YMCA-Silver Oak, 5000 Farnsworth Dr., (408) 223-4524
YMCA-Simonds, 6515 Grapevine Way, (408) 268-7125
YMCA-Terrell, 5925 Pearl Ave., (408) 226-9622
YMCA-Vinci Park, 1131 Vinci Park Way, (408) 259-0127
YWCA-Almaden, 1295 Dentwood Dr., (408) 295-4011
YWCA-Canoas, 880 Wren Dr., (408) 595-2208
YWCA-Lynhaven, 881 S. Cypress Ave., (408) 247-1693
YWCA-Villa Nueva, 375 S. 3rd St., (408) 295-4011
YWCA-West Valley, 4343 Leigh Ave., (408) 269-7534

San Martin
San Martin Head Start, 13570 Depot Ave., (408) 683-0402
San Martin State Presch. & Sch. Age CDCtr., 100 North St., (408) 683-2808

Santa Clara
A Special Place, 5041 Stevens Creek Blvd., (408) 248-0148
Action Day Nursery, 2001 Pruneridge Ave., (408) 244-2909
Angels Montessori Presch., 1000 Kiely Blvd., (408) 241-8434
Bowers State Presch., 2755 Barkley Ave., (408) 423-1117
Bracher Center, 2401 Bowers Ave., (408) 423-1215
Briarwood Children's Ctr. State Presch., 1940 Townsend Ave., (408) 423-1315
Bright Beginnings Presch. & DC, 2445 Cabrillo Ave., (408) 247-7777
Carden El Encanto Day Sch., 615 Hobart Terr., (408) 244-5041
Challenger School, 890 Pomeroy Ave., (408) 243-6190
First Step Presch., 1515/1525 Franklin St., (408) 554-6692
Haman Dist. Presch., 435 Saratoga Ave., (408) 423-1443
Happy Days CDCtr., 220 Blake Ave., (408) 296-5770
Hughes State Presch., 4949 Calle de Escuela, (408) 983-2174
Jubilee Acad., 2499 Homestead Rd., (408) 244-9777
Kids on Campus, 2705 The Alameda, (408) 554-5563
Kidsville Presch. & DCCtr., 1247 Benton St., (408) 296-7442
KinderCare, 840 Bing Dr., (408) 246-2141
Laurelwood Presch., 955 Teal Dr., (408) 241-8626
Martinson CDCtr., 1350 Hope Dr., (408) 988-8296
MCA Granada Islamic Sch., 3003 Scott Blvd., (408) 980-1161
Mission College CDCtr., 3000 Mission College Blvd., (408) 855-5176
Montague State Presch., 750 Laurie Ave., (408) 423-1917
Monticello Acad., 3345 Lochinvar Ave., (408) 365-1561
Monticello CDCtr., 3401 Monroe St., (408) 261-0494
Neighborhood Christian Ctr., 3111 Benton Ave., (408) 984-3418
Noah's Ark, 2545 Warburton Ave., (408) 296-2774

One World Montessori Sch., 2495 Cabrillo Ave., (408) 615-1254
Pomeroy District Presch., 1250 Pomeroy Ave., (408) 423-3817
Santa Clara Christian Presch., 3421 Monroe St., (408) 246-5423
Santa Clara Parents Nursery Sch., 471 Monroe St., (408) 248-5131
Scott Lane-Wilson, 1840 Benton St., (408) 423-3670
Small World-Sutter Sch. Age, 3200 Forbes Ave., (408) 985-5990
St. Lawrence Presch., 1971 St. Lawrence Dr., (408) 248-1966
St. Mark's Episcopal Ch., 1957 Pruneridge Ave., (408) 247-2223
Tican Institute, 220 Blake Ave., #D, (408) 554-8787
Wahaha Sch., 220 Blake Ave., (408)247-0286
YMCA-Eisenhower, 277 Rodonovan Dr., (408) 249-5330
YMCA- Millikin, 2720 Sonoma Pl., (408) 243-6577

Saratoga

Action Day Nursery, 13560 S. Saratoga-Sunnyvale Rd., (408) 867-4515
Challenger Presch., 18811 Cox Ave., (408) 378-0444
Creative Corner CC, 20300 Herriman Dr., (408) 354-8700
Marshall Lane Sch. Age CDCtr., 14114 Marilyn Ln., (408) 371-9900
My Preschool, 1472 Saratoga Ave., (408) 376-0385
Nature's Classroom, 19010 Austin Way, (408) 399-3071
Primary Plus, 18720 Bucknall Rd., (408) 370-0357
Sacred Heart Presch., 13718 Saratoga Ave., (408) 867-9241
Saratoga Presby. Presch., 20455 Herriman Ave., (408) 741-5770
St. Andrew's School, 13601 Saratoga Ave., (408) 867-3785
Village Presch., 20390 Park Pl., (408) 867-3181
West Valley College CDCtr., 14000 Fruitvale Ave., (408) 741-2409
World of Discovery Presch., 20300 Herriman Dr., (408) 867-4683
YMCA-Blue Hills, 12300 De Sanka Ave., (408) 257-7160

Stanford

Bing Nursery, 850 Escondido Rd., (650) 723-4865
Children's Creative Lrng. Ctr., 1711 Stanford Ave., (650) 493-6006
Children's Ctr. of Stanford, 695 Pampas Ln., (650) 853-3090
Rainbow Sch. at Escondido Village, 859 Escondido Rd., (650) 723-0217
Stanford Arboretum Children's Ctr., 215 Quarry Rd., (650) 725-6322

Sunnyvale

Amazing Creations Presch., 1025 The Dalles Ave., (408) 730-0365
Appleseed Montessori Sch., 1302 Warner Ave., (408) 245-7338
Appleseed Montessori Sch., 1095 Dunford Way, (408) 260-7333
Bishop CDCtr., 440 N. Sunnyvale Ave., (408) 739-2611
Calif. Young World #5, 1110 Fairwood Dr., (408) 245-7285
Calif. Young World-Ellis, 550 East Olive St., (408) 774-0405
Calif. Young World-Lakewood, 750 Lakechime Dr., (408) 245-7976
Calif. Young World-San Miguel, 777 San Miguel Ave., (408) 738-1385
Caring Hearts CDCtr., 645 W. Fremont Ave., (408) 245-6356
Challenger Sch., 1185 Hollenbeck Ave., (408) 245-7170
Cherry Chase Presch., 1138 Heatherstone Way, (408) 523-4887
Cherry Chase Sch. Age CDCtr., 1138 Heatherstone Way, (408) 736-0168
Children's Creative Lrng. Ctr., 794 E. Duane Ave., (408) 732-2288
Community Presch., 1098 Remington Dr., (408) 739-2022
Cumberland Sch. Age CDCtr., 824 Cumberland Ave., (408) 736-0179
Cupertino Coop. Nursery Sch., 563 W. Fremont Ave., (408) 739-8963
De Lor Montessori Sch., 1510 Lewiston Dr., (408) 773-0200
Early Horizons, 1510 Lewiston Dr., (408) 746-3020
French-American Sch. of Silicon Valley, 1510 Lewiston Dr., (408) 746-0460
Jamil Islamic Ctr., 1095 Dunford Way, (650) 326-0400
Little Rascals CCCtr., 494 S. Bernardo Ave., (408) 730-9900

Montessori House of Children, 582 Dunholme Way, (408) 749-1602
Mother's Day Out, 728 W. Fremont Ave., (408) 736-2511
My Dream Acad., 1500 Partridge Ave., (408) 730-9600
New World CDCtr., 730 E. Homestead Rd., (408) 255-5330
Nimitz Sch. Age CDCtr., 545 E. Cheyenne Dr., (408) 736-6176
Ponderosa Dist. Presch., 804 Ponderosa Ave., (408) 423-4017
Presby. Early Lrng. Ctr., 728 W. Fremont Ave., (408) 245-2253
Prodigy CDCtr., 1155 E. Arquez Ave., (408) 245-3276
Rainbow Montessori CDCtr., 790 Duane Ave., (408) 738-3261
Resurrection Sch., 1395 Hollenbeck Ave., (408) 245-4571
South Peninsula Hebrew Day Sch., 1030 Astoria Dr., (408) 738-3060
St. Martin Sch., 597 Central Ave., (408) 736-5534
Stocklmeir Sch. Age CDCtr., 592 Dunholme Way, (408) 732-2008
Stratford Sch., 820 W. McKinley Ave., (408) 737-1500
Sunnyvale Christian Sch., 445 S. Mary Ave., (408) 736-3286
Sunnyvale Parent Presch., 1515 Partridge Ave., (408) 736-8043
Sunnyvale Sch. Dist. State Presch., 739 Morse Ave., (408) 522-8213
Triumphant Lrng. Ctr., 420 Carroll St., (408) 737-7450
Vargas Sch. Age CDCtr., 1054 Carson Dr., (408) 736-0174
Village Campus CDCtr., 649 E. Homestead Rd., (408) 732-5611
YMCA-West Valley, 1635 Belleville Way, (408) 245-6775

Santa Cruz County
Aptos
Apple After School, 221 Thunderbird Dr., (831) 685-0629
Aptos Christian CCCtr., 7200 Freedom Blvd., (831) 688-3312
Cabrillo College Children's Ctr., 6500 Soquel Dr., (831) 479-6352
Calvary Chapel Children's Ctr., 8065 Valencia St., (831) 662-3470

Children's Enrichment Ctr., 2701 Cabrillo College Dr., (831) 475-4899
Rose Blossom Nursery Sch., 6401 Freedom Blvd., (831) 662-8458
Santa Cruz Montessori Sch., 6230 Soquel Dr., (831) 476-1646
Simcha Presch., 3055 Porter Gulch Rd., (831) 479-3449
St. Andrew Presch., 9850 Monroe Ave., (831) 688-7095
Ben Lomond
Children's Ctr. of San Lorenzo Valley, 8500 Hwy. 9, (831) 336-2857
Glen Arbor Sch., 9393 Glen Arbor Rd., (831) 336-2932
St. Andrew's Presch., 101 Riverside & Glen Arbor, (831) 336-5994
Boulder Creek
Little People's Sch., 13171 Railroad Ave., (831) 338-4112
YMCA-Boulder Creek, 400 Lomond St., (831) 338-6788
Capitola
Capitola Christian CDCtr., 4575 Capitola Rd., (831) 475-7484
Capitola CKC, 504 Monterey Ave., (831) 462-1718
Lifespring Presch., 1255 41st Ave., (831) 477-0584
Neighborhood DC, 875 Monterey Ave., (831) 462-7494
Corralitos
Santa Cruz Co. Head Start, 26 Browns Valley Rd., (831) 761-8894
Davenport
Pacific Presch., 50 Ocean St., (831) 425-7002
Felton
Redwood Mountain State Presch., 7103-A Hwy. 9, (831) 335-3222
Freedom
Freedom Children's Ctr., 37 Holly Dr., (831) 728-6274
Freedom Migrant Head Start, 37 Holly Dr., (831) 761-6669
Vista Verde CDCtr., 1936 Freedom Blvd., (831) 724-3749
La Selva Beach
Secret Garden, 26 Florido, (831) 688-7790
Mount Hermon
Mount Hermon Play Sch., Parkview, (831) 335-9420

Santa Cruz

A Child's Reflection, 327 Church St., (831) 426-3655
Blanche's House, 3420 Lillian Way, (831) 479-1964
Bonny Doon Presch., 1492 Pine Flat Rd., (831) 459-7795
Branciforte CKC, 840 Branciforte Ave., (831) 462-9822
Calvary Presch., 532 Center St., (831) 425-1332
City of Scotts Valley 2, 151 Brook Knoll Dr., (831) 427-0671
Common Threads Montessori, 208 Rankin St., (831) 427-1316
Community Children's Ctr., 301 Center St., (831) 425-8668
De La Veaga CKC, 1145 Morrissey Blvd., (831) 426-7402
Del Mar State Presch., 1959 Merrill St., (831) 462-1247
Discoveryland, 532 Rodriguez, (831) 476-9684
Downtown Children's Ctr., 303 Walnut Ave., (831) 426-3062
El Rancho Day Sch., 2474 El Rancho Dr., (831) 438-5437
Emeline CCCtr., 1030 Emeline Ave., (831) 459-8866
Family Network Presch., 1225 Brommer St., (831) 462-2535
Gateway Presch., 720 17th Ave., (831) 479-7545
Gault CKC, 1320 Seabright Ave., (831) 462-9822
Good Shepherd Sch., 2727 Mattison Ln., (831) 476-4000
Granary CDCtr., 1156 High St., (831) 426-3831
Green Acres State Presch., 984 Bostwick Ln., (831) 462-1116
Growing Years Presch., 3205 Salisbury Dr., (831) 462-4453
Harvey West Children's Ctr., 191-B Harvey West Blvd., (831) 469-9358
Holy Cross Presch., 170-A High St., (831) 425-1782
Johnny Crow's Garden, 548 Highland Ave., (831) 426-7620
Kids' Klub, 1114 Water St., (831) 469-0403
Kinder Cottage, 3834 Gross Rd., (831) 475-0899
Live Oak Presch., 1916 Capitola Rd., (831) 462-1116
Loving & Learning, 2091 17th Ave., (831) 464-1915
Messiah Luth. Presch. & DC, 801 High St., (831) 423-8330
Neighborhood CCCtr., 904 Western Dr., (831) 423-9073
Nuevo Dia CDCtr., 135 Leibrandt AVe., (831) 426-1276
Pride-n-Joy Children's Ctr., 1215 Chanticleer Ave., (831) 464-2121
Santa Cruz Co. Head Start, 255 Swift St., (831) 457-8506
Santa Cruz Garden CKC, 8005 Winkle Ave., (831) 475-5925
Sweet Dreams DC, 454 Roxas St., (831) 426-0834
Swift Street CDCtr., 255 Swift St., (831) 458-2348
Sycamore Street CDCtr., 121 Sycamore St., (831) 454-9920
UCSC Children's Ctr., 599 Koshland Way, (831) 459-2967
Westlake CKC, 1000 High St., (831) 458-2259

Scotts Valley

A Child's Reflection, 106 Vine Hill School Rd., (831) 438-4813
Baymonte Christian Presch., 5000-B Granite Creek Rd., (831) 438-5657
Baymonte Christian Presch. Too, 4901 Scotts Valley Dr., (831) 440-9248
Circle of Friends, 111 N. Navarra Dr., (831) 461-1366
City of Scotts Valley-Vine Hill, 151 Vine Hill School Rd., (831) 438-6529
Early Childhood Lrng. Ctr., 570 Bethany Dr., (831) 438-3800
Montessori Scotts Valley, 123 S. Navarra Dr., (831) 439-9313
Scotts Valley Children's Ctr., 255 Mt. Hermon Rd., (831) 461-9330

Soquel

Lion Cubs CDCtr., 3060 Cunnison Ln., (831) 476-0924
Main St. CKC, 3400 Main St., (831) 475-5758
Mid County Children's Ctr., 305 Alturas Way, (831) 476-8890
Mountain After Sch. DC, 3042 Old San Jose Rd., (831) 475-3274
Rocking Horse Ranch DC, 4134 Fairway Dr., (831) 462-2702

Santa Cruz Montessori Sch., 2645 Park Ave., (831) 465-7681

Soquel CKC, 2700 Porter St., (831) 475-2302

Watsonville

Bradley Migrant Presch., 321 Corralitos Rd., (831) 728-6955

Buena Vista Children's Ctr., 201 Tierra Alta, (831) 728-6428

Calabasas Presch. Ctr., 202 Calabasas Rd., (831) 786-1870

Comm. Interplay Presch., 95 Alta Vista Ave., (831) 722-7075

Cope Centro Familiar, 2667 E. Lake Ave., (831) 761-6295

Green Valley Christian Sch., 376 Green Valley Rd., (831) 724-6505

H.A. Hyde Presch., 125 Alta Vista Ave., (831) 761-6179

Hall Migrant Head Start, 300 Sill Rd., (831) 728-6604

Heart & Hands Christ. CC & Presch., 40 Blanca Ln., (831) 724-0175

Linscott State Presch., 220 Elm St., (831) 728-0365

Louise Blanchard CCCtr., 175 Lawrence Ave., (831) 724-9234

Macquiddy After Sch. CC Prog., 330 Martinelli, (831) 763-0624

Mt. Madonna Presch., 445 Summit Rd., (831) 847-2717

Noah's Ark Presch., 710 Green Valley Rd., (831) 722-7811

Ohlone Presch. Ctr., 21 Bay Farms Rd., (831) 761-6180

Pajaro Valley Children's Ctr., 234 Montecito St., (831) 722-3737

Pajaro Head Start, 41 Jonathan St., (831) 784-4172

Pajaro Valley Shelter Svcs. CCCtr., 115 Brennan St., (831) 728-5649

Salsipuedes Head Start Ctr., 115 Casserly Rd., (831) 728-6913

Santa Cruz Co. Head Start, 1936 Freedom Blvd., (831) 566-2478

Santa Cruz Co. Head Start, 235 Hammer Dr., (831) 724-7134

Santa Cruz Co. Head Start, 340-B E. Beach St., (831) 763-0780

Santa Cruz Co. Head Start, 201 Brewington Ave, (831) 722-8663

Santa Cruz Co. Head Start, 15 Madison Ave., (831) 728-1102

Santa Cruz Co. Head Start, 140 Herman Ave., (831) 722-3644

Santa Cruz Co. Head Start, 441 Rogers Ave., (831) 761-9009

United Presby. Sch., 112 E. Beach St., (831) 722-1859

Viste Verde CDCtr., 1936 Freedom Blvd., (831) 724-8725

Watsonville Children's Ctr., 32 Madison St., (831) 728-6280

YMCA-Bradley Sch., 321 Corralitos Rd., (831) 728-9622

YWCA CCCtr., 118 2nd St., (831) 768-0900

San Benito County
Aromas

YMCA-Aromas, 365 Vega St., (831) 726-2970

Hollister

The Children's House Montessori Sch., 720 Monterey St., (831) 630-3038

Countryside DC & Presch. Ctr., 331 Gateway Dr., (831) 638-0599

Fairview CDCtr., 5381 Fairview Rd., (831) 637-9204

Go Kids Club-Ro Hardin, 761 South St., (831) 636-8171

Herman Fehl Head Start, 1101 Community Pkwy., (408) 453-6900

Kinderville, 433 7th St., (831) 637-3199

Little Baler Presch., 1520 Sunnyslope Rd., (831) 636-5706

Methodist Presch., 521 Monterey St., (831) 637-4240

Paddington Sch., 1431 Santa Ana Rd., (831) 637-5065

Presby. Coop. Presch., San Benito at Cienega Rd., (831) 637-5816

Rosa Morada Migrant Head Start, 5381 Fairview Rd., (831) 636-1975

Sacred Heart Parish Presch., 670 College St., (831) 637-4157

San Felipe-Herman Fehl Head Start, 1101 Community Pkwy., (408) 453-6900

Southside Migrant CDCtr., 3235 Southside Rd., (831) 637-1125

Spring Grove Pre-K & Presch., 500 Spring Grove Rd., (831) 637-5574

San Juan Bautista

ASJUSD-Miescuelita Presch., 300 The Alameda, (831) 623-2627

San Juan State Presch., 1112 3rd St., (831) 623-4032

Chapter 11

Hospitals &Health Care

GOOD HEALTH CARE. You want it. Where, how, do you get it? The question is particularly puzzling these days because so many changes are taking place in medicine and medical insurance.

The "operations" of a few years ago are the "procedures" of today, done in the office not the surgery room, completed in minutes not hours, requiring home care, not hospitalization. Large insurance companies, through their health maintenance plans, are setting limits on what doctors and hospitals can charge, and — critics contend — interfering with the ability of doctors to prescribe what they see fit. The companies strongly deny this, arguing they are bringing reforms to a profession long in need of reforming.

Many hospitals are merging, the better to avoid unnecessary duplication and to save money by purchasing supplies and medicine in larger amounts.

Universal health insurance having failed to clear congress, about 44 million Americans are not covered by any medical plan. Unable to afford medical bills, many ignore ailments and illnesses. The state legislature has passed a law that makes it easier for patients to sue Health Maintenance Organizations and insurers.

This chapter will give you an overview of Northern California health care and although it won't answer all your questions — too complex a business for that — we hope that it will point you in the right directions.

For most people, health care is twinned with insurance, in systems that are called "managed care." But many individuals, for a variety of reasons, do not have insurance. This is a good place to start: with nothing, all options open. Let's use as our seeker for the best of all health care worlds — on a tight budget — a young woman, married, one child. Her choices:

No Insurance — Cash Care

The woman is self-employed or works at a small business that does not offer health benefits. She comes down with the flu. When she goes into the doctor's office, she will be asked by the receptionist, how do you intend to pay? With no insurance, she pays cash (or credit card), usually right there. She takes her prescription, goes to the pharmacy and pays full cost.

Population by Age & Sex
Santa Clara County

Age	Male	Female	Total
0-4	69,034	65,394	134,428
5-9	71,032	67,576	138,608
10-14	62,647	59,040	121,687
15-19	56,161	53,241	109,402
20-24	52,151	48,957	101,108
25-29	61,667	56,301	117,968
30-34	75,486	66,379	141,865
35-39	91,298	79,492	170,790
40-44	85,725	76,290	162,015
45-49	67,453	63,470	130,923
50-54	54,943	55,677	110,620
55-59	42,623	44,341	86,964
60-64	33,032	34,129	67,161
65-69	26,143	27,618	53,761
70-74	19,901	23,764	43,665
75-79	14,666	20,261	34,927
80-84	8,010	12,708	20,718
85-plus	4,976	11,666	16,642
All	896,948	866,304	1,763,252
Median age	35	36	35

Source: Census 2000

If her child or husband gets sick and needs to see a doctor, the same procedure holds. Also the same for treatment of a serious illness, to secure X-rays or hospitalization. It's a cash system.

Medi-Cal

If an illness strikes that impoverishes the family or if the woman, through job loss or simply low wages, cannot afford cash care, the county-state health system will step in. The woman fills out papers to qualify for Medi-Cal, the name of the system (it's known elsewhere as Medicaid), and tries to find a doctor that will treat Medi-Cal patients. If unable to find an acceptable doctor, the woman could turn to a county hospital or clinic. There she will be treated free or at very low cost.

Drawbacks-Pluses of Medi-Cal

County hospitals and clinics, in the personal experience of one of the editors — who has relatives who work at or use county facilities — have competent doctors and medical personnel. If you keep appointments promptly, often you will be seen with little wait. If you want immediate treatment for, say, a cold, you register and you wait until an urgent-care doctor is free.

If you need a specialist, often the county facility will have one on staff, or will be able to find one at a teaching hospital or other facility. You don't choose the specialist; the county physician does.

County facilities are underfunded and inconveniently located — a major drawback. Some counties, lacking clinics and hospitals, contract with adjoining counties that are equipped. You have to drive some distance for treatment.

County hospitals and clinics are not 100 percent free. If you have money or an adequate income, you will be billed for service. Some county hospitals run medical plans designed for people who can pay. These people can ask for a "family" doctor and receive a higher (usually more convenient) level of care.

Let's say the woman lacks money but doesn't want to hassle with a long drive and, possibly, a long wait for treatment of a minor ailment. She can sign up for Medi-Cal to cover treatment of serious illnesses, and for the colds, etc., go to a private doctor for treatment and pay in cash, ignoring Medi-Cal. There are many ways to skin the cat, and much depends on circumstances. For the poor and low-income, Medi-Cal is meant to be a system of last resort.

Medicare — Veterans Hospital

If our woman were elderly, she would be eligible for Medicare, the federal insurance system, which covers 80 percent, with limitations, of medical costs or allowable charges. Many people purchase supplemental insurance to bring coverage up to 100 percent (long-term illnesses requiring hospitalization may exhaust some benefits.) If the woman were a military veteran with a service-related illness, she could seek care at a Veteran's clinic or hospital.

Indemnity Care

Usually the most expensive, this insurance allows complete freedom of choice. The woman picks the doctor she wants. If her regular doctor recommends a specialist, she can decide which one, and if she needs hospital treatment, she can pick the institution. In reality, the choice of hospital and specialist will often be strongly influenced by her regular doctor but the patient retains control. Many indemnity plans have deductibles and some may limit how much they pay out in a year or lifetime. Paperwork may be annoying.

Managed Care

This divides into two systems, Preferred Provider Organizations (PPO) and Health Maintenance Organizations (HMO). Both are popular in California and if your employer provides health insurance, chances are almost 100 percent you will be pointed toward, or given a choice of, one or the other.

PPOs and HMOs differ among themselves. It is beyond the scope of this book to detail the differences but you should ask if coverage can be revoked or rates increased in the event of serious illness. Also, what is covered, what is not. Cosmetic surgery might not be covered. Psychiatric visits or care might be limited. Ask about drug costs and how emergency or immediate care is provided.

Preferred Provider

The insurance company approaches certain doctors, clinics, medical facilities and hospitals and tells them: We will send patients to you but you must agree to our prices — a method of controlling costs — and our rules. The young woman chooses her doctor from the list, often extensive, provided by the PPO.

The physician will have practicing privileges at certain local hospitals. The young woman's child contracts pneumonia and must be hospitalized. Dr. X is affiliated with XYZ hospital, which is also signed up with the PPO plan. The child is treated at XYZ hospital.

If the woman used an "outside" doctor or hospital, she would pay extra — the amount depending on the nature of the plan. It is important to know the doctor's affiliations because you may want your hospital care at a certain institution.

Hospitals differ. A children's hospital, for instance, will specialize in children's illnesses and load up on children's medical equipment. A general hospital will have a more rounded program. For convenience, you may want the hospital closest to your home.

If you need specialized treatment, you must, to avoid extra costs, use the PPO-affiliated specialists. The doctor will often guide your choice.

Complaints are surfacing from people who started out with a general physician, who was affiliated with their PPO, then moved on to a specialist who was not affiliated with the PPO. When the second doctor submits a bill, people are shocked. Each time you see a doctor you should ask if he or she is affiliated with your PPO.

Besides the basic cost for the policy, PPO insurance might charge fees, co-payments or deductibles. A fee might be $5 or $10 a visit. With co-payments, the bill, say, comes to $100. Insurance pays $80, the woman pays $20.

Deductible example: The woman pays the first $250 or the first $2,000 of any medical costs within a year, and the insurer pays bills above $250 or $2,000. With deductibles, the higher the deductible the lower the cost of the policy. The $2,000 deductible is really a form of catastrophic insurance.

Conversely, the higher the premium the more the policy covers. Some policies cover everything. (Dental care is usually provided through a separate insurer.) The same for prescription medicines. You may pay for all, part, or nothing, depending on the type plan.

The PPO doctor functions as your personal physician. Often the doctor will have his or her own practice and office, conveniently located. If you need to squeeze in an appointment, the doctor usually will try to be accommodating.

Drawback: PPOs restrict choice.

Health Maintenance Organization (HMO)

Very big in California because Kaiser Permanente, one of the most popular medical-hospital groups, is run as an HMO. The insurance company and medical provider are one and the same. All or almost all medical care is given by the HMO. The woman catches the flu. She sees the HMO doctor at the HMO clinic or hospital. If she becomes pregnant, she sees an HMO obstetrician at the HMO hospital or clinic and delivers her baby there.

With HMOs you pay the complete bill if you go outside the system (with obvious exceptions; e.g., emergency care).

HMOs encourage you to pick a personal physician. The young woman wants a woman doctor; she picks one from the staff. She wants a pediatrician as her child's personal doctor; the HMO, usually, can provide one.

HMO clinics and hospitals bring many specialists and services together under one roof. You can get your eyes examined, your hearing tested, your prescriptions filled, your X-rays taken within an HMO facility (this varies), and much more.

If you need an operation or treatment beyond the capability of your immediate HMO hospital, the surgery will be done at another HMO hospital within the system or at a hospital under contract with the HMO. Kaiser recently started contracting with other facilities to provide some of the services that it used to do in its own hospitals or clinics.

HMO payment plans vary but many HMO clients pay a monthly fee and a small ($5-$15) per visit fee. Often the plan includes low-cost or reduced-cost or free prescriptions.

Drawback: Freedom of choice limited. If HMO facility is not close, the woman will have to drive to another town.

Point of Service (POS)

Essentially, an HMO with the flexibility to use outside doctors and facilities for an extra fee or a higher deductible. POS systems seem to be popular with people who don't feel comfortable limiting themselves to an HMO. They pay extra but possibly not as much as other alternatives.

Tiered Plans

One of the latest wrinkles. Because hospital stays make up a large part of insurance bills, insurers are shifting some of these costs onto employers and consumers. This approach divides hospitals, based on their costs, into three tiers or price levels. When a patient is admitted to a hospital, he or his plan pays extra, the amount depending on the tier rating.

Choices, more information

If you are receiving medical insurance through your employer, you will be limited to the choices offered. In large groups, unions often have a say in what providers are chosen.

Some individuals will base their choice on price, some on convenience of facilities, others on what's covered, and so on.

Many private hospitals offer Physician Referral Services. You call the hospital, ask for the service and get a list of doctors to choose from. The doctors will be affiliated with the hospital providing the referral. Hospitals and doctors will also tell you what insurance plans they accept for payment and will send you brochures describing the services the hospital offers.

For Kaiser and other HMOs, call the local hospital or clinic.

A PPO will give you a list of its member doctors and facilities.

Ask plenty of questions. Shop carefully.

Here's some advice from a pro on picking a health plan: Make a chart with a list of prospective health plans in columns across the top.

Down the left side of the chart, list the services or attributes that you think are important. Review the health plans and check off the "important" services in each plan. Choose or investigate further those plans that have the most check marks.

Common Questions

• *The young woman is injured in a car accident and is unconscious. Where will she be taken?*

Generally, she will be taken to the closest emergency room or trauma center, where her condition will be stabilized. Her doctor will then have her admitted into a hospital. Or she will be transferred to her HMO hospital or, if indigent, to a county facility.

If her injuries are severe, she most likely will be rushed to a regional trauma center. Trauma centers have specialists and special equipment to treat serious injuries. Both PPOs and HMOs offer urgent care and emergency care.

• *The young woman breaks her leg. Her personal doctor is an internist and does not set fractures. What happens?*

The personal doctor refers the case to a specialist. Insurance pays the specialist's fee.

In PPO, the woman would generally see a specialist affiliated with the PPO. In an HMO, the specialist would be employed by the HMO.

• *The young woman signs up for an HMO then contracts a rare disease or suffers an injury that requires treatment beyond the capability of the HMO. Will she be treated?*

Often yes, but it pays to read the fine print. The HMO will contract treatment out to a facility that specializes in the needed treatment.

• *The young woman becomes despondent and takes to drink. Will insurance pay for her rehabilitation?*

Depends on her insurance. And often her employer. Some may have drug and alcohol rehab plans. Some plans cover psychiatry.

• *The woman becomes pregnant. Her doctor, who has delivered many babies, wants her to deliver at X hospital. All the woman's friends say, Y Hospital is much better, nicer, etc. The doctor is not cleared to practice at Y Hospital. Is the woman out of luck?*

With a PPO, the woman must deliver at a hospital affiliated with the PPO — or pay the extra cost. If her doctor is not affiliated with that hospital, sometimes a doctor may be given courtesy practicing privileges at a hospital where he or she does not have staff membership. Check with the doctor.

With HMOs, the woman must deliver within the HMO system.

Incidentally, with PPOs and HMOs you should check that the doctors and specialists listed in the organization's booklets can treat you. Some plans may restrict access to certain doctors. Some booklets may be out-of-date and not have an accurate list of doctors.

• *The young woman goes in for minor surgery, which turns into major surgery when the doctor forgets to remove a sponge before sewing up. Upon reviving, she does what?*

Some medical plans require clients to submit complaints to a panel of arbitrators, which decides damages, if any. But the courts are taking a dim view of this policy. Read the policy.

• *The woman's child reaches age 18. Is she covered by the family insurance?*

All depends on the insurance. Some policies will cover the children while they attend college. (But attendance may be defined in a certain way, full-time as opposed to part-time.) You should read the plan thoroughly.

• *At work, the woman gets her hand caught in a revolving door and is told she will need six months of therapy during which she can't work. Who pays?*

Insurance will usually pay for the medical costs. Workers Compensation, a state plan that includes many but not all people, may compensate the woman for time lost off the job and may pay for medical costs. If you injure yourself on the job, your employer must file a report with Workers Comp. Ask also how emergency or immediate care is provided.

• *The woman wakes up at 3 a.m. with a sore throat and headache. She feels bad but not bad enough to drive to a hospital or emergency room. She should:*

Many hospitals and medical plans offer 24-hour advice lines. This is something you should check on when you sign up for a plan.

• *While working in her kitchen, the woman slips, bangs her head against the stove, gets a nasty cut and becomes woozy. She should:*

Call 9-1-1, which will send an ambulance. 9-1-1 is managed by police dispatch. It's the fastest way to get an ambulance — with one possible exception. San Jose Police Dept. has opened an easy-dial line for non-emergencies. Phone 3-1-1.

• *What's the difference between a hospital, a clinic, an urgent-care center and a doctor's office?*

The hospital has the most services and equipment. The center or clinic has several services and a fair amount of equipment. The office, usually, has the fewest services and the smallest amount of equipment but in some places "clinic-office" means about the same.

Hospitals have beds. If a person must have a serious operation, she goes to a hospital. Hospitals have coronary-care and intensive-care units, emergency care and other specialized, costly treatment units. Many hospitals also run clinics for minor ailments and provide the same services as medical centers.

Urgent care or medical centers are sometimes located in neighborhoods, which makes them more convenient for some people. The doctors treat the minor, and often not-so-minor, ailments of patients and send them to hospitals for major surgery and serious sicknesses.

Some doctors form themselves into groups to offer the public a variety of services.

Some hospitals have opened neighborhood clinics or centers to attract patients. Kaiser has hospitals in some towns and clinic-offices in other towns.

The doctor in his or her office treats patients for minor ailments and uses the hospital for surgeries, major illnesses. Many illnesses that required hospitalization years ago are now treated in the office or clinic.

Major Hospitals & Medical Facilities

Santa Clara-Southern Alameda County

Columbia Good Samaritan Hospital, 2425 Samaritan Dr., San Jose, 95124. Phone: (408) 559-2011.

Columbia Breast Center on the Mission Oaks Hospital Campus, 15400 National Ave., Los Gatos. For physician referral, call 1-800-COLUMBIA.

Community Hospital of Los Gatos, 815 Pollard Rd., Los Gatos, 95032. Phone: (408) 378-6131.

El Camino Hospital, 2500 Grant Rd., Mountain View, 94040. Ph: (650) 940-7000.

Kaiser Medical Center, 900 Kiely Blvd., Santa Clara, 95051. Phone: (408) 236-6400.

Kaiser Permanente-Santa Teresa Medical Center, 250 Hospital Pkwy., San Jose, 95119. Phone: (408) 972-3000.

Kaiser Permanente Medical Offices—Gilroy, 7520 Arroyo Cir., Gilroy, 95020. Ph. (408) 848-4630. Outpatient medical office.

Kaiser Permanente Medical Offices—Milpitas, 770 E. Calaveras Blvd., Milpitas, 95035. Ph. (408) 945-2900. Outpatient medical office.

Kaiser Permanente Medical Offices—Mountain View, 555 Castro St., Mountain View, 94041. Ph. (650) 903-3000.

Lucille Salter Packard Children's Hospital at Stanford, 725 Welch Rd., Palo Alto, 94304. Phone: (650) 497-8000. Parent Information & Referral Center (PIRC), Kidcall program.

Mission Oaks & Good Samaritan Hospital, 15891 Los Gatos Almaden Rd., Los Gatos, 95032. Ph. (408) 356-4111.

O'Connor Hospital, 2105 Forest Ave., San Jose, 95128. Phone: (408) 947-2500.

Regional Medical Center of San Jose, 225 N. Jackson Ave., San Jose, 95116. Phone: (408) 259-5000.

Saint Louise Regional Hospital, 9400 No Name Uno, Gilroy, 95020. Phone: (408) 848-2000 or (800) 423-2032.

Santa Clara Valley Health & Hospital System, 751 S. Bascom Ave., San Jose, 95128. Phone: (408) 885-5000.

Stanford University Hospital, 300 Pasteur Dr., Stanford, 94305. Ph: (650) 723-4000.

Washington Hospital Healthcare System, 2000 Mowry Ave., Fremont, 94538-1716. Ph. (510) 797-1111.

Veterans Affairs Palo Alto Health Care System, 3801 Miranda Ave., Palo Alto, 94304. Phone: (650) 493-5000.

Santa Cruz County

Dominican Hospital, 610 Frederick St., Santa Cruz, 95065. Phone: (831) 462-7700.

Sandy Warren - Cypress Outpatient Surgical, 1665 Dominican Way #120, Santa Cruz, 95065. Phone: (831) 476-6943.

Santa Cruz Surgery Center, 3003 Paul Sweet Rd., Santa Cruz, 95065. Phone: (831) 462-5512.

Sutter Maternity & Surgery Ctr., 2900 Chanticleer Ave., Santa Cruz, 95065. Phone: (831) 477-2200.

San Benito County

Hazel Hawkins Medical Center 911 Sunset Dr., Hollister, 95023. Phone: (831) 637-5711.

Chapter 12

Rental Housing

AFTER SEVERAL YEARS of sharp increases, rents have fallen in Silicon Valley — but newcomers will still find them shockingly high.

The average rents and rent sampler in this chapter will give you the flavor of rents in Silicon Valley.

In north San Jose and Santa Clara, large new apartment complexes are opening, putting more competition into the market.

In Santa Cruz County, the situation is trickier. In the City of Santa Cruz, many apartments are taken by students at the university. Housing got so tight that the university purchased a Holiday Inn and an apartment complex. The university guarantees freshmen an apartment on campus and sophomores are tossed into a lottery for a campus unit. Juniors and seniors fend for themselves.

With the economic downturn, pressures have eased but probably not by much. Santa Cruz County wants to control growth; it's not building many new apartments.

For those new to the region and shopping for homes, a hotel might do the trick — short term. The major chains have built large and small hotels in the suburbs, many of them near freeway exits and a few smack in the middle of residential neighborhoods.

Residency (extended stay) hotels offer a different experience. They combine the conveniences of a hotel — maid service, continental breakfast, airport shuttle — with the pleasures of home: a fully-equipped kitchen and a laundry room (coin-operated). They may also have a pool, a spa, a sports court, a workout room. Some offer free grocery shopping and a social hour.

Residency hotels welcome families. Typically, guests remain at least five days and often much longer. At a certain stage, a discount will kick in.

In Silicon Valley, apartments come in all sizes and settings. If you're strapped for funds, you can find single bedrooms and studios for under $800 a month. No pool, no spa, no extras. What goes for $1,900 in Palo Alto may rent for $1,200 in San Jose. If the neighborhood is safe and nice, if the apartment complex is close to light rail, you probably will pay extra.

Average Rents

Santa Clara County

City	Average Rent
Campbell	$1,148
Cupertino	1,592
Gilroy	1,159
Los Gatos	1,362
Milpitas	1,350
Mountain View	1,318
Palo Alto	1,831
Santa Clara	1,363
San Jose	1,262
Sunnyvale	1,256

Santa Cruz County

Santa Cruz	$1,436

Source: REALFACTS, Novato, California. Average rents as of December 2004.

Renters pay for cable service, electricity or gas and phone (in some instances, deposits may be required to start service.)

The landlord will ask for a security deposit and for the first month's rent up front. State law limits deposits to a maximum two months rent for an unfurnished apartment and three months for a furnished (this includes the last month's rent.) If you agree to a lease, you might get an extra month free. If you move out before the lease is up, you pay a penalty.

Some apartments forbid pets, some will accept only cats, some cats and small dogs. Many will ask for a pet deposit (to cover possible damage.)

To protect themselves, landlords will ask you to fill out a credit report and to list references. If you want help or are striking out with the classified ads, you might try a rental agency. Some complexes supposedly are renting only through agencies.

The Fair Housing laws will apply: no discrimination based on race, sex, family status and so on. But some complexes will be designed to welcome one or several kinds of renters.

A complex that wants families, for example, might include a tot lot. One that prefers singles or childless couples might throw Friday night parties or feature a large pool and a workout room but no kiddie facilities.

Some large complexes will offer furnished and unfurnished apartments or corporate setups, a variation of the residency hotel.

If hotels or apartments are not your cup of tea, you might take a look at renting a home or townhouse. See classified ads or Real Estate Rentals in

Yellow Pages. Many owners turn the maintenance and renting over to a professional property manager.

In older towns, many of the cottages and smaller homes in the older sections will often be rentals. If you see a "For Sale" sign in front of a home that interests you, inquire whether the place is for rent.

San Jose and Hayward — where major universities are located — all possess a thriving market in shared rentals. For information, consult the campus housing office. Some universities run housing departments that try to line up homes and apartments for single students, married students and staff and faculty. The larger universities have dorms. Community colleges will sometimes support, just off campus, a small shared-rental neighborhood.

Many mature adults who never dreamed they would be sharing their home and apartments are in fact doing just that. Newspapers routinely carry ads from people looking to share a rental. Preferences are stated: no smokers, women only, no pets, etc. If you really want to save the bucks and possibly pick up a friend or two, a shared rental might be just the thing.

A word on furniture. If you don't want to buy it, you can rent it. Check the Yellow Pages under furniture rental. For cheap furniture, check out the garage sales. Usually they are advertised on weekends in the local newspapers.

Rent Sampler from Classified Ads
Santa Clara County

Almaden Valley (San Jose)
- Condo, 1BR/1BA, $1,075
- Home, 3BR/2.5BA, $1,875

Berryessa (San Jose)
- Home, 4BR/2BA, $1,795
- Home, 4BR/2.5BA, $2,050

Cambrian (San Jose)
- Apt., 2BR/2BA, $950
- Home, 4BR/4BA, $2,250

Campbell
- Apt., 1BR/1BA, $1,095
- Home, 3BR/2.5BA, $2,300

Cupertino
- Apt., 1BR/1BA, $1,295
- Home, 3BR/2.5BA, $2,800

Gilroy
- Apt., 2BR/1BA, $895
- Home, 4BR/3BA, $2,400

Los Altos
- Apt., 1BR/1BA, $1,450
- Townhouse, 2BR/2BA, $1,995

Los Gatos
- Apt., 2BR/1BA, $1,050
- Home, 3BR/2BA, $2,425

Milpitas
- Apt., 2BR/1BA, $1,000
- Home, 4BR/2.5BA, $2,100

Morgan Hill
- Apt., 3BR/1BA, $1,100
- Home, 3BR/2BA, $1,800

Mountain View
- Apt., 1BR/1BA, $1,279
- Home, 3BR/2.5BA, $1,975

North Valley (San Jose)
- Apt., 1BR/1BA, $969
- Home, 4BR/3BA, $2,500

Palo Alto
- Apt., 1BR/1BA, 00
- Home, 3BR/2BA,000

Rose Garden (San Jose)
- Apt., 1BR/1BA, $850
- Home, 2BR/1BA, $1,700

San Jose (South)
- Apt., 1BR/1BA, $1,042
- Home, 4BR/2.5BA, $2,300

San Jose (West)
- Apt., 2BR/2BA, $999
- Home, 2BR/1BA, $1,775

Santa Clara
- Apt., 1BR/1BA, $1,095
- Home, 3BR/2BA, $1,995

Saratoga
- Apt., 1BR/1BA, $1,100
- Home, 3BR/2BA, $2,500

Sunnyvale
- Apt., 1BR/1BA, $1,095
- Home, 3BR/2BA, $2,050

Rent Sampler from Classified Ads

Santa Cruz County

Aptos
- Apt., 2BR/1BA, $1,195
- Home, 3BR/2BA, $1,975

Bonny Doon
- Cabin, 1BR/1BA, $950
- Cottage, 1BR/1BA, $800

Boulder Creek
- Apt., 1BR/1BA, $800
- Home, 2BR/2BA, $1,350

Ben Lomond
- Apt., 3BR/1BA, $1,575
- Home, 2BR/2BA, $1,300

Capitola
- Apt., 1BR/1BA, $1,050
- Home, 2BR/2BA, $1,700

Felton
- Apt., 1BR/1BA, $895
- Home, 3BR/2BA, $1,925

La Selva Beach
- Apt., 2BR/1BA, $1,200
- Home, 4BR/2BA, $2,800

Live Oak
- Apt., 2BR/1BA, $1,050
- Home, 3BR/2.5BA, $2,000

Santa Cruz
- Apt., 2BR/1BA, $1,395
- Apt., 1BR/1BA, $1,195
- Home, 3BR/3BA, $3,200

Scotts Valley
- Apt., 2BR/1BA, $1,200
- Home, 4BR/2BA, $2,800

Soquel
- Apt., 2BR/1BA, $1,295
- Home, 3BR/2BA, $1,950

Watsonville
- Apt., 2BR/2BA, $1,050
- Home, 3BR/2BA, $1,650

When you're out scouting for a rental, check out the neighborhood, do a little research, and think about what you really value and enjoy.

If you want the convenient commute without the hassle of a car, pick a place near a light-rail line or bus stop.

If it's the active life, scout out the parks, trails and such things as bars and restaurants and community colleges. Say the first thing you want to do when you arrive home is take a long run. Before you rent, get a map of local trails. City recreation departments usually will be able to give you information.

For parents, your address usually will determine what public school your child will attend. If you want a high-scoring school, see the scores in this book before making a decision. Always call the school before making a rental decision. See the chapter on how public schools work.

The same advice applies to day care. Make sure that it is available nearby before signing a lease.

Many of the larger apartment complexes offer some kind of security: parking lot lights, gates, guards. Happy hunting!

Chapter 13

New Housing

SHOPPING FOR A new home? This chapter gives an overview of new housing. Smaller projects are generally ignored. The same with in-fill units, which pop up all around the county. If you know where you want to live, drive that town or ask the local planning department what's new in housing. Or check newspapers and housing magazines.

Prices change. Incidentals such as landscaping fees may not be included. In the 1980s, to pay for services, cities increased fees on home construction. Usually, these fees are included in the home prices but in what is known as Mello-Roos districts, the fees are often assessed like tax payments (in addition to house payments).

Nothing secret. By law, developers are required to disclose all fees and, in fact, California has some of the toughest disclosure laws in the country. But the prices listed below may not include some fees.

After rocketing in the 1980s, home prices, new and resale, stabilized and in many instances dropped but about five years ago started to rise again, sharply. In 2001, prices stabilized and at the upper end, dropped. But thanks to low interest rates, prices increased again in 2002, 2003, 2004 and 2005.

This information covers what's available at time of publication. For latest information, call the developers for brochures.

If you have never shopped for a new home, you probably will enjoy the experience. In the larger developments, the builders will decorate models showing the housing styles and sizes offered. You enter through one home, pick up the sales literature, then move to the other homes or condos. Every room is usually tastefully and imaginatively decorated — and enticing.

An agent or agents will be on hand to answer questions or discuss financing or other aspects of interest to you. Generally, all this is done low-key. On Saturdays and Sundays, thousands of people can be found visiting developments around the Bay Area and Northern California. Developers call attention to their models by flags. When you pass what appears to be a new development and flags are flying, it generally means that units are available for view and for sale.

ALAMEDA COUNTY

Livermore

Cresta Blanca, Signature Properties, 2394 Peregrine St., (925) 960-9220, single family homes, 3-6 bedrooms, from high $800,000.

Station Square, Signature Properties, 1832 Railroad Ave., (925) 245-0760, townhomes, 2-3 bedrooms, from low $500,000.

Private Reserve, Signature Properties, 5436 Stockton Loop, (925) 373-3440, single family homes, 4-5 bedrooms, from low $1 million.

Oakland

Harborwalk, Signature Properties, 3090 Glascock St., (510) 532-8843, townhomes, 1-3 bedrooms, from high $400,000.

The Estuary, Signature Properties, 2909 Glascock St., (510) 535-0120, townhomes, 2-3 bedrooms, from low $600,000.

SAN JOAQUIN COUNTY

Stockton

Fox Hollow, Morrison Homes, 2352 Etcheverry Dr., (209) 954-1305, single family homes, 3-4 bedrooms, from high $300,000.

Tracy

Redbridge, Standard Pacific, 2624 Redbridge Rd., (209) 833-7000, single family homes, 3-4 bedrooms, from mid $500,000.

CONTRA COSTA COUNTY

Brentwood

Cedarwood, Signature Properties, 502 Richdale Ct., (925) 513-1057, single family homes, 3-5 bedrooms, from low $600,000.

Garin Landing, Signature Properties, 570 Almanor St., (925) 240-1585, single family homes, 3-4 bedrooms, from mid $500,000.

San Pablo

Abella Villas, Signature Properties, 102 Carmel St., (510) 236-8215, condominiums, 2-3 bedrooms, from mid $400,000.

SOLANO COUNTY

Fairfield

Andalucia, Standard Pacific, 3001 Pebble Beach Cir., (707) 422-3199, single family homes, 2-4.5 bedrooms, from $700,000.

Vacaville

Lantana at Alamo Place, Standard Pacific, call for address, (707) 450-0178, single family homes, 4-6 bedrooms, from lower $600,000.

She's Not Just Coming For A Little Stay

Life is really full of surprises. But we don't think home buying should be. So we do all we can to ease you through every step of buying your new home. From selecting your floor plan through closing escrow. Even after move in. Which shouldn't be surprising, considering we've spent over 39 years doing our best to make home buying as easy as possible.

STANDARD PACIFIC HOMES
Making You Right At Home™

1-877-STNDPAC (786-3722)
www.standardpacifichomes.com

  HomeAid America. *Home Loans Provided by* FAMILY LENDING   Prices, terms, and specifications subject to change without notice. Models do not reflect racial preferences.

MARIN COUNTY

San Rafael

The Forest at Redwood Village, Signature Properties, 36 Apricot Ct., (415) 479-8808, townhomes, 2-3 bedrooms, from high $500,000.

PLACER COUNTY

Lincoln

Traditions, Morrison Homes, 1603 Allenwood Cir., (916) 434-6927, single family homes, 4-5 bedrooms, from high $400,000.

Woodbury Glen, Standard Pacific, call for location, (916) 826-7129, single family homes, 3-5 bedrooms, from $400,000.

Rocklin

Claremont, Signature Properties, 2103 Wyckford Blvd., (916) 434-7787, single family homes, 4-5 bedrooms, from mid $600,000.

Roseville

Willow Creek, Standard Pacific, call for location, 1 (877) STNDPAC, single family homes, 4-6 bedrooms, from mid $400,000.

STANISLAUS COUNTY

Patterson

Bella Flora at Patterson Gardens, Morrison Homes, 1256 Fawn Lily Dr., (209) 895-4034, single family homes, 4-5 bedrooms, from mid $400,000.

Turlock

Ventana, Morrison Homes, 4077 Enclave Dr., (209) 632-0025, single family homes, 3-4 bedrooms, from high $300,000.

MERCED COUNTY

Merced

University Park, Morrison Homes, 1339 Irvine Ct., (209) 388-0611, single family homes, 3-4 bedrooms, from mid $300,000.

SACRAMENTO COUNTY

Rancho Cordova

Anatolia, Morrison Homes, 4008 Kalamata Way, (916) 869-5779, single family homes, 3-4 bedrooms, from high $300,000.

Sacramento

Silver Hollow, Morrison Homes, 8151 Stallion Way, (916) 525-3945, single family homes, 4-5 bedrooms, from high $800,000.

Chapter 14

Newcomer's Guide

Voter Registration

You must be 18 years and a citizen. Go to post office and ask for a voter registration postcard. Fill it out and pop it into the mail box. Or pick up the form when you register your vehicle or secure a driver's license. Before every election, the county will mail you a sample ballot with the address of your polling place.

Change of Address — Mail

The change-of-address form can also be picked up at the post office. To assure continuity of service, fill out this form 30 days before you move.

Dog Licensing-Spaying

If you live in a city, call city hall for information about dog licensing and pet vaccinations and spaying-neutering. City hall numbers are listed at the beginning of your phone book. If you live in the Santa Clara County jurisdiction, phone (800) 215-2555. For licensing, bring proof of rabies vaccination. Some jurisdictions will discount the license fee if Rover or Fifi has been fixed.

Driving

California has the most stringent smog requirements in the country. If your car is a few years old, you may have to spend a couple of hundred dollars to bring it up to code. You have 20 days from the time you enter the state to register your vehicles. After that you pay a penalty, and face a ticket-fine.

For registration, go to any office of the Department of Motor Vehicles. Bring your smog certificate, your registration card and your license plates.

If you are a California resident, all you need to do is complete a change-of-address form, which can be obtained by calling (800) 777-0133 or visiting one of the following Dept. of Motor Vehicles offices:

Santa Clara County

• Campbell: 430 Darryl Dr.

• Los Gatos: 600 N. Santa Cruz Ave.

• Mountain View: 595 Showers Dr.

• San Jose: 111 W. Alma Ave.

• San Jose (south): 180 Martinvale Ln.

• Santa Clara: 3665 Flora Vista Ave.

• Gilroy: 8200 Church St.

Santa Cruz County
• Capitola: 4200 Capitola Rd.

• Watsonville: 90 Alta Vista Ave.

San Benito County
• Hollister: 80 N. Sally St.

Driver's License

To obtain a driver's license, you must be 16 years old, pass a state-certified Driver's Education (classroom) and Driver's Training (behind-the-wheel) course, and at Department of Motor Vehicles a vision test and written and driving tests.

Once you pass the test, your license is usually renewed by mail. Retesting is rare, unless your driving record is poor. High schools used to offer free driving courses but these have all but disappeared due to state budget cuts. Private driving schools have moved in to fill the gap, at a cost of $100 to $200.

Teenagers older than 15 1/2 years who have completed driver's training can be issued a permit. Law restricts driving hours for young teens to daylight hours and, unless supervised, forbids them for six months to drive other teens. Law also requires more parental training and extends time of provisional license. Purpose is to reduce accidents.

If no driver's education program has been completed, you must be at least 18 years old to apply for a driver's license. Out-of-state applicants must supply proof of "legal presence," which could be a certified copy of a birth certificate. Foreign applicants must supply other documents. If going for a driver's license, ask to have the booklet mailed to you or pick it up. Study it. All the questions will be taken from the booklet but be warned: the state has introduced a new written exam. Even though it's easy to prepare for - read the booklet — many people are flunking it. So many that the state has revised the test.

Turning Rules. If signs don't say no, you can turn right on a red light (after making a full stop) and make a U-turn at an intersection.

Stop for pedestrians. Stop for discharging school buses, even if on opposite side of road. Must have insurance to drive and to register vehicle.

Earthquakes

They're fun and great topics of conversation, until you get caught in a big one. Then they are not so funny. At the beginning of your phone book is some advice about what to do before, during and after a temblor. It's worth reading.

Garbage Service

The garbage fellows come once a week. Rates vary by city and lately a lot of competition has been coming into this business. Figure $20 a month for one-cart-a-week service. Besides the cart, almost every home will receive recycling bins for plastics, glass and cans, and a cart for lawn trimmings.

Pickup weekly, usually the same day as garbage. Garbage companies have switched to wheeled carts that can be picked up by mechanical arms attached to truck.

Don't burn your garbage in the fireplace or outside. Don't burn leaves. Against the law. To get rid of car batteries, motor oils and water-soluble paints, call your local garbage firm and ask about disposal sites. Or call city hall.

Property Taxes

The average property tax rate in California is 1.25 percent. If you buy a $600,000 home this year, your property tax will be $7,500. Once the basic tax is established, it goes up about 2 percent annually in following years.

"Average" needs to be emphasized. Some jurisdictions have tacked costs on to the property tax; some have not. Some school districts, in recent years, have won approval of annual parcel taxes.

Property taxes are paid in two installments, due by April 10 and December 10. They are generally collected automatically through impound accounts set up when you purchase a home, but check your sale documents carefully. Sometimes homeowners are billed directly. Some cities, to fund parks and lights and other amenities in new subdivisions, have installed what is called the Mello-Roos tax. Realtors are required to give you complete information on all taxes.

Sales Tax

Varies by county. In Santa Clara County, it is 8.25 percent. In Santa Cruz, 8 percent with the exception of Capitola and Scotts Valley, 8.25 percent. If an item costs $100, you will pay $108.25 in Santa Clara and for most of Santa Cruz County, $108. Food, except when sold in restaurants, is exempted.

State Income Taxes

See chart page 224

Disclosure Laws

California requires homes sellers to give detailed reports on their offerings, including information on flood, fire and earthquake zones. For information on registered sex offenders by town, go to meganslaw.ca.gov

Cigarette-Tobacco Tax

California has laid some extra taxes on cigarettes to discourage smoking and raise money for social causes. Many smokers load up on cigarettes in Nevada or buy over the internet.

Grocery Prices

Item	Store one	Store two	Average
Apple Juice, 1 gal. store brand	$4.79	$3.96	$4.38
Almonds, whole, 2.25 oz.	2.49	2.17	2.33
American Cheese, Kraft, 1 lb.	5.19	5.19	5.19
Apple Pie, Sara Lee	6.49	5.99	6.24
Apples, Red Delicious, 1 lb.	1.99	1.00	1.50
Aspirin, cheapest, 250 count	4.49	4.99	4.74
Baby Shampoo, Johnson's, 15 fluid oz.	4.39	4.19	4.29
Bacon, Farmer John Sliced, 1 lb.	4.99	5.79	5.39
Bagels, store brand, half doz.	2.99	3.08	3.04
Bananas, 1 lb.	.79	.79	.79
Beef, round tip boneless roast, 1 lb.	4.59	4.49	4.54
Beef, ground round, 1 lb.	4.49	2.49	3.49
Beer, O'Douls 6-pack bottles	5.99	5.99	5.99
Beer, Coors, 12-pack, cans	10.99	10.69	10.84
Bisquick batter, 2 lbs. 8 oz.	2.99	2.99	2.99
Bleach, Clorox, 96 oz.	2.69	2.59	2.64
Bok Choy, 1lb.	.99	.99	.99
Bread, sourdough, Colombo, 1.5 lb.	3.89	3.87	3.88
Bread, wheat, cheapest 1.5 lb.	.99	.99	.99
Broccoli, 1 lb.	1.99	1.00	1.50
Butter, Challenge, 1 lb.	5.49	5.49	5.49
Cabbage, 1 lb.	.99	.69	.84
Cantaloupe, 1 lb.	.99	1.29	1.14
Carrots, fresh, 1 lb.	.59	.69	.64
Cat Food, store brand, small can	.49	.55	.52
Cereal, Grapenuts, 18 oz.	4.89	4.99	4.94
Cereal, Wheaties, 18 oz.	4.99	4.89	4.94
Charcoal, Kingsford, 10 lbs.	4.99	4.99	4.99
Cheese, Cream, Philadelphia, 8 oz.	2.89	2.59	2.74
Cheese, Mild Cheddar, 1 lb.	4.99	3.69	4.34
Chicken breasts, Foster Farms bone/skinless, 1 lb.	5.99	5.99	5.99
Chicken, Foster Farms, whole, 1 lb.	1.59	1.29	1.44
Chili, Stagg, with beans, 15 oz. box	2.29	2.29	2.29
Cigarettes, Marlboro Lights, carton	48.99	48.99	48.99
Coca Cola, 12-pack, 12 oz. cans	4.99	5.29	5.14
Coffee, Folgers Instant Coffee, 6 oz.	5.99	5.99	5.99
Cafe latte, Starbucks, 1 cup	2.30	2.30	2.30
Coffee, Starbucks, 1 cup	1.35	1.35	1.35
Cookies, Oreo, 18 oz. pkg.	3.99	3.99	3.99
Diapers, Huggies, size 2, (42-pack)	16.99	9.99	13.49
Dishwashing Liquid, Dawn, 25 oz.	3.99	3.69	3.84
Dog Food, Pedigree, 22-oz. can	1.39	1.54	1.47
Eggs, large, Grade AA, 1 doz.	3.19	2.69	2.64
Flour, Gold Medal, 5 lbs.	2.39	2.39	2.39
Flowers, mixed	4.99	4.99	4.99
Frozen Dinners, Marie Callendar's	4.59	4.59	4.59
Frozen Yogurt, Dreyer's, half gallon	5.99	5.99	5.99
Gatorade, 64 oz.	3.29	2.99	3.14
Gerber's baby food, fruit or veg., 4 oz.	.57	.50	.54
Gerber's baby food, meat, 2.5 oz.	.79	.79	.79
Gerber's baby food, cereal, 8 oz.	1.69	2.08	1.89
Gin, Gilbeys, 1.75 Ltrs.	18.99	18.99	18.99
Ginger Root, 1 lb.	2.99	1.99	2.49
Granola Bars, 10-bar box	3.99	3.79	3.89
Grapes, Red Seedless, 1 lb.	2.99	2.99	2.99

Grocery Prices

Item	Store one	Store two	Average
Ham, Dubuque, 5 lb., canned	$14.39	$13.99	$14.19
Ice Cream, Dreyers, half gal.	5.99	5.99	5.99
Ice Cream, Haagen Daaz, 1 pint	3.99	3.99	3.99
Jam, Mary Ellen, strawberry, 18 oz.	4.99	3.86	4.43
Ketchup, Del Monte, 36 oz.	2.99	3.11	3.05
Kleenex, 144-count box	2.59	2.53	2.56
Laundry Detergent, Tide, 87 oz.	9.29	8.99	9.14
Lettuce, Romaine, head	1.29	1.49	1.39
Macaroni & Cheese, Kraft, 14.5 oz	2.25	2.29	2.27
Margarine, tub, Brummel & Brown	2.39	2.39	2.39
Mayonnaise, Best Foods, 1 qt.	3.99	3.49	3.74
Milk, 1% fat, half gal.	1.29	1.29	1.29
Milk, soy, half gal.	2.99	2.39	2.69
M&M Candies, plain, 2 oz.	.65	.65	.65
Mushrooms, 8 oz. package	2.29	2.29	2.29
Olive Oil, cheapest, 17 oz.	6.39	5.99	6.19
Onions, yellow, 1 lb.	.99	1.69	1.34
Oranges, Navel, 1 lb.	.69	.99	.84
Orange Juice, Tropicana, 64-oz., Original Style	4.59	4.79	4.69
Paper Towels, single pack	.99	1.18	1.09
Peanuts, cocktail, Planter's, 12 oz.	4.19	4.19	4.19
Peas, frozen, 16 oz.	2.39	3.00	2.70
Peanut Butter, Jiff, 18 oz.	3.19	3.29	3.24
Pizza, Frozen, Di Giorno, 1 lb. 13 oz.	7.59	6.29	6.94
Popcorn, Orville Reddenbacher, 3-pack	3.49	3.55	3.52
Pork chops, center cut, 1 lb.	4.99	3.99	4.49
Potato Chips, Lays, 12 oz.	2.99	2.99	2.99
Potatoes, Russet, 10 lbs.	2.99	2.99	2.99
Raisins, 2 lbs.	4.99	3.99	3.49
Reese's Mini-Peanut Butter Cups, 13 oz.	3.99	3.29	3.39
Rice, cheapest, 5 lbs.	3.69	3.39	3.54
Salmon, fresh, 1 lb.	4.49	5.99	5.24
Seven-Up, 6-pack, cans	2.99	2.99	2.99
Soap, bar, Zest, 3-pack	2.89	2.89	2.89
Soup, Campbell, chicken noodle, 10-oz. can	.99	1.85	1.42
Soup, Top Ramen	.25	.37	.31
Soy Sauce, Kikkoman, 10 oz.	2.29	2.19	2.24
Spaghetti, Golden Grain, 2 lbs.	2.79	2.79	2.79
Spaghetti Sauce, Prego, 12 oz.	1.99	1.99	1.99
Sugar, cheapest, 5 lbs.	1.99	1.99	1.99
Tea, Lipton's, 48-bag box	2.99	4.21	4.10
Toilet Tissue, 4-roll pack, cheapest	1.79	3.29	2.54
Tomatoes, on the vine, 1 lb.	3.69	3.49	3.59
Toothpaste, Colgate 6.4 oz.	2.99	2.99	2.99
Tortillas, flour, cheapest, 10-count pack	2.59	1.99	2.29
Tuna, Starkist, Chunk Light, 6 oz.	1.99	.99	1.49
Vegetable Oil, store brand, 64 oz.	3.79	4.41	4.10
Vegetables, mixed, frozen, 1 lb.	2.39	2.50	2.45
Vinegar, 1 gallon	3.39	3.83	3.61
Water, 1 gallon	1.49	1.29	1.39
Whiskey, Seagrams 7 Crown, 750ml.	13.49	13.49	13.49
Wine, Cabernet, Glen Ellen	9.99	9.99	9.99
Yogurt, Frozen, Dreyers, half gal.	5.99	5.99	5.99
Yogurt, Yoplait Original, single	.99	.85	.92

CALIFORNIA TAX RATES 2005

Single Married Filing Separate Returns

Taxable Income		Basic Tax	Plus
Over	But Not Over		
$0	$6,147	$0.00 +	1% over $0.00
$6,147	$14,571	$61 +	2% over $6,147
$14,571	$22,997	$230 +	4% over $14,571
$22,997	$31,925	$567 +	6% over $22,997
$31,925	$40,346	$1,103 +	8% over $31,925
$40,346	And Over	$1,776 +	9.3% over $40,346

Married Filing Jointly & Qualified Widow(er)s

Taxable Income		Basic Tax	Plus
Over	But Not Over		
$0	$12,294	$0.00 +	1% over $0.00
$12,294	$29,142	$123 +	2% over $12,294
$29,142	$45,994	$460 +	4% over $29,142
$45,994	$63,850	$1,134 +	6% over $45,994
$63,850	$80,692	$2,205 +	8% over $63,850
$80,692	And Over	$3,553 +	9.3% over $80,692

Heads of Households

Taxable Income		Basic Tax	Plus
Over	But Not Over		
$0	$12,300	$0.00 +	1% over $0.00
$12,300	$29,143	$123 +	2% over $12,300
$29,143	$37,567	$460 +	4% over $29,143
$37,567	$46,494	$797+	6% over $37,567
$46,494	$54,918	$1,332 +	8% over $46,494
$54,918	And Over	$2,006 +	9.3% over $54,918

Example

John and Jackie Anderson have a taxable income of $125,000.

Taxable Income	Basic Tax	Plus
$125,000	$3,553 +	9.3% over $80,692

They subtract the amount at the beginning of their range from their taxable income.

```
    $125,000
    -80.692
    $44,308
```

They multiply the result by the percentage for their range.

```
    $ 44,308
    x .093
    $ 4,121
```

Total Tax

Basic	$3,553
% +	+4,121
Total	$7,674

Note: Amounts rounded off. This chart is not a substitute for government forms. If you have questions, consult tax authorities or your tax advisor.

'06

Gas and Electricity

Most homes are heated with natural gas. No one, or almost no one, uses heating oil. Up until recently, Pacific Gas and Electric (PG&E) reported that gas bills, year round, averaged about $30 a month, and electric bills $60 a month. The bill for an average three-bedroom home ran $130 to $140 a month.

Rates have been increased but structured to reward conservation. Low consumption will see zero increases, medium 7 percent, medium plus 18 percent, heavy 37 percent. Read your utility bill to see how the system works.

Almost never between May and September, and rarely between April and October, will you need to heat your home. Air conditioners are used in the summer but on many days they are not needed.

Cable-DSL TV Service

Almost all South Bay homes are served by cable, and DSL services are available throughout much of the county. Cable rates vary according to channels accessed. For clear FM radio reception, often a cable connection is required. Many people subscribe to cable packages with over 100 channels.

Bottled Water

If the direct source for your town's water is the Sierra, then you may not need bottled water. If the source is wells, many people take the bottled.

Tipping

It's not done in the Bay Area as much as it is done in other parts of the country. Tip the newspaper delivery person, cab or limo drivers, waiters and waitresses and, at the holidays, people who perform regular personal services: yard maintenance, child care, housekeeping.

Don't tip the supermarket employee who carries bags to your car. Don't tip telephone or cable TV installers. Your garbage collector will usually be a Teamster. No beer. No money. Maybe a little cake or box of candy at Christmas. If a garbage collector gets nailed for drunk driving, it will probably cost him his job. Some people give the mail carrier a little holiday gift; many don't. Let your conscience guide: Coffee shops. Many are sprouting "tip" cups.

Smoking

In 1998 a state law took effect forbidding smoking in saloons, one of the last bastions of smoking. Bars in restaurants comply. Neighborhood saloons used to enforce sporadically but more are complying. Some people light up and hide the cigarette under the table. If visiting socially, you are expected to light up outside.

Love and Society

San Francisco often flaunts its sexuality, hetero and homo, bi and trans. Except in rare instances, the suburbs don't but the cosmopolitan virtues apply. In the Bay Area, consenting adults, in sexual matters, are generally free to do what they want as long as it doesn't harm others.

In professional society in Santa Clara and Santa Cruz counties and the Bay Area, same-sex couples attend office parties and social events, and no subterfuge is put up to disguise the relationship but what is accepted in San Francisco will often cock eyebrows in the suburbs. If you slobber over your loved one, no matter what the sexual orientation, you won't be stoned but you might be shunned.

If you want the society of men or the society of women or both, numerous groups exist to help to make connections.

Ages

You must be 18 to vote and smoke and 21 to drink alcohol. Watch the booze. California has a drunken-driving law so stringent that even a drink or two can put you in violation. Clerks are supposed to ask you for ID if you look under 27 for smokes and under 30 for booze.

Mountain Lions and Coyotes

They are out there, in the forests of the county, especially in the western hills. The pumas prefer deer but will eat pets and farm animals. The coyotes, not in the least sentimental, love to dine on puppies, doggies and pussy cats. Take care!

Chapter 15

Commuting

FREEWAYS AND PARKWAYS, light rail, trains and buses — in ways of getting around, Santa Clara County does very well. Nonetheless, commuting is often an irritating, time-consuming business.

The reasons why can be summed up with a few numbers.

Irritating Statistics

Annual surveys done by RIDES, a local transit group, show that solo drivers make up 77 or 78 percent of all Santa Clara County commuters, the highest percentage in the state, surpassing Orange and Los Angeles counties.

The 2000 census counted 1,682,585 residents in the county. Of these, 351,576 were under age 14 and 17,987 were over age 85. Another 10,975 were institutionalized. Subtracting these numbers from the total population and taking out another 20,000 for teens 14 to 15. 5 years old, you come up with, rounded off, 400,000 people who, for whatever reason, can't drive and 1,282,585 who can, if they choose to, secure a driver's license.

In 2000, the California Dept. of Motor Vehicles reported that licensed drivers in Santa Clara County numbered 1,181,103 — which means that except for about 100,000 residents, just about everyone eligible for a driver's license has secured one.

In 2000, the Dept. of Motor Vehicles registered within the county 1,132,059 autos, 218,570 trucks, and 28,000 motorcycles — a total 1,378,629 vehicles. Many of the trucks will be owned by businesses but even allowing for this, the numbers suggest that just about every licensed driver has something to drive.

With these numbers and this attitude — drive alone — it's no wonder commuting is often an exasperating chore. Three other factors worsen matters:

Santa Clara County, having so many jobs, attracts thousands of commuters from other counties.

Many work places provide free parking, which encourages travel by motor vehicle. In the Bay Area, 78 percent of residents have free parking at work, reported RIDES. For Santa Clara County, the number is 88 percent.

Jobs north, homes south. This used to be cited as one of main reasons for the lousy commute. The homes were on the south side of the county, the jobs on the north side, which created jams in the central area and at interchanges. This is still a problem but not as big a factor as in the past.

Santa Cruz Commute

Santa Cruz subscribes to the Star Trek school of commuting. Its residents have classified the motor vehicle as an interim and destructive phase in the evolution of travel and await the day when people can say, OK Scotty, beam me down to the Boardwalk or Aptos or wherever.

Three main roads connect the county to Silicon Valley and the Bay Area: Highway 17, Highway 1, and last and least, Highway 9. The first has at least four lanes; the second, two and four lanes; the third, two lanes only.

Improvements have been made to Highway 17 and Highway 1 — turning lanes, turnouts, safer asphalt and access points, more cops and patrols. All this made a big difference in accidents and moving traffic.

But residents refuse to do the one thing that would make these highways more effective: add lanes.

The county has buses. Minor improvements to the roads will continue to be made. One of these years, Highway 101 will get car-pool lanes. Beyond that ... very little. Residents are willing to endure the inconvenience because they believe it protects the environment of the region. In late 2004, Santa Cruz voters again shot down a measure to impose an half-cent sales tax for transit.

Silicon Valley Improvements

About 20 years ago, Santa Clarans concluded that they had to build more freeways, widen those they had and overhaul the interchanges. A lot of this work has been done. And people figured out that they had do something besides building more streets and freeways.

Since then, the central cities, notably San Jose, have constructed a light-rail system that serves the towns with the most jobs. Almost every few years, the line is extended to another city. The line arrived at East San Jose in 2004 and at Campbell in 2005. Fingers crossed, transit officials are predicting that these two extensions might boost the number of riders on the light-rail line by 65 percent.

More trains and more funding have improved service on Caltrain, the commute rail that runs from Gilroy to San Francisco.

In 2004, Caltrain started "Baby Bullet" service on this line. It cuts travel time between San Jose and San Francisco from 90 minutes to just under an hour, mainly by eliminating some station stops.

Voters are taxing themselves to bring BART (high-speed, commute rail) from Fremont to the east side of county and San Jose Airport but this is a very expensive undertaking that has been delayed and delayed.

City halls and businesses leaders have woken up to what is called "smart growth," building condos and apartments near transit-business centers. Many apartments were recently build in North San Jose and the City of Santa Clara near light-rail stations.

In the late 1990s, a rail service called the Altamont Commuter Express was started. It runs trains from Stockton/Manteca/Tracy to San Jose, with stops along the way, including two in the City of Santa Clara.

Amtrak has a service–Capitols or the Capitol Corridor — with commute trains from Sacramento to Silicon Valley. Stops in many East Bay towns.

More buses have been added to the roads. Almost all freeways have marked off diamond lanes for buses and high-occupancy vehicles.

In 2000, Santa Clara County put its money where its mouth was. Voters said OK to extending a half-cent sales tax, which will raise an extra $7 billion.

The Comforting Secret

If you have a local job, it may take you a half-hour to land in the old easy chair but compared to the wretches who are driving to Tracy and Manteca and Merced, you're in hog heaven. Many people in the county have a local job.

If you are going nuts with driving, you might think about other ways of commuting. Alternatives out are there: bus, light rail, train, car-pooling.

Timesaving Strategies

- Buy a good map book and keep it in the car. The editors favor Thomas Guides, which are updated annually. Sooner than later you will find yourself jammed on the freeway and in desperate need of alternate routes. They're out there. As for the fold-out maps that are sold at service stations, many are several years old and don't show the new subdivisions.

- Avoid trouble–listen to traffic reports on the radio for news of jams. road. For freeway info, dial 511. Or go Highway Patrol web site.

- Buy bridge ticket books and, for buses and light rail, flash passes (good for a month) or ticket books. All will save you time and money.

- Join a car pool. RIDES, 511, will help you find a car pool in your town — no charge. Passengers meet and get dropped off at one or two spots. Pools go all over. About 15 percent of commuters car pool. To set up your own pool, RIDES will help with passengers and van arrangements. Passengers split the cost, which is based on the type of van, mileage and operating expenses. The driver gets a free commute and use of the van.

- Avoid peak hours. If you can leave for work — it gets earlier every year — about 6:30 a.m. and hit the freeway home before 4 p.m., your kids might not greet you, "Hey, stranger."

- Take public transportation. Yes, the car is flexible, so handy, so private. But if other, easier, cheaper ways of commuting are at hand, why ignore them?
- Break out the bicycle. Miles of bike trails run through Silicon Valley.

Buses

Santa Clara Valley Transportation Authority runs all over county: Gilroy, Milpitas, Palo Alto, San Jose, Los Gatos. During morning commute, express buses travel from Gilroy and Santa Cruz to destinations in Silicon Valley. Wheelchair access. Stops at Park & Ride lots, Caltrain stations, shopping malls, hospitals, San Jose State, other colleges, city halls, parks, airports, Fremont BART station. Connections in Alameda and San Mateo counties.

Historic trolleys circle the downtown transit mall, a 1.5-mile route. 9 a.m. to 5 p.m. Weekends and holidays. The transportation authority puts out a handy map. To obtain one and for more information, phone 511.

For information on Santa Cruz buses, call (831) 425-8600. Express buses shuttle between downtown San Jose and Scotts Valley-Santa Cruz.

SamTrans

Bus system for San Mateo County. Many high-tech firms have set up in San Mateo County, the location of San Francisco International Airport. For bus information, 511.

• Highway 237 from Milpitas to Santa Clara. Long a nightmare, it is getting major improvements.

• Bay Area bridges have opened Fastrak portals on their toll plazas. Scanners read sticker on vehicle and debit your account. Sign-up flyers at toll booths.

Light Rail

From South San Jose (and other neighborhoods) to downtown San Jose to Great America and the city of Santa Clara. A sleek ride. The system recently was extended to Mountain View, Milpitas and East San Jose (Alum Rock Road).

Bus connections at each station. The line also provides service to the San Jose neighborhoods of Blossom Valley (Santa Teresa Boulevard and San Ignacio Avenue) and to Almaden (Winfield and Coleman).

Run by Santa Clara Valley Transportation Authority. All tickets sold from machines, none on board. Day passes can be used for bus and light rail. For information, 511. Ask for light-rail brochure.

Caltrain

This system runs from Santa Clara County through San Mateo County and up the peninsula to San Francisco. The new "Baby Bullet" trains zips from San Jose to downtown S.F. in just under an hour, stops in Mountain View, Palo Alto, Hillsdale, Millbrae (San Francisco International Airport).

Caltrain also offers localized service between Gilroy and SF. In addition to above stations, these trains stop at Morgan Hill, Santa Clara, Sunnyvale, Menlo Park, Redwood City, San Carlos, Belmont, San Mateo, Burlingame, San Bruno, South San Francisco.

Transfers are available for buses from SamTrans, Santa Clara County Transportation Agency and Muni. Riders can also transfer to BART in Millbrae, providing access to other locales in San Francisco and East Bay. Caltrain tickets must be purchased before boarding. For schedules and more information, call (800) 660-4287

Bullet Train Schedule	A.M.	P.M.
Gilroy	6:07	7:07
Morgan Hill	7:22	6:48
San Jose (transfer)	6:57	6:11
Mountain View	7:23	5:56
Palo Alto	7:36	5:49
Hillsdale (San Mateo)	7:51	5:38
Millbrae	7:59	5:30
4th & King (S.F.)	8:19	5:14

Amtrak

Amtrak is used more for excursions, especially during ski season, than commuting but for some people it can work as a commute train. Stations in San Jose and Santa Clara. Check the schedule. (800) 872-7245.

BART

This system doesn't go into Santa Clara County yet but buses connect end of the line (Fremont) with Milpitas. Bullet Train passengers can also catch BART from the Millbrae Caltrans station. BART schedules and info, 817-1717.

Altamont Commuter Express (ACE)

This commute train starts in Stockton and stops in Manteca, Tracy, Livermore, Pleasanton, Fremont, Santa Clara, San Jose. Phone 800-411-7245.

Chapter 16

Job Training & Colleges

IF YOU ARE LOOKING for a job but need training or additional education, local colleges, public adult schools and private institutions have put together a variety of programs, ranging from word processing to MBA degrees.

Many institutions have devised programs for working adults or parents who must attend the duties of school and child rearing.

In many instances jobs and careers are mixed in with personal enrichment. At some colleges, you can take word processing, economics and music.

This chapter lists the major local educational and training institutes. All will send you literature (some may charge a small fee), all welcome inquiries.

Adult Schools

Although rarely in the headlines, adult schools serve thousands of Santa Clara County residents. Upholstery, microwave cooking, ballroom dancing, computers, cardiopulmonary resuscitation, aerobics, investing in stocks, art, music, digital photography, Quicken, how to raise children — all these and more are offered in the adult schools. These schools and programs are run by school districts and by cities. Many schools also run adult sports programs, basketball, volleyball, tennis. Call your local school or city for a catalog.

Older Students

As the public's needs have changed, so have the colleges. The traditional college audience — high school seniors — is still thriving but increasingly colleges are attracting older students and working people.

Many colleges now offer evening and weekend programs, especially in business degrees and business-related subjects. Some programs —like the MBA — can take years, some classes only a day. The Bay Area is loaded with educational opportunities. Here is a partial list of local colleges. As with any venture, the student should investigate before enrolling or paying a fee.

Universities and Colleges

- San Jose State University. The largest university in Santa Clara County and one of the largest in the Bay Region. Located in downtown San Jose. Bachelor's and master's degrees. Schools of Business, Education,

Engineering, Applied Arts and Sciences, Science, Humanities and the Arts, Social Work, Social Science. State universities also run extension schools — one-shot classes or short programs generally aimed at building business skills but many cultural offerings are mixed in. For admissions information, call (408) 283-7500. For extension classes, call (408) 924-2630 or (408) 985-7578.

- Santa Clara University. Located in city of Santa Clara. Enrollment about 7,500, half undergrads. Run by Jesuits. Founded in 1851. One of the oldest colleges in the state. Site of Mission Santa Clara de Asisi, which has been rebuilt. Pretty campus. Good scholastic reputation. Traditional university, bachelor to doctorate degrees. Undergraduate programs include engineering, business and arts and sciences. Other graduate programs popular with the over-25 age group: Engineering, Counseling, Psychology, Education, Law, Catechetics-Liturgy-Spirituality. Phone (408) 554-4000 for information.

- Stanford. Located in Palo Alto. One of the great universities of the planet. About 13,500 students are enrolled in seven schools: Earth Sciences, Education, Engineering, Graduate School of Business, Humanities and Sciences, Law, Medicine. Has bachelors, masters and Ph D programs. Continuing studies, (650) 725-2650.

- University of California Extension. UC Extension in Santa Clara County is run by the University of California at Santa Cruz. Professional development classes are taken by about 30,000 adults each year at the Extension's facility at 3120 De La Cruz Blvd. in the city of Santa Clara (Trimble Road at Hwy. 101). Computer science, engineering, business and management, environmental sciences, arts and humanities, English

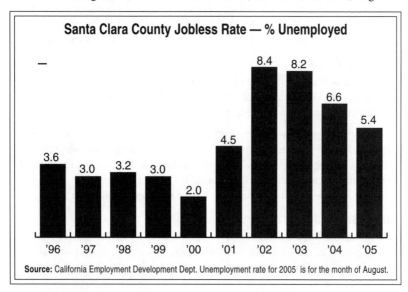

Santa Clara County Jobless Rate — % Unemployed

'96	'97	'98	'99	'00	'01	'02	'03	'04	'05
3.6	3.0	3.2	3.0	2.0	4.5	8.4	8.2	6.6	5.4

Source: California Employment Development Dept. Unemployment rate for 2005 is for the month of August.

language, teacher education and behavioral sciences. Seminars. Certificates in professional programs. Phone (831) 427-6600.

• University of San Francisco. Offers bachelor's and master's programs at its South Bay Center in Cupertino at 7337 Bollinger Rd. For information call (408) 255-1701.

• Golden Gate University. Based in Los Altos. Phone (408) 573-7300 For working adults. Bachelor's degrees in Human Relations, Management, Telecommunications. Master's in Banking and Finance, Management, Human Resources Management, Information Systems, International Management, Marketing, Taxation, Telecommunications.

• National Hispanic University, 14271 Story Rd., San Jose. (408) 254-6900. AA and Bachelor's degrees in arts. Master's in education and bus admin. English as second language. Learning Center opened in 2004.

• University of California, Santa Cruz. 1156 High St., Santa Cruz 95064. Phone (831) 459-0111.

Community Colleges

Four community college districts with campuses located throughout Santa Clara County: San Jose-Evergreen, Foothill-De Anza, Gavilan Joint and West Valley-Mission community college districts. Academic and vocational subjects, day and evening classes.

Santa Clara County

• San Jose City College, 2100 Moorpark Ave., San Jose, 95125. Phone (408) 298-2181.

• Evergreen Valley College, 3095 Yerba Buena Rd., San Jose, 95135. Phone (408) 274-7900.

• De Anza College, 21250 Stevens Creek Blvd., Cupertino, 95014. Phone (408) 864-5678.

• Foothill College, 12345 El Monte Rd., Los Altos Hills, 94022. Phone (650) 949-7777.

• Gavilan College, 5055 Santa Teresa Blvd., Gilroy, 95020. Phone (408) 847-1400

• West Valley College, 14000 Fruitvale Ave., Saratoga, 95070. Phone (408) 867-2200.

• Mission College, 3000 Mission College Blvd., Santa Clara, 95054. Phone (408) 988-2200.

Santa Cruz County

• Cabrillo College, 6500 Soquel Dr., Aptos, 95003. Phone (831) 479-6100.

Chapter 17

Fun & Games

SANTA CLARA COUNTY is bulging with places to visit and things to do but, with some exceptions, it is not oriented toward tourists.

No battle monuments summon visitors simply because there were no battles. Only the Indians suffered catastrophe and they went quietly and quickly, mostly through disease, leaving little behind. The Spanish built missions at Santa Clara, later destroyed and rebuilt, and Mission San Jose, now part of Fremont. Both well worth a visit but little else of great interest remains from the ranchero era.

For most of its "American" history, Santa Clara County has been run by farmers and shopkeepers — people who for the most part doted on grapes, raisins and prunes; it welcomed settlers but saw little need to encourage tourism. Indeed, some of the early settlers' actions — the cutting of great redwood groves — later worked against the tourist trade.

In recent decades, the county has built a few wineries, museums and amusements that attract outsiders. And such places as downtown San Jose and Palo Alto have put together clubs, galleries, restaurants and cultural events that have made the county much more palatable to the business visitor.

For its own residents, however, the county, in parks, culture, recreation and amusements, the county and its cities have done very well. Where there have been gaps, the county has inventively filled them. Of note are the celebrations of the stomach, the food festivals which flow nicely out of the county's history.

San Benito County has a few attractions, most notably the mission at San Juan Bautista (a location for the Hitchcock film "Vertigo") and the Pinnacles, unusual rock formations.

Santa Cruz County, with its Boardwalk amusement park, deep-sea fishing, miles of beaches, and train rides through the redwoods, attracts many tourists but if you live in the county, you may sample the Boardwalk occasionally and take the trouble to identify some favorite beaches, and ignore the rest.

Here is some advice about making the most of local activities.

City Recreation Departments

Just about all cities have recreation departments that sponsor their own activities and coordinate or assist private groups. Chambers of commerce are excellent sources for club and activity lists. School districts occasionally run after-school programs and other activities. Adult schools and community colleges are loaded with recreational, exercise, cultural classes and activities.

Softball thrives in many communities, complete with umpires, schedules, playoffs and trophies. Many teams are organized through jobs. Some live wire will recruit fellow employees and field a team. There are men's and women's leagues and mixed teams.

Private Classes and Clubs

What the public sector lacks, the private sector provides — racquetball, golf, bowling, tennis, movies, special-activity classes. Also shopping, an unsung, often-maligned pursuit but one that brings pleasure to thousands. Santa Clara County has some delightful malls and shopping centers.

Club life is varied and, as might be expected, computer clubs abound, great fun for the many enthusiasts. There are also model sailboat, powerboat, airplane and rocketry groups, water skiing, sailboating, powerboat racing, hiking, horseback and hunting trails, trap, skeet, pistol and rifle ranges, car clubs, even hang-gliding and hot-air balloon groups.

Church and Home

Many people organize their lives around the area's numerous church activities. See Yellow pages, under Churches.

Watching television may be the most popular local pastime ("going online" is a close second). Thanks to extensive cable TV service and satellite dishes, the stations are many and the diversity of choices great, from schlock to Stravinsky. Lots of DVD rental stores. Libraries are also plentiful.

City Parks, Sports, the Arts

Regional parks tend to get most of the attention, but city parks can be counted in the dozens and draw many people. Bicycle and jogging trails wind their way throughout the county.

Of the many children's activities, soccer is probably the most popular, attracting kids by the thousands. Little League, Pop Warner football, basketball, swimming — almost every town will have a league or several leagues. Some sports — gymnastics — may attract more girls than boys.

Art guilds and galleries, dance schools, bands, a symphony, choral groups, college football and basketball, little theater — Santa Clara County has them.

And if the local offerings are not to your liking, San Francisco and Monterey are within an hour's drive and the Sierra Nevada (skiing, hiking and gambling) a few hours off.

Sorting It All Out

Sometimes hard to know just what to do. Here are suggestions to help with the sorting out.

- Find out who is organizing activities in your town and in nearby towns. Usually this can be accomplished by calling or visiting the chambers of commerce, the city recreation departments and the school districts. Some activities take more digging than others.

- Soccer and baseball leagues are occasionally put together by parents' groups with no connection to City Hall. A phone call to the city recreation department will usually turn up a phone number that will lead to another phone number that will pan out.

- Get on mailing lists. Adult schools and recreation departments change their classes about every three months. Theaters and orchestras issue calendars every season.

- Find out the rules. Some cities provide minimal support for certain activities. You may have to sign up players on your softball team and collect the fees and meet application deadlines. Baseball and soccer leagues usually guarantee the younger children, no matter what their skill, two innings or two quarters of play. But other sports (football) often go by skill. Ask about playing time.

- Ignore city boundaries. If you live in Campbell and want to take a class in San Jose, go ahead. A person with a Mountain View job might want to tackle an aerobics class in that city before hitting the freeway.

- Do a little investigation and spadework before making choices. This sounds obvious, but many people, to their unhappiness, do not.

  If you are new to the county and wish to make friends, almost assuredly you will mingle with people if you attend movies, art shows and concerts. But the opportunities for conversation may be few.

  The trick is to put yourself in a situation where you can meet and talk to people who share your interests or might in other ways make good friends. This could be a book club, the PTA, a bridge group, a wine tasting club, even the local Democrat or Republican clubs.

- Subscribe to a local newspaper, of which there are many. Almost all will have calendars of events, lists of local attractions and hours of operation.

- Visit or call the San Jose Visitors and Convention Bureau, 333 West San Carlos St., San Jose. Phone (408) 295-9600. For Gilroy (south Santa Clara County), call (408) 842-6436. For Santa Cruz, call (831) 425-1234. All will have maps, pamphlets or magazines.

Santa Clara County, Places to Visit, Things to Do

Please phone ahead to find out hours of operation. Many of these places charge for admission.

Bonfante Gardens. New horticultural theme park on Highway 152 in Gilroy. Rides, trees, picnics. Has been struggling to make a go. For information, call Gilroy Visitors Bureau, (408) 842-6436.

Children's Discovery Museum. Hands-on exhibits with themes of "community, connection and creativity," with technology, science, humanities and the arts interwoven. Third-largest such museum in the nation, largest in the west. 180 Woz Way, San Jose. Phone (408) 298-5437.

Great America. Located in city of Santa Clara, off Great America Parkway. First-class amusement park. Over 100 attractions, many of spine-tingling, stomach-churning variety.

Great place for kids. Enjoyable for adults. Entertaining musical reviews. When the kids poop out, take them inside for a show. (408) 988-1776.

Intel Museum. Located at Intel complex in the Robert Noyce Building at 2200 Mission College Blvd., Santa Clara. How computer chips are made and used and other aspects of high tech. Changing exhibits. Phone (408) 765-0503.

Lick Observatory. Atop Mt. Hamilton, southeast of San Jose, one of the most powerful observatories in the world, although in modern times its effectiveness has diminished because of background light from San Jose.

The history of Santa Clara County has been blessed by two benevolent screwballs, Sarah Winchester and James Lick. An adventurer and land speculator, Lick purchased a good deal of downtown San Francisco at the time of the gold rush and, as a consequence, became one of the richest men in the state.

Withdrawn, inclined to lawsuits and shabby dress, Lick was also an admirer of Tom Paine and determined to do good, particularly by encouraging education. Someone suggested a great telescope to study the heavens, to which Lick replied with the 19th century equivalent of "right on" and advanced the money to build the observatory, which was bequeathed to the University of California.

Scenic but slow and winding ride to the top. Tours. For schedules, phone (408) 274-5061.

Mission Santa Clara de Asis. Located on Santa Clara University campus, at 500 El Camino Real, Santa Clara. Old California, a good introduction to the Franciscan padres and what they tried to accomplish in pioneer days. Fires and other calamities destroyed early buildings. In 1929, Mission Santa Clara was rebuilt. While there, tour the university, a pretty campus. Phone (408) 554-4023.

Raging Waters. Your typical wild and wet water-slide and swimming park. Picnic areas, video arcade, shops, entertainment. Open May to September, exact dates depending on weather. In Lake Cunningham Park, San Jose, on the east side, at Tully Road and Capitol Expressway. Phone (408) 238-9900.

Rose Garden. Naglee and Dana avenues, in San Jose. Park planted with 5,000 rose bushes in 150 varieties.

Rosicrucian Museum. Park and Naglee avenues, San Jose. The Rosicrucians are a fraternal order of men and women who encourage the study of ancient learning. At their world headquarters in San Jose, the Rosicrucians built a striking museum that houses a large collection of ancient Egyptian artifacts. Highlights include a mummy gallery, a full-sized rock tomb, and exhibits on the Assyrians and the Babylonians.

The planetarium, one of the first in the U.S., explores the universe and pays particular attention to the mythologies and star lore of the ancients. Phone (408) 947-3635.

San Jose Flea Market. 12000 Berryessa Rd., between Highway 101 and Interstate 680, San Jose. One of the great bazaars of the West Coast. Open Wednesdays through Sundays. Draws 50,000 to 75,000 on weekends. Also includes farmers' markets and kiddie amusements. (408) 453-1110.

San Jose Historical Museum. 635 Phelan St., San Jose. Old Santa Clara County recreated at Kelley Park — an Indian acorn granary, the Pacific Hotel, a candy store, an electric tower, a 1920s gas station, a dental building, stables and more. Much memorabilia from the old days, also exhibits on Costanoan Indians, the rancheros, the high-wheeler bicycles. Well worth a visit, especially with kids. Petting zoo nearby. Also nearby, the Japanese Friendship Park, six acres of waterfalls, stone bridges, bonsai plants — peaceful, restful, inviting. Phone (408) 287-2290.

San Jose Museum of Art. Market and San Fernando streets. 20th century and contemporary art. Photography, paintings, sculpture, drawings. Many classes in art for children and adults. Taught by working artists. Phone (408) 294-2787.

San Jose Sharks. Professional ice-hockey team. San Jose Arena. For information on events and sports schedules, phone (800) 755-5050. Sharks tickets are sold at the arena and through Ticketmaster. Phone (408) 998-8497.

Stanford University. Palo Alto. A beautiful campus, a delight to tour. Spanish architecture. Hoover Tower (good view). Rodin Sculpture Garden, museums, galleries. Daily walking tours. For information on campus and group tours, and Hoover Tower, call (650) 723-2560. Palo Alto is also a good shopping town, lots to choose from.

Tech Museum of Innovation. San Jose, helped by Silicon Valley firms, opened a new tech museum. The museum features 250 exhibits divided into the following galleries, "Life Tech; The Human Machine"; "Innovation: Silicon Valley and Beyond"; "Communication: Global Connections"; "Exploration: New Frontiers." Located at 201 S. Market St., San Jose. For more info call (408) 294-8324.

Triton Museum. 1505 Warburton Ave., Santa Clara. Folk, contemporary, classic art. Pastoral scenes and wildlife of the early valley. Phone (408) 247-3754.

Villa Montalvo. Located just outside Saratoga on Saratoga-Los Gatos Road. Italian Renaissance villa built by politician with an artistic soul. James Phelan, a three-term mayor of San Francisco and a U.S. senator, was a patron of the arts. He left his beloved Villa Montalvo as a retreat for artists, writers and musicians. Many shows and programs on cultural subjects. The grounds, 175 acres, are maintained as a public arboretum. For information about programs, call (408) 741-3421.

Winchester Mystery House. 525 S. Winchester Blvd., San Jose. Sarah Winchester, heiress of the shooting Winchesters, pumped about $5 million into this four-story, 160-room house.

A reclusive, whimsical eccentric with a perverse eye for beauty, Mrs. Winchester ordered carpenters to build doors that opened to walls, staircases that lead nowhere and a window that peered out of a floor. Excellent rifle collection. Beautiful garden. Cafe. Banquet facilities. Tours. Phone (408) 247-2101.

Musical and Cultural Events

Music and culture buffs should get on mailing lists of four "must" places:

Flint Center, De Anza College, 21250 Stevens Creek Blvd., Cupertino. Phone (408) 864-8816.

San Jose Center for the Performing Arts, Almaden Boulevard and Park Avenue. Phone (408) 277-3900.

Shoreline Amphitheater at Mountain View, phone (650) 967-3000.

Stanford University, Palo Alto, Musical and cultural events, phone (650) 725-ARTS; athletic events, phone (650) 723-1021.

Regional Parks

Alum Rock Park. Old favorite of San Jose. In east hills, via Penitencia Creek Road. Dappled sycamores. Hiking, bike trails, picnicking, falls and springs. A spa, now long gone, used to attract people to Alum Rock for the cure.

Anderson Lake County Park. East of Morgan Hill, off East Dunne Avenue or Coyote Road. About 2,000 acres of park around north and east sides of Anderson Reservoir, which is occasionally drained. Views. Picnic tables.

Coe State Park. A big one, 68,000 acres, east of Morgan Hill. Take East Dunne Avenue. Hiking, backpacking, about 100 miles of trails. Nature center.

Grant County Park. 9,522 acres on the road to Mt. Hamilton, east of San Jose. Hiking, horseback riding trails. Many natural history exhibits. Four lakes.

Mount Madonna County Park. West of Gilroy. Take Highway 152. Redwoods and bay, oak and large madrone trees among 3,093 acres of hilly land. Rewarding but strenuous trails.

Monterey and Santa Cruz–Places to Visit, Things to Do

Please phone ahead to find out hours of operation.

Agricultural History Project Museum. 2601 East Lake Ave., Watsonville. On display are early farming equipment and methods of the central coast. Special activities for children. (831) 724-5898.

Annual Watsonville Antique Fly-In and Air Show. Watsonville Municipal Airport, This show on Memorial Day weekend features over 500 classic aircrafts and aerobatic performances. (831) 763-5600.

Aptos History Museum. 7605-A Old Dominion Court, Aptos—Located inside Aptos Chamber of Commerce with collection of photographs and artifacts representing area history. (831) 688-1467.

Capitola Wharf, 1400 Wharf Rd. Capitola. Pier fishing, boat rentals, restaurants, weekend live music. (831) 462-2208.

Davenport Cash Store. Restaurant and inn with gift shop that features artisan crafts from around the world. (800) 870-1817, www.davenportinn.com

Davenport Jail Museum. 705 Front St., Davenport. This 1917 county jail was only used twice and then abandoned in 1936. It houses an exhibition of north coast history. Open some weekends, and by appointment. (831) 429-1964.

Downtown Santa Cruz Antique Faire. Lincoln and Cedar Sts., Downtown Santa Cruz—A monthly fair featuring 50 vendors of antiques and collectibles from before 1950.

Many Hands Gallery. 1510 Pacific Ave., Santa Cruz—Acryllic paintings. (831) 429-8696.

Many Hands Gallery Capitola. 510 Bay Ave., Capitola—Acryllic paintings. (831) 475-2500.

McPherson Center for Art & History 705 Front Street, Santa Cruz— Features exhibits of local history and the art of modern times.

Monterey Bay Aquarium. 886 Cannery Row, Monterey. In Monterery's historic Cannery Row, features million-gallon indoor ocean aquarium, jellyfish exhibit, sea otter tank, kelp forest, pedestrian tunnel through aquarium and more. Recent addition: great white shark. (831) 644-7548.

Mystery Spot. 465 Mystery Spot Road, Santa Cruz. Discovered in the Santa Cruz redwoods in 1940. Experiences unique variations in gravity, balance, perception, height and light. Mystifying! (831) 423-8897.

Pajaro Valley Historical Association. 332 East Beach St., Watsonville. Exhibits and archives pertaining to Watsonville and the Pajaro Valley. (831) 722-0305.

Rancho Del Oso Nature and History Center. Big Basin Redwoods State Park, Davenport. Former country estate features exhibits of native flora and fauna, local history and nature-oriented work. Hiking, backpacking, biking, beachcombing, horseback riding, windsurfing and more. (831) 427-2288.

Roaring Camp Railroads. Graham Hill Rd., Felton—Ride two historic railroads through redwood forests at Roaring Camp, an 1880s logging town, general store, steam-powered saw mill, recreation of great train robberies, Easter egg hunt, Memorial Day weekend Civil War Reenactments, steam festival, jumping frog contest, Chuckwagon Barbecue. (831) 335-4484, www.roaringcamp.com.

San Lorenzo Valley Historical Museum. 12547 Highway 9, Boulder Creek. Located in an Episcopal Church built in 1885. Regularly changing museum displays feature artifacts, photographs and documents related to the varied history of the San Lorenzo Valley. (831) 338-8382.

Santa Cruz Beach Boardwalk. 400 Beach St., Santa Cruz—Major seaside amusement park featuring 30 rides, Neptune's Kingdom (mini golf, arcade, pool tables, historium, restaurant), Casino Fun Center (virtual reality games), outdoor summer concerts, shopping. (831) 426-7433, www.beachboardwalk.com.

Santa Cruz Harley-Davidson Museum. 1148 Soquel Ave., Santa Cruz. Santa Cruz County's only Harley-Davidson dealership featuring a museum of antique motorcycles and factory-authorized memorabilia. (831) 421-9600.

Santa Cruz Museum of Natural History. 1305 East Cliff Dr., Santa Cruz—Exhibits on native peoples, geology, area animal life. (831) 420-6115

Santa Cruz Surfing Museum. Lighthouse on West Cliff Dr., Santa Cruz—One hundred years of surfing history. (831) 420-6289.

UCSC Arboretum. High Street near Western, Santa Cruz. Known for its plant collections from Australia, South Africa and New Zealand. Gift shop. (831) 427-2998.

UCSC Seymour Marine Center. 100 Shaffer Rd., Santa Cruz. Aquarium, exhibits and activities dedicated to educating children and families in marine science and research programs conducted by UCSC. (831) 459-3800.

Parks

Ben Lomond Park/Dam. 9525 Mill St., Ben Lomond. Historical creekside park offers seasonal swimming, picnic/barbecue areas, playground, basketball court, horseshoe pit and nature area. (831) 454-7956.

Big Basin Redwoods State Park. 21600 Big Basin Way, Boulder Creek—First state park in California. Camping, picnics, over 50 miles of trails for hiking through forests, waterfalls. (831) 338-8860.

Camp Evers Fishing Park. Glen Canyon Rd., half-mile from Mt. Hermon Rd., Scotts Valley. Ideal fishing hole for youths. Stocked with native steelhead. Free seasonal fishing May-September for youths ages 15 and under. Picnic areas and barbecue. (831) 438-3251.

Elkhorn Slough Reserve. 1700 Elkhorn Rd., Watsonville—Five miles of hiking trails through grassland adjoining fresh and saltwater marshes. Great place to view shorebirds. (831) 728-2822.

Fall Creek State Park. 101 Big Trees Park Rd., Felton. Heavily forested park has a lime kiln, barrel mill and 20 miles of hiking trails along old wagon and logging roads. No bikes or dogs. (831) 335-4598.

Felton Covered Bridge Park. Graham Hill Rd. and Mt. Hermon Rd., Felton. The park's covered bridge is a California State Historical Landmark. Park offers volleyball, picnic area with barbecue and playground. (831) 454-7956.

Forest of Nisene Marks State Park. Aptos Creek Rd., Aptos—Hike, bike or jog through 10,000 acres of redwood forest. Picnic tables and BBQ pits available. (831) 763-7064.

Gray Whale Ranch. Hikers walk an unbroken trail across scenic public land. Trail leads from Graham Hill Road through Henry Cowell State Park, the University of California, Gray Whale Ranch and then Wilder Ranch to the ocean.

Henry Cowell Redwoods State Park. 101 North Big Trees Park Rd., Felton—Giant redwoods, self-guided trails, picnic areas and nature center. (831) 335-4598.

Santa Cruz Mission State Historic Park. Mission Hill, overlooking downtown Santa Cruz. It preserves some of the earliest Spanish history in the region. An adobe built in 1824 is all that remains of the original 17-structure site built by Yokuts Indians. It is the only surviving Indian mission housing in all of California. During some weekends, Mission docents conduct tours in authentic period costumes, and also offer living history craft activities such as adobe brick making and tortilla making. (831) 429-2850

Seacliff Beach State Park. 201 State Park Dr., Aptos. Site of the abandoned ship Palo Alto which saw its glory days as a nightclub in the 1920s. Now used as a fishing pier. (831) 685-6500.

Wilder Ranch State Park. 1401 Coast Rd., Santa Cruz. Historic ranch has hiking, bike and horseback riding trails. On bluffs overlooking Monterey Bay between Davenport and Santa Cruz, the park has old farm buildings dating back to the 1880s containing historic exhibits of interest to kids and adults. Live farm animals. (831) 426-0505.

Beaches

Capitola Beach. The Esplanade in Capitola. Lined with shops and restaurants, beach area. (831) 475-7300.

Davenport Beach. Davenport Landing in Davenport. Original site of Davenport, a thriving whaling town. Strictly a day-use beach, it is generally less crowded than many of the north coast beaches and is a favorite for windsurfers. (831) 454-7956.

Lighthouse Field State Beach. West Cliff Dr. & Pelton Ave., Santa Cruz—Steamer Lane, widely considered the birthplace of mainland American surfing, is here. Also, the Surfing Museum is located in the lighthouse. (831) 420-5270

Manresa Uplands State Beach. 205 Manresa Rd., La Selva Beach. Enjoy the surf, sand and sun. Fire rings on beach. Picnic tables available. Day-use fee. Tent camping only, no RVs. Reservations required in the summer. (831) 724-3750.

Natural Bridges State Beach. West Cliff Dr., west of Swift St., Santa Cruz—Natural rock formations here, a mecca for surfers and windsurfers. Named for the two natural sandstone arches that stood at the entrance. A winter storm several years ago collapsed one of them and the local residents nicknamed the beach "Fallen Arches Beach" (831) 423-4609

New Brighton State Beach. 1500 State Park Rd., Capitola. Towering cypress and pine provides a sense of isolation and privacy between campsites. Surf fishing, dump station, camping, no RV hookups. Day-use fee. Reservations required. (831) 464-6330.

Red, White and Blue Beach. 5021 Coast Rd., Santa Cruz. Clothing-optional beach featuring day-use facilities and overnight camping. Closed November-January. (831) 423-6332.

Rio Del Mar Beach. Rio Del Mar Blvd., Aptos. A wide strip of clean sand and a jetty. Nearby shopping and restaurants. Dogs allowed on leashes. Lifeguards in the summer. (831) 685-6500

Sunset State Beach. 201 Sunset Beach Blvd., Watsonville. A secluded stretch of coast surrounded by farms. Camping reservations required in the summer. Day-use fee. No RV hookups. (831) 763-7063.

Twin Lakes State Beach. East Cliff at 7th Ave., Santa Cruz. One of the area's warmest beaches due to its location at the entrance of Schwann Lagoon. Fire rings, outdoor showers and restrooms available. (831) 429-2850.

Waddell State Beach. Highway 1, Davenport. Windy beaches preclude sunbathing much of the year, but attract hang gliders, windsurfers and tidepool explorers. (831) 427-2288.

San Benito, Places to Visit, Things to Do

Please phone ahead to find out hours of operation.

Bolado Park Fairgrounds and Grandstand Arena. The site for the county fair and Saddle Horse Show and Rodeo and a variety of other activities. Facilities include swimming, pavilion, RV camping, picnic and barbecue areas. (831) 628-3421.

Bolado Park Golf Course. 9-hole public course on Hwy 25 south of Hollister. (831) 628-9995.

Casa de Fruta Orchard Resort. Live entertainment with country line dancing every weekend in the Spring and Summer, special festival events, wine tasting, campgrounds, RV park, restaurant, picnic areas, petting zoo, and train rides. (408) 842-7282.

El Teatro Campesino. Nationally renown theater company. Call for current programming. (831) 623-2444.

Hollister Hills State Vehicular Recreation Area. 2,400 acre motorcycle activity area with 800 acres set aside for four-wheel-drive vehicles. Campsites are available. (831) 637-3874.

Ridgemark Golf and Country Club. Two semi-private 18-hole championship courses, ten lighted tennis courts, lodging and conference facilities. (831) 637-8151.

Saint Francis Retreat. Just outside of downtown San Juan Bautista with a view of Rancho Justo Valley. Indoor and outdoor conference facilities. (831) 623-4234.

San Andreas Brewery Company. Nachos rated on a Richter scale of hotness and home of the famous earthquake burger. Also brews cream soda, ginger beer, and sarsparilla. (831) 637-7074.

Mission San Juan Bautista. Founded 1797, it is still an active church with activities and festivals. Across from the mission is the State Historical Park with original buildings like the Castro Adobe, the Plaza Hotel and stable with a collection of buggies and wagons, and the old blacksmith shop. (831) 623-2127.

Chapter 18

Weather

"HE HAD BEEN suddenly jerked from the heart of civilization and flung into the heart of things primordial. No lazy, sun-kissed life was this ...."

Jack London, in "The Call of the Wild," was describing the great dog, Buck, stolen from the Santa Clara Valley and secreted to Alaska to work as a sled dog. Compared to frigid Alaska, Santa Clara was cream cheese, Jack thought, an arguable proposition, but there was no denying he caught the gist of the local weather, "sun-kissed."

One of Life's Joys

Rarely very hot or cold, always finding its way back to balmy tranquillity.

Although appearing somewhat erratic, the weather proceeds logically, responding to broad patterns and local topography. Easily learned, these patterns will make you somewhat of a weather expert, a reliable source on what to wear, when to have a picnic and when to drive slowly.

For starters, it can be safely said that rain will rarely fall between May and September, that Pacific swimming will be warmer in October than in June, that the San Lorenzo Valley (Santa Cruz County) to the south and Berkeley to the north will receive more rain or moisture than the Santa Clara Valley.

Five great actors star in the Bay Area weather extravaganza: the sun, the Pacific, the Golden Gate, the Central Valley and the hills.

The Sun

In the spring and summer, the sun moves north bringing a mass of air called the Pacific High. The Pacific High blocks storms from the California Coast and dispatches winds down the coast. In the fall, the sun moves south, taking the Pacific High with it. The winds slough off for a while, then in bluster the storms. Toward spring, the storms abate as the Pacific High settles in.

The Pacific

Speeding across the Pacific, spring and summer winds pick up moisture and, at the coast, strip the warm water from the surface and bring up the frigid.

Average Daily Temperature

Location	Ja	Fb	Mr	Ap	My	Ju	Jy	Au	Sp	Oc	No	Dc
Ben Lomond	49	52	54	57	61	65	68	68	66	61	53	49
Gilroy	50	54	56	60	65	69	72	72	70	65	55	49
Hollister	49	52	54	57	60	65	66	67	67	63	55	49
King City	50	53	56	59	63	67	69	69	68	63	55	50
Los Gatos	49	52	54	57	62	67	70	70	68	63	54	48
Mt. Hamilton	44	43	43	47	56	64	70	71	66	57	47	43
Palo Alto	49	53	55	58	62	66	68	68	66	62	54	49
San Francisco	49	53	54	56	58	62	63	64	63	61	55	50
San Jose	51	54	57	60	64	69	71	71	69	64	56	50
Santa Cruz	50	53	54	57	59	62	64	65	63	62	55	51

Source: National Climatic Data Center, Ashville, NC, 1971-2000

Cold water exposed to warm, wet air makes a wonderfully thick fog. In summer, San Francisco, Monterey, Half Moon Bay and Pacifica, among others, often look like they are buried in mountains of cotton.

The Golden Gate

This fog would love to scoot inland to the Santa Clara Valley and Bay shore cities such as Palo Alto and Mountain View. But the coastal hills and mountains stop or greatly impede its progress — except where there are openings. Of the half dozen or so major gaps, the biggest is that marvelous work of nature, the Golden Gate.

The fog shoots through the Golden Gate in the spring and summer, visually delighting motorists on the Bay Bridge, bangs into the East Bay hills and eases down toward San Jose, where it takes the edge off temperatures. The Crystal Springs gap, located northwest of Palo Alto, also allows cooling air into the South Bay.

The Central Valley

Also known as the Sacramento and San Joaquin valleys and located about 75 miles inland, the Central Valley is influenced more by continental weather than coastal. In the summer, this means heat. Hot air rises, pulling in cold air like a vacuum. The Central Valley sucks in the coastal air through the Golden Gate and openings in the East Bay hills, until the Valley cools.

Then the Valley says to the coast: no more cool air, thank you.

With the suction gone, the inland pull on the ocean fog drops off, often breaking down the fog-producing apparatus and clearing San Francisco and the coastline. Meanwhile, lacking the cooling air, the Valley heats up again, creating the vacuum that pulls in the fog.

This cha-cha between coast and inland valley gave rise to the Bay Region's boast of "natural air conditioning." In hot weather, nature works to bring in cool air; in cool weather, she works to bring in heat.

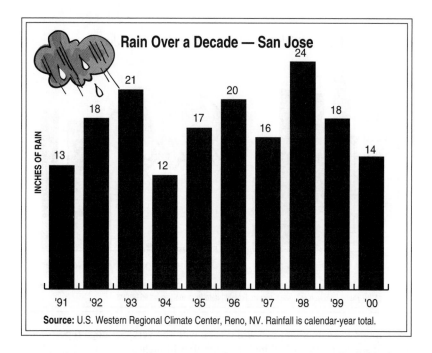

Rain Over a Decade — San Jose

INCHES OF RAIN

'91: 13
'92: 18
'93: 21
'94: 12
'95: 17
'96: 20
'97: 16
'98: 24
'99: 18
'00: 14

Source: U.S. Western Regional Climate Center, Reno, NV. Rainfall is calendar-year total.

In Santa Clara County, this push-pull phenomenon has a diminutive counterpart. At night, fog will occasionally creep over the coastal mountains only to be burned off the following morning by the robust sunlight.

The Hills

Besides blocking the fog, the hills also greatly determine how much rain falls in a particular location. Many storms travel south to north, so a valley that opens to the south (San Lorenzo) will receive more rain than one that opens to the north (Santa Clara).

When storm clouds rise to pass over a hill, they cool and drop much of their rain. Some towns in the Bay Region will be deluged during a storm, while

San Jose Temperature Patterns

Month	Avg. Max.	Avg. Min.	Record High	Record Low
January	58	41	79	22
April	69	47	93	30
July	81	56	108	43
October	74	51	97	31
Year	70	49	108	20

Source: San Jose Municipal Weather Station.

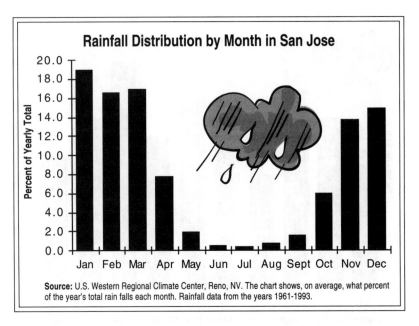

Rainfall Distribution by Month in San Jose

Percent of Yearly Total

Jan Feb Mar Apr May Jun Jul Aug Sept Oct Nov Dec

Source: U.S. Western Regional Climate Center, Reno, NV. The chart shows, on average, what percent of the year's total rain falls each month. Rainfall data from the years 1961-1993.

a few miles away another town will escape with showers. Saratoga reports an average annual rainfall of 29 inches, Cupertino 14 inches.

That basically is how the weather works in the Bay Area. Unfortunately for regularity's sake, the actors often forget their lines or are upstaged by minor stars.

Rainfall at San Jose over 10 years (1975-84) demonstrates the mildly erratic nature of Mother Nature. From 12 inches in 1975, rainfall dropped to 7 and 9 inches in the drought years of 1976 and 1977 and after bouncing between 16 and 20 over the next five years, zoomed to 33 inches in storm-wracked 1983.

In 1987, a drought began that in subsequent years forced rationing. It ended with the 1992 winter, which soaked all, loaded the Sierra with snow and filled local reservoirs.

Swimming

September and October are often best months to swim in the Pacific. The upwelling of the cold water has stopped. Often the fog has departed. Sunshine glows upon the water and the coast. Almost every year the summer ends with hot spells in September and October.

Sunshine

Like sunshine? You are in the right place. Records show that during daylight hours the sun shines in New York City 60 percent of the time; in Boston, 57 percent; in Detroit, 53 percent and in Seattle, 43 percent. San Jose averages 63 percent.

Temperatures for Selected Cities
Number of Days Greater than 90 Degrees in Typical Year

City	Ja	Fb	Mr	Ap	My	Ju	Jy	Au	Sp	Oc	No	Dc
Gilroy	0	0	0	0	1	3	4	19	11	0	0	0
Los Gatos	0	0	0	0	1	6	6	12	7	0	0	0
Mount Hamilton	0	0	0	0	0	0	1	5	2	0	0	0
Palo Alto	0	0	0	0	0	1	3	7	3	0	0	0
San Jose	0	0	0	0	2	3	8	12	8	0	0	0
Santa Cruz	0	0	0	0	0	0	0	1	1	0	0	0

Source: National Weather Service.

Temperatures for Selected Cities
Number of Days 32 Degrees or Less in Typical Year

City	Ja	Fb	Mr	Ap	My	Ju	Jy	Au	Sp	Oc	No	Dc
Gilroy	2	1	0	0	0	0	0	0	0	0	0	12
Los Gatos	11	5	0	0	0	0	0	0	0	0	0	10
Mount Hamilton	6	11	19	13	1	1	0	0	0	0	3	10
Palo Alto	6	0	0	0	0	0	0	0	0	0	0	10
San Jose	0	0	0	0	0	0	0	0	0	0	0	6
Santa Cruz	1	2	0	0	0	0	0	0	0	0	0	9

Source: National Weather Service.

The gloomiest month: January, 42 percent sunshine. The brightest, the summer months, e.g. July, 83 percent.

Humidity

Heat Santa Clara County does experience but rarely muggy weather. When hot spells arrive, the air usually has little moisture — dry heat. When the air is moist (the fog), the temperatures drop.

Fog

Of the Bay Area's two types of fog, one is more dangerous than the other. The coastal fog often forms well above the Pacific and, pushed by the wind, generally moves at a good clip. In thick coastal fog, you will have to slow down but you can see the tail lights of a car 50 to 75 yards ahead.

Valley or tule fog blossoms at shoe level when cold air pulls moisture from the earth. Found mostly in the Central Valley, tule fog hugs the ground and generally stays put. When you read of 50- and 75-car pileups in the Central Valley, tule fog is to blame.

Occasionally, tule fog is pulled down into the Bay — an effect of the pull of heat on cold air. The ocean being warmer than the land, the Bay Area in winter will occasionally suck in the colder air and fog of the interior — the reverse of the summer pattern.

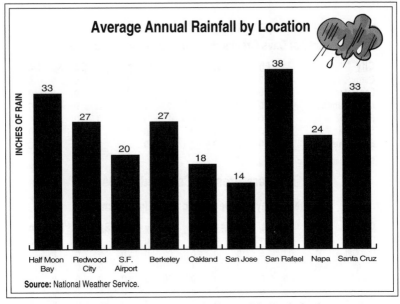

Average Annual Rainfall by Location

INCHES OF RAIN

Location	Inches
Half Moon Bay	33
Redwood City	27
S.F. Airport	20
Berkeley	27
Oakland	18
San Jose	14
San Rafael	38
Napa	24
Santa Cruz	33

Source: National Weather Service.

If you are planning a redwoods excursion to Big Basin in the summer, bring a jacket and an umbrella. Redwoods are creatures of the fog, need it to thrive. Where you find a good redwood stand, you will, in summer, often find fog, cold thick fog, that will usually burn off by noon.

Scorchers

During the summer and fall, the Pacific High will occasionally loop a strong wind down from Washington through the Sierra and the hot valleys, where it loses its moisture, and into the Bay Area.

Extremely dry, these northeasters, which are now called "Diablos," will tighten the skin on your face, cause wood shingle roofs to crackle and turn the countryside into tinder. The October 1991 fire that destroyed 2,500 homes and apartments in the Berkeley-Oakland hills and killed 25 was caused by a Diablo. If you buy in the hills, if your home is surrounded with brush and trees, take a look at fire-retardant shingles and fire-prevention tactics.

Storms

Rain is rain, generally welcome all the time in dry California. But some rains are more welcome than others. Storms from the vicinity of Hawaii turn Sierra Nevada slopes to slush and, in the upper elevations, deposit soft snow that sinks under the weight of skis.

Alaskan storms bring snow to the lower mountains and deposit a fine powder, ideal for skiing. Some Alaskan storms occasionally bless the Bay Region with snow on the mountain tops. The air will be crystal clear, with a shiver of cold. Mt. Hamilton and the other mountains, green for the winter, will overnight don a lovely mantle of white.

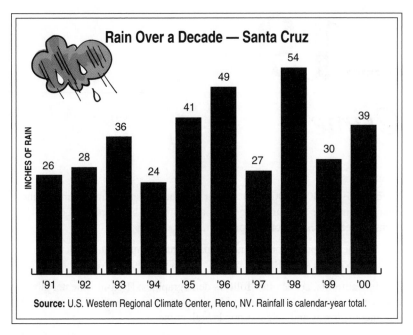

Rain Over a Decade — Santa Cruz

INCHES OF RAIN

Year	Inches
'91	26
'92	28
'93	36
'94	24
'95	41
'96	49
'97	27
'98	54
'99	30
'00	39

Source: U.S. Western Regional Climate Center, Reno, NV. Rainfall is calendar-year total.

Allergies

They often kick in during the spring and in October. During the spring, the grasses pop their buds and many trees release pollen. In the fall, the Diablos dry out the trees and cones and pollen fills the air. Hanky time.

Santa Cruz Weather

Santa Cruz is open to the ocean but the middle and lower half shelter in the wide curve of Monterey Bay. The Bay takes the edge off of the foggy blasts but on many days you will catch them in full force.

As for summer heat, there are differences from city to city in the region but overall we're still talking California balmy. During one heat wave in summer 2000, the weather people recorded these highs: Monterey 80, Santa Cruz 82, Watsonville 85, Mountain View 87, Hollister 98, Gilroy 102.

Chapter 19

Crime

EVERY NEIGHBORHOOD and city in this country suffers from some crime. Even communities surrounded by gates and patrolled by guards will on occasion see domestic violence or pilfering by visitors.

So when shopping for a home or apartment, the question to ask is not: Is this neighborhood safe? But rather, how safe is it compared to other places?

In California, crime often follows demographics: High-income neighborhoods generally have low crime, middle-income places middling crime and low-income towns and neighborhoods high crime.

In many instances, these patterns mislead. You can take probably every high-crime city in the country and find within it low-crime neighborhoods. New York City seemingly is overrun with felons but the City includes Staten Island, generally suburban and probably low to middle in crime. The same for Oakland, San Francisco, San Diego and Los Angeles. These are not crime cities; they are cities with certain neighborhoods high in crime.

Theft is the most common crime. A city with many stores or a regional shopping mall will often have a high number of thefts — and consequently, a higher crime rate. Number of homicides, in some instances, gives a clearer picture of local crime. Many peaceful, law-abiding people live in the "worst" neighborhoods. But these neighborhoods also contain a disproportionate number of the troubled and criminally inclined.

Why does crime correlate with income and demographics? In many countries, it doesn't. Japan, devastated after World War II, did not sink into violence and thievery. Many industrialized nations with about the same or lower standards of living than the U.S. have far fewer murders. In 2000, France, about 54 million people, counted 503 homicides; in 2002, the United Kingdom (England, Wales, Scotland and Northern Island), 58 million people, recorded 513 homicides. By contrast, in 2004, the City of Los Angeles, 3.9 million people, tallied 518 homicides (and historically this was low for L.A.). In recent years Europeans have seen more burglaries, robberies, etc. In fact, in some categories, the U.S. is doing better than some Europe nations. The big exception: shootings.)

Crime Statistics by City
Santa Clara County

City	Population	Violent Crimes	Homicides
Campbell	38,415	66	1
Cupertino	53,452	60	0
Gilroy	47,671	181	0
Los Altos	27,614	10	0
Los Altos Hills	8,452	NA	0
Los Gatos	28,976	32	1
Milpitas	64,998	195	0
Monte Sereno	3,505	NA	0
Morgan Hill	36,423	50	0
Mountain View	72,033	263	1
Palo Alto	61,674	89	2
San Jose	944,857	3,379	24
Santa Clara	109,106	239	2
Saratoga	30,850	14	0
Sunnyvale	133,086	161	2
County	1,723,900	5,090	37

Santa Cruz County

City	Population	Violent Crimes	Homicides
Capitola	9,924	NA	NA
Santa Cruz	56,451	490	1
Scotts Valley	11,571	15	0
Watsonville	49,601	283	2
County	259,990	1,198	5

Crime in Other Northern California Cities

City	Population	Violent Crimes*	Homicides
Concord	126,539	393	5
Danville	43,012	49	0
Hillsborough	10,815	3	1
Fremont	210,445	454	5
Oakland	407,003	5,151	83
Sacramento	450,472	4,730	50
San Francisco	772,065	5,757	88
San Ramon	46,702	47	0
Stockton	265,593	3,700	40
Vacaville	94,555	331	2
Walnut Creek	66,031	115	1

Source: Annual reports from FBI, 2004 data. Homicides include murders and non-negligent manslaughter. *Number of violent crimes. NA (not available). The FBI doesn't track cities under 10,000 population. The state does but publishes its reports sometimes a year later. Sometimes we can track down the information. The three cities with NA entries — Monte Sereno, Los Altos Hills and Capitola — have for years been low in crime.

Crime in Other Cities Nationwide

City	Population	Violent Crimes*	Homicides
Anchorage	273,714	2,164	15
Atlanta	430,066	7,922	112
Austin	683,298	3,589	27
Birmingham	238,167	3,261	59
Boise	193,864	745	0
Boston	580,087	6,917	61
Chicago	2,882,746	NA	448
Cleveland	462,260	5,983	78
Dallas	1,228,613	16,165	248
Denver	563,688	4,490	87
Hartford, Conn.	125,109	1,514	16
Detroit, MI	914,353	15,913	385
Honolulu	906,589	2,507	26
Houston	2,043,446	23,427	272
Jacksonville, FLA	790,972	6,533	104
Las Vegas	1,239,805	9,783	131
Little Rock	185,870	3,048	40
Milwaukee	590,874	4,637	87
Miami	385,186	6,461	69
New York City	8,101,321	55,688	570
New Orleans	471,057	4,467	264
Oklahoma City	525,094	4,321	39
Philadelphia	1,484,224	20,902	330
Phoenix	1,428,973	9,465	202
Pittsburgh, PA	334,231	3,739	46
Portland, OR	543,838	4,034	29
Reno	201,981	1,480	9
St. Louis, MO	335,143	6,897	113
Salt Lake City	182,768	1,328	15
Scottsdale, AZ	224,357	468	4
Seattle	575,816	3,798	24
Tucson	522,487	4,873	55

Source: Annual 2004 FBI crime report. *Number of violent crimes.
Key: NA (not available).

Sociologists blame the breakdown of morals and the family in the U.S, the pervasive violence in the media, the easy access to guns, and other forces. Any one of these "causes" could be argued into the next century but if you're shopping for a home or an apartment just keep in mind that there is a correlation between demographics and crime.

Drive the neighborhood. The signs of trouble are often easily read: men idling around liquor stores, bars on many windows, security doors in wide use. Sometimes you may want to trade off. Troubled neighborhoods often carry low prices or rents and are located near job centers. Many towns and sections are in transition; conditions could improve, the investment might be worthwhile. What's intolerable to a parent might be acceptable to a single person.

Crime in States

States	Population	Homicides	Violent Crimes	Rate*
Alabama	4,530,182	254	19,324	427
Alaska	655,435	37	4,159	635
Arizona	5,743,834	414	28,952	504
Arkansas	2,752,629	176	13,737	499
California	35,893,799	2,392	198,070	552
Colorado	4,601,403	203	17,185	374
Connecticut	3,503,604	91	10,032	286
Delaware	830,364	17	4,720	568
Florida	17,397,161	946	123,754	711
Georgia	8,829,383	613	40,217	456
Hawaii	1,262,840	33	3,213	254
Idaho	1,393,262	30	3,412	245
Illinois	12,713,634	776	69,026	543
Indiana	6,237,569	316	2,294	325
Iowa	2,954,451	46	8,003	271
Kansas	2,735,502	123	10,245	375
Kentucky	4,145,922	236	10,152	245
Louisiana	4,515,770	574	28,844	639
Maine	1,317,253	18	1,364	104
Maryland	5,558,058	521	38,932	701
Massachusetts	6,416,505	169	29,437	459
Michigan	10,112,260	643	49,577	490
Minnesota	5,100,958	113	13,751	270
Mississippi	2,902,966	227	8,568	295
Missouri	5,754,618	354	28,226	491
Montana	926,865	30	2,723	294
Nebraska	1,747,214	40	5,393	309
Nevada	2,334,771	172	14,379	616
New Hampshire	1,299,500	18	2,170	167
New Jersey	8,698,879	392	30,943	356
New Mexico	1,903,289	169	13,081	687
New York	19,227,088	889	84,914	442
North Carolina	8,541,221	532	38,244	448
North Dakota	634,366	9	504	79
Ohio	11,459,011	517	39,163	342
Oklahoma	3,523,553	186	17,635	501
Oregon	3,594,586	90	10,324	298
Pennsylvania	12,406,292	650	50,998	411
Rhode Island	1,080,632	26	2,673	274
South Carolina	4,198,068	288	32,922	784
South Dakota	770,883	18	1,322	172
Tennessee	5,900,962	351	41,024	695
Texas	22,490,022	1,364	121,554	541
Utah	2,389,039	46	5,639	236
Vermont	621,394	16	696	112
Virginia	7,459,827	391	20,559	276
Washington	6,203,788	190	21,330	344
West Virginia	1,815,35	68	4,924	271
Wisconsin	5,509,026	154	11,548	210
Wyoming	506,929	11	1,163	230
Washington D.C.	553,523	198	7,590	1,371

Source: FBI 2004 Figures. *Violent crime rate is number of incidents per 100,000 residents.

Crime In Other California Cities

City	Population	Violent Crimes*	Homicides
Anaheim	345,317	1,530	10
Bakersfield	274,162	1,948	23
Fresno	456,663	3,496	53
Huntington Beach	200,763	421	6
Riverside	285,537	1,777	17
Los Angeles	3,864,018	42,785	518
San Diego	1,294,032	6,774	62
Santa Ana	351,697	1,858	25
Santa Barbara	89,269	264	0

Source: Annual reports from FBI, 2004 data. Homicides include murders and non-negligent manslaughter.
*Number of violent crimes.

U.S. Crime

• In 2004, the FBI reports, 16,137 people were murdered in the United States. Of these, the FBI was able to assemble data on 14,121. The following is based on these 14,121 deaths. Of them, 9,326 or 66 percent were shot, 1,866 stabbed, 663 beaten with a blunt instrument, 933 assaulted with feet, hands or fists, 11 poisoned, 15 drowned, 114 killed by fire and 155 strangled. Narcotics killed 76 and asphyxiation 105. In 856 homicides, weapons were not identified.

• Of total murdered, 10,990 were male, 3,099 female and 32 unknown.

• In murders involving guns, handguns accounted for 7,365 deaths, rifles 393, shotguns 507, and other guns or type unknown 1,161.

• Of the 14,121 murdered in 2004, the FBI reported that 3,976 lost their lives in violence stemming from arguments or brawls. The next largest category was robbery victims, 988 homicides. Romantic triangles led to 97 homicides, narcotic drug laws 554, juvenile gang violence 804, gangland violence 95, rape 36, arson 28, baby-sitter-killing-child 17, burglary 77, prostitution 9, gambling 7.

• In 2004, there were 666 justifiable homicides in the U.S. — 437 by police officers, 229 by private citizens.

• In 1993, the U.S. recorded 24,526 homicides. There then began dramatic decreases. By the year 2000, total homicides numbered 15,586. Among possible reasons for decline: better emergency-trauma care, locking up more people, prosperity, more cops and according to the author of the book, "Freaknomics," abortions.

California Crime

Of the 2,394 homicides in 2004, guns, mostly pistols, accounted 73 percent of the total, knives 12 percent, blunt objects such as clubs 4 percent, hands and feet other personal weapons 6 percent, and unidentified weapons 5.

Megan's Law

For a list of registered sex offenders by town or city, go to
www.meganslaw.ca.gov

Population by Age Groups
Santa Clara County

City or Area	Under 5	5-19	20-34	35-54	55+
Campbell	2,491	6,404	10,002	12,729	6,512
Cupertino	3,060	11,301	7,841	18,371	9,973
Gilroy	3,903	10,857	9,677	11,669	5,358
Los Altos	1,629	5,281	2,598	9,462	8,723
Los Altos Hills	355	1,611	664	2,640	2,632
Los Gatos	1,419	5,025	4,537	9,889	7,722
Milpitas	4,484	12,575	16,207	20.296	9,136
Monte Sereno	206	805	254	1,248	970
Morgan Hill	2,729	8,378	6,207	11,079	5,163
Mountain View	4,270	9,570	22,161	22,165	12,542
Palo Alto	2,970	10,162	10,680	19,827	14,959
San Jose	68,243	192,410	225,363	267,134	141,793
Santa Clara	6,688	16,872	30,771	29,596	18,434
Saratoga	1,597	6,649	2,430	10,613	8,554
Sunnyvale	9,270	19,861	38,565	39,570	24,494
County Total	119,418	340,194	411,830	515,598	295,545

Santa Cruz County

Aptos	456	1,518	1,667	3,483	2,272
Ben Lomond	127	543	447	944	303
Boulder Creek	201	874	714	1,770	522
Capitola	488	1,610	2,366	3,360	2,209
Felton	56	249	231	346	169
Santa Cruz	2,664	10,236	17,094	16,486	8,113
Scotts Valley	774	2,428	1,825	3,896	2,462
Soquel	273	1,106	972	1,839	891
Watsonville	4,100	12,460	10,984	10,532	6,189
County Total	15,544	54,646	57,676	82,760	44,976

San Benito County

Hollister	3,442	9,501	7,897	9,653	3,920
San Juan Bautista	116	348	293	464	328
County Total	4,705	13,933	10,995	15,606	7,995

Source: 2000 Census.

Subject Index

Advertisers' Index

Developers

Information Services

Major Employers

Private Schools

Realtors & Relocation Services

Transit

To advertise in McCormack's Guides, call 1-800-222-3602

BUY 10 OR MORE & SAVE!